THE EXPERT
CLUB PLAYER

DANNY ROTH is a writer and coach who specializes in teaching bridge to beginners and intermediates. An experienced and successful player at club, country and tournament level, he represented Great Britain in the European Pairs' Championships in 1987. He has written several other books on bridge, and is author of *The Expert Beginner*, *The Expert Improver* and *The Expert Advancer*, all published by HarperCollins.

COLLINS
WINNING BRIDGE

THE EXPERT
CLUB PLAYER

DANNY ROTH

CollinsWillow

An Imprint of HarperCollins*Publishers*

First published in 1993 by
Collins Willow
an imprint of HarperCollins*Publishers*, London

© Danny Roth, 1993

**A CIP catalogue record for this book
is available from the British Library**

ISBN 0 00 218529 6

Printed and bound in Great Britain
by Cox & Wyman Ltd

Contents

Introduction

Welcome – or welcome back – whichever is appropriate! My readers will now fall into a number of categories.

I started the *Expert* series a couple of years ago after years of dissatisfaction with long-established teaching methods. In the beginners' book, I explained that evening classes, bridge teachers and schools are trying to achieve the impossible in explaining the game in a dozen or so lessons by the 'Let's start playing and we'll learn as we go along' approach. Students are taught a long series of 'parrot-type rules', with little or no explanation, and then go out and play the game in social, club and tournament circles, almost totally unaware of the reasoning behind them. Even worse, they do not appreciate that, while these rules work a fair proportion of the time, the exceptions almost outnumber them. As a result the overall standard of bridge, and therefore the level of enjoyment and satisfaction derived from it, is well below what it should be. This seems a great pity, when a player who is prepared to put aside a few hours for private study and practice could improve out of all recognition. Yes, it does need some effort, but – barring luck in the lotteries – you do not get anything for nothing in this life.

My Expert series enables players to do the bulk of their learning in the privacy of their own homes, without having to bother better players. They can then go to the table with what I call a solid 'platform' of knowledge on which to build up their experience. In *The Expert Beginner*, I introduced the three basic elements of that platform:

1   Familiarization with a pack of cards;
2   Knowledge of the language and procedure of the game;
3   A full understanding of the scoresheet.

Basic play and simple bidding followed, and there were countless practice examples with a brief introduction to the world of conventional partnership communication in bidding and defence. I am a great believer in learning by repetition and mistakes and the place to make those mistakes is away from the table where they cost nothing and annoy no one.

In the two sequels, *The Expert Improver* and *The Expert Advancer*, I built on the platform and introduced more complicated examples in both play and bidding, adding to the short list of conventional bids and defensive signals. The major part of *The Expert Advancer* is devoted to play and defence, the section on bidding being proportionately shorter. In this book, the imbalance will be rectified in that the play and defence section will be relatively short and the lion's share will be devoted to bidding. We shall learn about the various procedures in duplicate bridge, which will involve meeting a large variety of opponents, each bidding in their own chosen language.

Readers who have studied any, or all, of the first three books will be familiar with my approach. Throughout, I have insisted on discussing every bid made and each card played in full detail, so that it is fully absorbed and comprehended. It all took time, and as a result each book runs to three hundred or more pages. This invited the inevitable criticism of being long-winded, but I offer little apology. A job well begun is a job half done, and I attach great importance to thoroughness, particularly at the foundation stage. My building will not collapse – not even after an earthquake!

Those who are joining now will have learnt by traditional methods and probably had a few years' playing experience. You will see that I periodically offer certain 'guides', but stress that they are no more than that. Common sense, at all times, must take priority. The play and defence section is divided up as before into trump and no-trump contracts. The section on duplicate bridge involves a revision and adaptation of our knowledge of the scoresheet and an understanding of how club evenings, matches and tournaments are run. The third section introduces some more advanced bidding systems. By the end, I hope that you will be in a position to play in any kind of game, fully conversant with what is happening.

For the time being, however, you need no more than the usual equipment. You should be sitting at a table about two feet square, with a pack of cards, pen and paper, and a stop-watch.

SECTION 1:
Play and Defence

Declarer Play at No-trump Contracts

As we discussed in the earlier books, no-trump contracts usually involve a race between the declarer and defenders to establish and cash long suits. With the defenders on lead, they will often be a move ahead, but we learnt that declarer has obstructive tactics such as holding up his stop(s) and blocking. If, despite all his efforts, the defenders still manage to set up their suit first, the hand with long cards will still need an entry to gain the lead and cash his winners and it may be that declarer can play his own suit in such a way as to keep the dangerous hand out of mischief. Let us look at an example.

Hand No. 1
Dealer North
N–S vulnerable

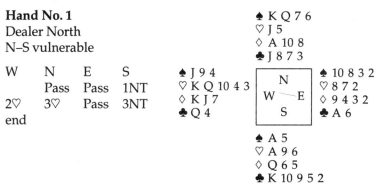

♠ K Q 7 6
♡ J 5
◇ A 10 8
♣ J 8 7 3

W	N	E	S
	Pass	Pass	1NT
2♡	3♡	Pass	3NT
end			

♠ J 9 4
♡ K Q 10 4 3
◇ K J 7
♣ Q 4

N
W E
S

♠ 10 8 3 2
♡ 8 7 2
◇ 9 4 3 2
♣ A 6

♠ A 5
♡ A 9 6
◇ Q 6 5
♣ K 10 9 5 2

North's unassuming cue-bid of 3♡ suggests a near-opening bid (remember he has already passed) and offers 3NT (if South can stop hearts) or 4♠ (if South has a four-card suit) as possible final contracts.

West leads the ♡K and South holds up to the third round, exhausting East of the suit. How does South continue? It is clear that, with only three spade tricks, one diamond and one heart on top, the club suit will have to be brought in for four tricks – without West being allowed to regain the lead. South therefore realizes that, if West has the ♣A, there is nothing to be done. He therefore credits that card to East and considers his line in that light. The aim now must be to keep West off play if he has the ♣Q. He therefore crosses to dummy in spades, and plays a low club, intending to go up with the ♣K if East plays low. This gives a chance of success if West has a stiff ♣Q or a doubleton as above. Note that, if West has ♣ Q x x, there is again nothing to be done.

Let us juggle the club suit around and look at other positions in which South is trying to keep West off play. Suppose the king is missing:

10 x x x

```
    +-------+
    |   N   |
    | W   E |
    |   S   |
    +-------+
```

A Q J x x

In normal circumstances, the percentage play to catch him is a finesse against East and, if we need five tricks, that is what we should do. However, where we only need four, we can afford to play the ace on the first round in case West has a stiff king. We do not mind losing an 'unnecessary' trick to East. Where the king and jack are missing, we can introduce a further refinement.

10 x x x

```
    +-------+
    |   N   |
    | W   E |
    |   S   |
    +-------+
```

A Q x x x

Playing the ace, to cover a stiff king with West, would be an unnecessary losing play here:

```
            10 x x x
           ┌─────────┐
           │    N    │
     J x x │ W     E │ K
           │    S    │
           └─────────┘
            A Q x x x
```

East's king would drop and now nothing could prevent West's gaining the lead with the jack. In this case, we go over to dummy in another suit and observe the guide of leading 'from weakness through strength to strength' by starting with a low card from there. When East puts in the king, we let him hold the trick, subsequently picking up West's jack with the ace and queen.

Having seen the idea, I should like you to do an example in match conditions. Having reached this standard, you should be aiming to be able to play hands with less than a minute's thought, approaching the speed expected in a normal game of reasonable standard. Start your stop-watch.

Problem 1

Hand No. 2

Dealer South

N–S vulnerable

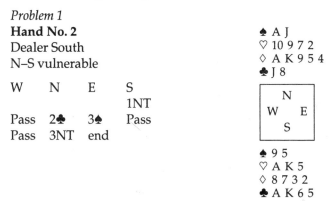

W	N	E	S
			1NT
Pass	2♣	3♠	Pass
Pass	3NT	end	

♠ A J
♡ 10 9 7 2
◊ A K 9 5 4
♣ J 8

♠ 9 5
♡ A K 5
◊ 8 7 3 2
♣ A K 6 5

West leads the ♠10 to the ♠J, ♠Q and ♠5. East returns the ♠7, all following. How do you continue?

Solution

We have two top tricks each in clubs and hearts, in addition to the ♠A, to total five so far. That implies the need for four in diamonds. We can therefore afford to lose one trick as long as it is to West.

East must be kept off play at all costs as he waiting with five spade winners. It is unlikely that there will be any problem as, with spades splitting 7–2, the diamond length is likely to be with West, but it is wise to play safe. We cross to hand with a high heart and lead a low diamond. The intention is to duck if West produces the queen. We are saved in this layout:

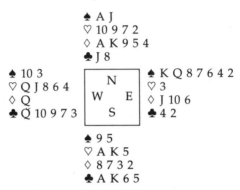

```
                    ♠ A J
                    ♡ 10 9 7 2
                    ◇ A K 9 5 4
                    ♣ J 8
  ♠ 10 3                          ♠ K Q 8 7 6 4 2
  ♡ Q J 8 6 4         N           ♡ 3
  ◇ Q              W     E        ◇ J 10 6
  ♣ Q 10 9 7 3        S           ♣ 4 2
                    ♠ 9 5
                    ♡ A K 5
                    ◇ 8 7 3 2
                    ♣ A K 6 5
```

Should West play low, we rise in dummy and carry on with the other diamond honour, hoping for a 2–2 break or the length with West.

We now turn to positions in which declarer has options in two suits. We studied some of these in *The Expert Advancer* and learnt the principle of *drop first; then finesse*. In other words, assuming again that defenders had an established suit ready to cash and we had two suits with honours missing, we would try to drop one of them, so that we could *hold* the lead if it failed and then take a finesse in the other. Suppose these were the two suits:

```
            ◇ A K J 8 6
            ♣ A J 7
            ┌─────────┐
            │    N    │
            │ W     E │
            │    S    │
            └─────────┘
            ◇ 9 7 3
            ♣ K 5 3
```

and we needed five tricks between them. The two aces and kings give four and the fifth could come from capturing the queen in either. If we choose one of the finesses, and it loses, we shall go down without having tried the other. The best line is to try for the drop in one and then take the finesse in the other. Here with eight diamonds but only six clubs, it is more likely that we can drop the ◇Q than the ♣Q, so we try the two top diamonds. If the queen does not appear, we take the finesse in clubs.

We can now extend that idea to positions where we have a choice of suits to play on. The break in another suit may provide a crucial clue.

Hand No. 3
Dealer South
E–W vulnerable

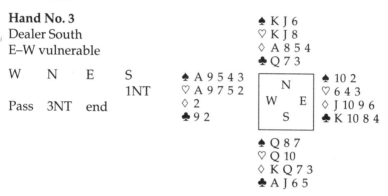

```
                              ♠ K J 6
                              ♡ K J 8
                              ◇ A 8 5 4
                              ♣ Q 7 3
W    N    E    S     ♠ A 9 5 4 3            ♠ 10 2
               1NT   ♡ A 9 7 5 2     N      ♡ 6 4 3
                     ◇ 2         W       E  ◇ J 10 9 6
Pass 3NT  end        ♣ 9 2           S      ♣ K 10 8 4
                              ♠ Q 8 7
                              ♡ Q 10
                              ◇ K Q 7 3
                              ♣ A J 6 5
```

West leads the ♡5. South can see that he has two tricks in each major, three top diamonds and the ♣A for eight tricks and has chances for a ninth in a 3–2 diamond split or the club finesse. However, playing on the majors involves the possibility of setting up long-suit cards for West. How does he set about it? Let us do a trial run with the 'drop first; then finesse' principle applying. Two rounds of diamonds will reveal the position. If they fail to break, as above, the club finesse will be needed. South plays on spades and, although West can duck and set up long cards in the major suit in which South persists, he can only take his two aces and two long cards – four in all – while South takes four major-suit tricks, three diamonds and two clubs. If, however, the diamonds do break, the club finesse is not needed. South plays on the majors exclusively, conceding four tricks as above but making four major-suit tricks, four diamonds and one club. Notice that taking the club finesse early would have been fatal had the deal been like this:

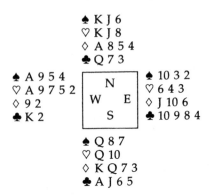

```
              ♠ K J 6
              ♡ K J 8
              ◊ A 8 5 4
              ♣ Q 7 3
♠ A 9 5 4                    ♠ 10 3 2
♡ A 9 7 5 2    N            ♡ 6 4 3
◊ 9 2       W     E         ◊ J 10 6
♣ K 2          S            ♣ 10 9 8 4
              ♠ Q 8 7
              ♡ Q 10
              ◊ K Q 7 3
              ♣ A J 6 5
```

West wins and plays a low heart, ensuring three heart tricks, the ♠A and ♣K before South can take more than four diamonds, two hearts and two clubs.

Having seen the idea, try this next problem in match conditions to the same time limit. Start your stop-watch.

Problem 2
Hand No. 4
Dealer East
Neither vulnerable

♠ 9 5 4
♡ Q 10 6
◊ K 5
♣ A Q 9 7 4

```
      N
   W     E
      S
```

W	N	E	S
		Pass	1◊
Pass	2♣	Pass	3◊
Pass	3♡	Pass	3NT
end			

♠ K 8
♡ K J
◊ A Q 8 7 3 2
♣ J 10 8

West leads the ♠2 to his partner's ♠A and East returns the ♠3, confirming the 4–4 break in the suit. Plan the play.

Solution
We have one spade trick, three diamonds and the ♣A on top to total five so far with several possibilities for more. If the diamonds break 3–2, we shall have six diamond tricks to bring the total up to eight and can knock out the ♡A to set up two heart tricks. That would be more than enough for the contract but we would only

make it exactly as we have to lose the ♡A and three spade tricks first.

The question thus arises of what happens if the diamonds do not break. There is now no time to knock out the ◊J, ensuring five tricks in the suit, because we should then lose the diamond, three spades and the ♡A for one off. The only hope now is to take the club finesse, hoping for five club tricks, three top diamonds and the spade. For that reason, diamonds must be tested first. If both defenders follow to two rounds, we can cash the rest and knock out the ♡A. If they do not, we cash the third diamond only and play on clubs.

The deal:

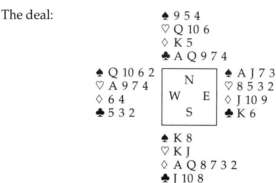

```
                    ♠ 9 5 4
                    ♡ Q 10 6
                    ◊ K 5
                    ♣ A Q 9 7 4
    ♠ Q 10 6 2     ┌─────────┐     ♠ A J 7 3
    ♡ A 9 7 4      │    N    │     ♡ 8 5 3 2
    ◊ 6 4          │ W     E │     ◊ J 10 9
    ♣ 5 3 2        │    S    │     ♣ K 6
                    └─────────┘
                    ♠ K 8
                    ♡ K J
                    ◊ A Q 8 7 3 2
                    ♣ J 10 8
```

Satisfy yourself that it would be a mistake to knock out the ♡A before testing the diamonds. West would win, and if the defenders arrange to play two more rounds of spades, finishing in the West hand, he can then play a club and we would have to take a decision whether to finesse or not *before* we know the diamond position. In the above diagram, we must rise with the ♣A. But exchange the positions of the ♣K and ◊4 and now we must finesse.

In the above deal, the North and South hands were of approximately equal strength and, in this situation, communications are usually fairly easy. Often, however, the bulk of the strength is concentrated in one hand and now, if the long suit to be cashed is sitting opposite, there are likely to be entry problems. In that event, low cards can be very important and possibly unnecessary tricks may have to be sacrificed to keep communications open. Here is an example:

Hand No. 5
Dealer North
E–W vulnerable

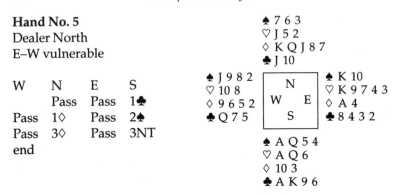

```
                            ♠ 7 6 3
                            ♡ J 5 2
                            ◊ K Q J 8 7
                            ♣ J 10
            ♠ J 9 8 2                     ♠ K 10
            ♡ 10 8           N            ♡ K 9 7 4 3
            ◊ 9 6 5 2    W       E        ◊ A 4
            ♣ Q 7 5          S            ♣ 8 4 3 2
                            ♠ A Q 5 4
                            ♡ A Q 6
                            ◊ 10 3
                            ♣ A K 9 6
```

W	N	E	S
	Pass	Pass	1♣
Pass	1◊	Pass	2♠
Pass	3◊	Pass	3NT
end			

West leads the ♠2 to the ♠K and ♠A. The ◊10 is allowed to hold, West commencing a peter (to show an even number) with the ◊6. On the second round, East wins and returns the ♠10. How should South continue? He has two spade tricks and can make two more in hearts and three in clubs. However, if he cannot reach the diamonds, he will be held to one trick in that suit to total eight only. Meanwhile, the defenders are threatening two spade tricks and one in each of the other suits to total five.

The diamonds must therefore be reached at all costs and the only sure way to do so is to use dummy's ♣ J 10. We effectively tuck the ♣A and ♣K under the table and consider this two-card position:

```
              J 10
               N
       Q 7  W       E  8 4
               S
               9 6
```

It is one trick each and, by leading a low card, we can ensure that the North–South trick is won by North. This holds even if East has the ♣Q. So South wins the spade and leads a low club. West can win and cash his two spades but South is subsequently able to cross to the ♣J to cash the long diamonds, discarding his losing hearts, to complete four diamond tricks, three clubs, two spades and a heart – ten in total but, as he has already lost two spades, a diamond and a club, there is a trick to burn at the end.

Satisfy yourself that, as long the defenders play accurately, the ♡J can never be an entry to dummy. This is the three-card position of the type we studied in *The Expert Beginner*:

J 5 2

```
        N
10 8  W     E   K 9 7
        S
```

A Q 6

A low heart towards the jack loses to the king, leaving the ace and queen to win the other two tricks for South. If South plays the ♡Q first, East lets her hold and again, South cannot reach dummy. Cashing the ♡A early makes no difference. Also it does not matter if West has the ♡K:

J 5 2

```
          N
K 10 8  W     E   9 7 4
          S
```

A Q 6

If South plays the six, West rises with the king, again forcing South to win the other two tricks. If South tries the ♡Q, again she is allowed to hold. North-South will always win two tricks to the defenders' one but the defenders can insist that South, rather than North, will win both tricks.

Having seen the idea, try this next one in match conditions. As there are several questions to answer, allow yourself three minutes. Start your stop-watch.

Problem 3
Hand No. 6
Dealer East
E–W vulnerable

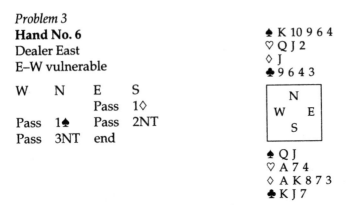

♠ K 10 9 6 4
♡ Q J 2
◇ J
♣ 9 6 4 3

W	N	E	S
		Pass	1◇
Pass	1♠	Pass	2NT
Pass	3NT	end	

♠ Q J
♡ A 7 4
◇ A K 8 7 3
♣ K J 7

West leads the ♣2 to his partner's ♣A. East returns the ♣5; you try the ♣J but West produces the ♣Q and plays a third round which you have to win with the ♣K while East discards the ◇2. On the ♠Q, West plays the ♠8 and East the ♠3. You continue with the ♠J, on which West completes a peter with the ♠2.

1 How do you play now?
2 How would you have played had East switched to the ♡6 at trick two?
3 How would you have played if, instead of a club, West had led the ♡3 at trick one?
4 How would you have played had West switched to the ♡3 at trick three?

Solution
We have one club trick, two top diamonds, and will take two hearts to total five so far, which means that the spades will have to be brought in for four tricks. There is a serious shortage of entries to dummy and the first hurdle must be to ensure that the only hope, in hearts, is kept intact until after the ♠A has been knocked out. For that reason, we must overtake the ♠Q with the ♠K to be able to continue the suit. Were we to play low, East would let the queen hold and we should be stuck in hand, unable to continue the suit without using the heart entry. Then we will never be able to return to dummy to cash the established spade winners.

We continue the spades until the ace is taken and return to

dummy by playing a low heart towards the queen-jack, ensuring that one of them will win. In the meantime, of course, the defenders are threatening to take three club tricks in addition to the spade and heart and, for full credit, you should have stated that we have to hope that the ♠A and ♡K are *both* in the hand with the short clubs:

The deal:

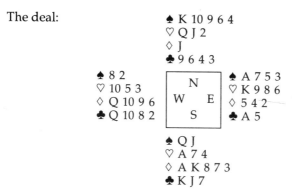

If the defenders attack hearts early, we must keep the entry in dummy intact and therefore, irrespective of who leads them or the position of the king, we must win the first round in hand with the ace! Let us tabulate the initial three-card position and possible resulting two-card positions:

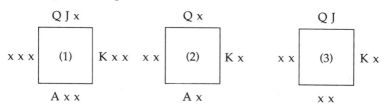

Diagram (1) is the initial three-card position from the main deal. If we play an honour from dummy on the first round, the king will be withheld and we shall be left with the two-card position in diagram (2); there is now no way we can reach dummy. However, if we play low from dummy on the first round, winning with the ace, then we cannot be prevented from reaching dummy in diagram (3). Satisfy yourself that the above argument equally applies if the ♡K is with West. In the case where the initial lead is a heart, South can set up four spade tricks, two hearts and two diamonds and must guess the clubs correctly to be successful.

Just as declarer must be careful to keep his entries intact, he should be equally determined to disrupt defenders' communications. In particular, declarer must be on his guard when he receives an unexpected lead.

Hand No. 7
Dealer West
E–W vulnerable

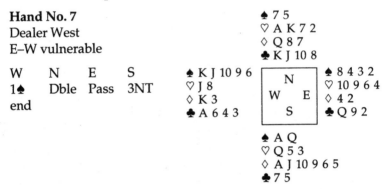

	♠ 7 5
	♡ A K 7 2
	♢ Q 8 7
	♣ K J 10 8

W	N	E	S
1♠	Dble	Pass	3NT
end			

♠ K J 10 9 6
♡ J 8
♢ K 3
♣ A 6 4 3

♠ 8 4 3 2
♡ 10 9 6 4
♢ 4 2
♣ Q 9 2

♠ A Q
♡ Q 5 3
♢ A J 10 9 6 5
♣ 7 5

A spade lead allows South time to knock out the ♢K to make the contract easily. But West, suspecting South's tenace, leads the ♣3.

A careless second-hand 'low', in practice putting on the jack, would be fatal here. East would win and return a spade. South, reduced to one stopper in the suit, would have to knock out the ♢K and would lose four spade tricks, the diamond and two clubs to finish three tricks short. With the dangerous spade position, it is vital to keep East off play at all costs. If he has the ♣A, there is nothing to be done but, if he has the ♣Q, putting up the ♣K from dummy at trick one saves the day. A diamond is lost to the king. The best defence is for West to cross to his partner with another low club, enabling East to push a spade through. But declarer is now a step ahead and takes five diamond tricks, the spade and three top hearts to add to the first club for an overtrick. At worst, he loses two clubs and the diamond.

Let us conclude this chapter with a four-problem test, covering the main topics studied, in match conditions. You should be aiming to get under seventy-five seconds for each one to complete them all in under five minutes. Start your stop-watch.

Problem 4

Hand No. 8
Dealer West
Both vulnerable

W	N	E	S
Pass	Pass	Pass	1◊
1♠	2♣	Pass	3NT
end			

♠ 7 5
♡ Q J 5 3
◊ 4 2
♣ A K 6 4 3

```
        N
    W       E
        S
```

♠ A 8 4
♡ A 2
◊ A K J 8 7 5
♣ 7 2

West leads top spades and you win the third round, East following. How do you continue?

Problem 5

Hand No. 9
Dealer West
N–S vulnerable

W	N	E	S
Pass	1♡	Pass	1NT
Pass	3♣	Pass	3NT
end			

♠ A J 10
♡ A Q 7 5 3
◊ Q
♣ A K 4 3

```
        N
    W       E
        S
```

♠ K 5
♡ 6 2
◊ A J 10 9 8 5
♣ 7 6 2

West leads the ♠3. How do plan the play?

Problem 6
Hand No.10
Dealer East
E–W vulnerable

♠ K Q 8
♡ A Q 8
◇ K J 3 2
♣ 10 9 7

W	N	E	S
		Pass	1NT
Pass	3NT	end	

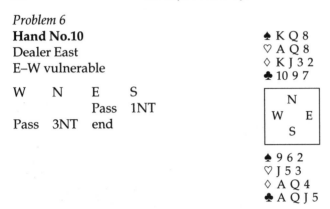

♠ 9 6 2
♡ J 5 3
◇ A Q 4
♣ A Q J 5

West leads the ♡4. How do you plan the play?

Problem 7
Hand No. 11
Dealer South
N–S vulnerable

♠ J 4 3
♡ J 5
◇ A J 9 8 7 4
♣ 6 2

W	N	E	S
			2NT
Pass	3NT	end	

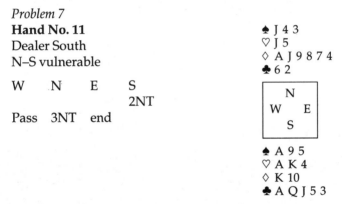

♠ A 9 5
♡ A K 4
◇ K 10
♣ A Q J 5 3

West leads the ♡10. Except in the unlikely event of East's holding a stiff queen, it will cost nothing to try the jack. You play it but East does produce the queen. How do plan the play?

Solutions

Problem 4
We have two club tricks, the spade and the ♡A on top, and therefore require at least five of our six diamonds. We can thus afford to lose one trick but it will have to be to East as West is waiting with two more spade winners. Clearly taking the diamond

finesse is out of the question and it is more sensible to play for the drop, banging down the ace and king. If West has three or more to the queen, there is nothing to be done. If East has the queen among three or more, we do not mind losing a trick to him. However, there is one further refinement and the guide of leading from weakness towards strength gives us an extra chance against this layout:

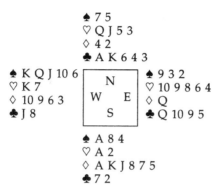

```
              ♠ 7 5
              ♡ Q J 5 3
              ◇ 4 2
              ♣ A K 6 4 3
♠ K Q J 10 6                    ♠ 9 3 2
♡ K 7          N                ♡ 10 9 8 6 4
◇ 10 9 6 3   W   E              ◇ Q
♣ J 8          S                ♣ Q 10 9 5
              ♠ A 8 4
              ♡ A 2
              ◇ A K J 8 7 5
              ♣ 7 2
```

We cross to dummy in clubs and lead a low diamond, intending to rise with the ace if East plays low. But when he produces the queen, we let her hold the trick! We win the heart return and cash nine tricks.

Problem 5
The lead has given us a free finesse for three spade tricks, two top clubs and two red aces, totalling seven so far. If the heart suit behaves reasonably – the finesse right and/or a 3–3 break – it could provide the extra two tricks necessary. However that is not guaranteed and, in fact, this contract is unbreakable against any defence and distribution provided we play carefully to bring the diamond suit in. With the shortage of entries to hand, we must not consider the finesse, which would only gain if East has exactly ◇ K x anyway. We must also see to it that the only side entry, the ♠K, is kept intact at all costs. For that reason, we must spurn the free spade finesse and go up with the ♠A. Although the lead suggests that the ♠Q is likely to be with West, we should not risk a layout like this (overleaf):

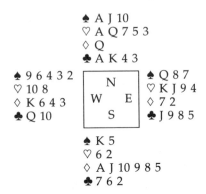

```
            ♠ A J 10
            ♡ A Q 7 5 3
            ◊ Q
            ♣ A K 4 3
♠ 9 6 4 3 2              ♠ Q 8 7
♡ 10 8          N        ♡ K J 9 4
◊ K 6 4 3    W     E     ◊ 7 2
♣ Q 10          S        ♣ J 9 8 5
            ♠ K 5
            ♡ 6 2
            ◊ A J 10 9 8 5
            ♣ 7 6 2
```

Now playing low from dummy at trick one allows East to play the queen, knocking out our king prematurely. (Allowing the ♠Q to hold does not help, as he simply plays another spade). At trick two, we overtake in diamonds and continue the suit – if we run the ◊Q, West simply ducks and the suit, apart from the ace, is dead.

Problem 6

There should be enough tricks; even with the club finesse wrong, we have three clubs, four diamonds and at least one in each major. The question, therefore, arises as to whether the defenders can take five tricks first. Irrespective of the position of the ♡K, we have a double stop in the suit but the spades are far from safe. If East has the ace, they could set up three tricks in that suit and we are in danger if both the ♡K and ♣K have to be lost.

The deal:

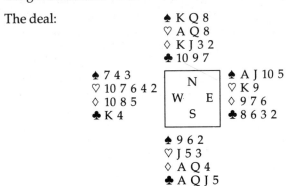

```
            ♠ K Q 8
            ♡ A Q 8
            ◊ K J 3 2
            ♣ 10 9 7
♠ 7 4 3                 ♠ A J 10 5
♡ 10 7 6 4 2    N       ♡ K 9
◊ 10 8 5     W     E     ◊ 9 7 6
♣ K 4           S        ♣ 8 6 3 2
            ♠ 9 6 2
            ♡ J 5 3
            ◊ A Q 4
            ♣ A Q J 5
```

If we innocently play low at trick one, East could win and switch to the ♠J, ensuring three tricks in the suit whether we win (after which West pushes through the second round) or not (after which East plays a low card to preserve communications with his partner). Admittedly, it would be very unlucky to find every important card as badly placed as above, but why take the risk? We simply rise with the ♡A and knock out the ♣K. That gives eight tricks on top and we have the choice of whether to set up our ninth in hearts or spades. Spades are better as there will be overtricks if West has the ace.

Problem 7
The first point is that there is little to be gained by ducking this trick and to do so would risk a spade switch, which could net three or more tricks for the defenders. So we must win trick one and consider how best to combine chances in the minors. To play the ◊K and then finesse the second round risks disaster on two counts. If the finesse loses, we shall have been restricted to one trick in the suit and all entries to dummy, needed to take club finesses, are lost. For these reasons, it is better to play for the slightly inferior chance of the diamond drop. That, at least, ensures two diamond tricks and the chance to take one club finesse.

However, we can be greedier still. Suppose we play the ◊10 and overtake with the ◊J. If this loses, we are able to overtake the ◊K with the ace on the second round to take five diamond tricks. We have two top hearts, one spade and at least one club to total nine. If the diamond holds, we can take an immediate club finesse and, if that holds, we can cross again to dummy by overtaking the ◊K. If the ◊Q does not appear, we can take another club finesse. We are now safe if the clubs break 3–3 or if they are 4–2 and the finesse succeeds, as here:

The deal:

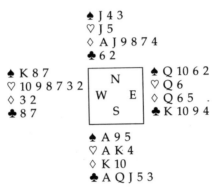

```
                    ♠ J 4 3
                    ♡ J 5
                    ◇ A J 9 8 7 4
                    ♣ 6 2
   ♠ K 8 7                            ♠ Q 10 6 2
   ♡ 10 9 8 7 3 2    ┌─────────┐      ♡ Q 6
   ◇ 3 2             │    N    │      ◇ Q 6 5
   ♣ 8 7             │ W     E │      ♣ K 10 9 4
                     │    S    │
                     └─────────┘
                    ♠ A 9 5
                    ♡ A K 4
                    ◇ K 10
                    ♣ A Q J 5 3
```

East must refuse the first diamond or allow the whole suit to be cashed. We take a successful club finesse, overtake in diamonds and take another successful club finesse. Now the ♣A followed by a fourth round ensures four club tricks, two diamonds and three top tricks in the majors for the contract.

As always, I urge you to play and replay these hands over and over again to ensure that you understand them before going on to the trump contracts in the next chapter.

Declarer Play
at Trump Contracts

We are going to start this section with trump control. A declarer is often in danger of losing it in two circumstances:

1 If he has a modest number of combined trumps in the first place;
2 If a hand short in a side-suit is likely to run out of trumps too early, after which losers in that suit can be cashed by the defenders.

Let us look at some examples and learn some counter-strokes:

Hand No. 12
Dealer South
E–W vulnerable

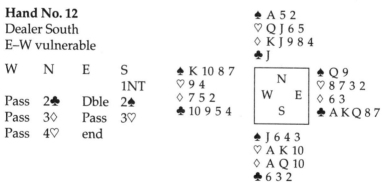

♠ A 5 2
♡ Q J 6 5
◊ K J 9 8 4
♣ J

♠ K 10 8 7
♡ 9 4
◊ 7 5 2
♣ 10 9 5 4

♠ Q 9
♡ 8 7 3 2
◊ 6 3
♣ A K Q 8 7

♠ J 6 4 3
♡ A K 10
◊ A Q 10
♣ 6 3 2

W	N	E	S
			1NT
Pass	2♣	Dble	2♠
Pass	3◊	Pass	3♡
Pass	4♡	end	

Let us first consider the bidding. After the Stayman enquiry was doubled for a club lead, North bid 3◊, an invitation that gave South a number of options:

1 To bid 3NT if he had the clubs well stopped;
2 To repeat his spades if he had a strong four-card suit (with a view to 4♠);

3 To show a three-card heart (with the possibility of 4♡);
4 To support the diamonds (with a view to 5◊).

West leads the ♣10; East wins and continues the suit. How should
South play? There will be no problem if the hearts break 3–3. We
can ruff and draw trumps, completing four trump tricks, and play
the diamonds for five more, the ♠A making the tenth. However, if
the trumps break 4–2 (more likely), we could be in trouble. Ruffing
the second club leaves us with only three trumps in each hand.
After drawing trumps, a defender (here East) will still have a
trump. He will ruff in as soon as he runs out of diamonds and cash
the clubs.

To avoid this, we must delay ruffing clubs until the *South* hand
is exhausted. We trade unavoidable spade losers for avoidable
club losers. At trick two, we discard a spade from dummy (loser
on loser) and, on the next round of clubs, we discard another
spade. Now any further club can be ruffed in the *short-trump* hand,
keeping dummy's long trumps all intact, after which we can draw
all the trumps and cash the diamonds uninterrupted.

An alternative counter-stroke to the defenders' forcing game is
to give them a taste of their own medicine.

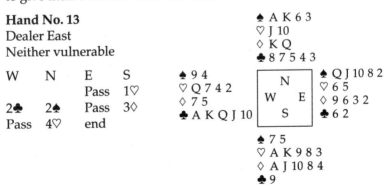

Hand No. 13
Dealer East
Neither vulnerable

♠	A K 6 3		
♡	J 10		
◊	K Q		
♣	8 7 5 4 3		

W	N	E	S
		Pass	1♡
2♣	2♠	Pass	3◊
Pass	4♡	end	

West: ♠ 9 4   ♡ Q 7 4 2   ◊ 7 5   ♣ A K Q J 10

East: ♠ Q J 10 8 2   ♡ 6 5   ◊ 9 6 3 2   ♣ 6 2

South: ♠ 7 5   ♡ A K 9 8 3   ◊ A J 10 8 4   ♣ 9

For North, this is a difficult hand to bid. 3NT would be on top if the
clubs split 4–3 but the bidding rules this out. With 13 working
points opposite an opening bid, he really ought to insist on game
and the best chance is the 5–2 heart fit.

West leads top clubs and South sees that, if East has the ♡Q, a slam is on. However, this kind of situation is most dangerous as it is easy to overlook the fact that the actual contract is in danger. South only needs to cross to dummy to take the trump finesse and he is doomed. West wins and returns a third club, forcing South again to leave West with a trump majority. South cannot now cash the diamonds and finishes at least one trick short.

South should foresee the danger of West's holding four trumps to the queen and cash two top trumps before starting on the diamonds. West can ruff but now *he* is the one to lose trump control. He can continue the force with clubs but now a further diamond forces him to ruff again. All South loses are two trump tricks in addition to the first club.

Now let us turn to the position where the declarer has long trumps but losers in another suit which need to be discarded on dummy's long suit. Obviously that long suit cannot be cashed until after trumps are drawn and now there could be a problem in timing. Here is an example.

Hand No. 14
Dealer East
N–S vulnerable

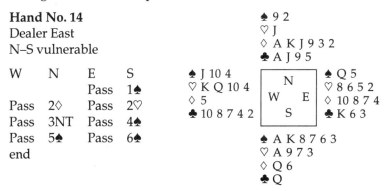

W	N	E	S
		Pass	1♠
Pass	2◇	Pass	2♡
Pass	3NT	Pass	4♠
Pass	5♣	Pass	6♠
end			

West leads the ♡K. South wins and could try the following: ruff a heart; return to the ♣A and ruff another heart; return to hand with a club ruff; draw two rounds of clubs and play on diamonds, hoping that two rounds stand up. On the third diamond, he discards his last losing heart, conceding one trump trick.

However, this line fails when the diamonds split 4–1 and the hand with the singleton has the long trump. Now a heart will be lost. It will also fail in the (admittedly unlikely) event that the hearts are 6–2 or worse and the hand with the short hearts also has only two trumps. Now two trump tricks will be lost.

The safe line, on the necessary assumption that the trumps are 3–2, is to ensure that the diamonds can be cashed uninterrupted. Therefore trumps must be drawn first. That involves losing a trick and the trick must be lost while a trump remains on dummy to look after the hearts. Let us look at the three-card position:

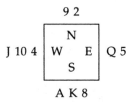

```
              9 2
           ┌───────┐
           │   N   │
  J 10 4   │ W   E │   Q 5
           │   S   │
           └───────┘
             A K 8
```

Clearly declarer will win two tricks for one lost but he can insist on losing the first round by playing low from both hands. He wins any return, draws the remaining trumps and cashes six rounds of diamonds. Therefore he makes five trump tricks, six diamonds and the other two aces – thirteen in all; with the trump trick lost, there will be a trick to burn in the end.

Having seen the idea, you should be able to do the next three examples in match conditions. You should aim for well under ninety seconds for each, to complete the test in about four minutes. Start your stop-watch.

Problem 1
Hand No. 15
Dealer East
Neither vulnerable

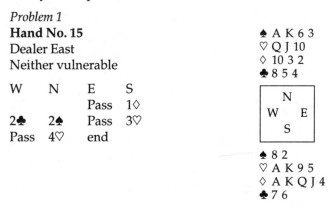

♠ A K 6 3
♡ Q J 10
◇ 10 3 2
♣ 8 5 4

```
┌───────┐
│   N   │
│ W   E │
│   S   │
└───────┘
```

♠ 8 2
♡ A K 9 5
◇ A K Q J 4
♣ 7 6

W	N	E	S
		Pass	1◇
2♣	2♠	Pass	3♡
Pass	4♡	end	

This is slightly indisciplined bidding by North; he ought to give preference to 4◇, leading to the safer contract of 5◇. However, with good heart support, there is a case for going for the cheaper game.

West leads three top clubs, East following. How do you plan the play?

Problem 2
Hand No. 16
Dealer North
Both vulnerable

♠ 10 9
♡ 6 5 2
◊ 8 7 2
♣ A K J 3 2

W	N	E	S
	Pass	Pass	1♠
Pass	1NT	Pass	2NT
Pass	3♣	Pass	3◊
Pass	3♠	Pass	4♠
end			

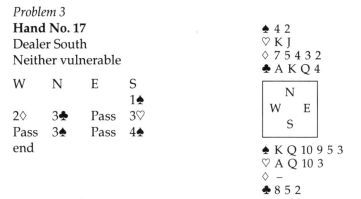

♠ A K Q 6 3
♡ J 7
◊ A Q 4
♣ Q 6 4

Arguably, South is strong enough for 3NT over 1NT and this is a reasonable contract, purely dependent on a 4–4 heart break. Over 2NT, the partnership has the scope to discuss the final contract and, once the heart weakness is pinpointed, they find the superior contract of 4♠.

West leads out three top hearts. How do you plan the play?

Problem 3
Hand No. 17
Dealer South
Neither vulnerable

♠ 4 2
♡ K J
◊ 7 5 4 3 2
♣ A K Q 4

W	N	E	S
			1♠
2◊	3♣	Pass	3♡
Pass	3♠	Pass	4♠
end			

♠ K Q 10 9 5 3
♡ A Q 10 3
◊ –
♣ 8 5 2

West leads the ◊A and you ruff. You cross to the ♡K to lead a spade to the ♠8, ♠K and ♠A. West returns the ◊K, East playing the

◊Q, and you ruff again. Crossing to the ♣A, you lead a second spade but East discards the ♡2. How do you continue?

Solutions

Problem 1

We learnt earlier that, where there is a danger of being reduced to embarrassingly short trumps, it pays to discard a loser in this kind of position rather than accept the force. Now a fourth round of clubs can be ruffed in dummy, trumps drawn and the diamonds cashed for ten tricks. The trouble here is that, with the diamonds solid and both spades covered, there is no loser to discard. Never mind – discard a *winner* instead! Play a spade or diamond at trick three and now nothing can happen.

The deal:

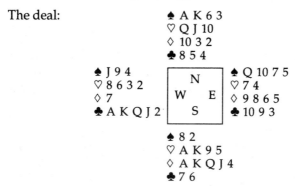

```
              ♠ A K 6 3
              ♡ Q J 10
              ◊ 10 3 2
              ♣ 8 5 4
 ♠ J 9 4                      ♠ Q 10 7 5
 ♡ 8 6 3 2        N           ♡ 7 4
 ◊ 7          W       E       ◊ 9 8 6 5
 ♣ A K Q J 2      S           ♣ 10 9 3
              ♠ 8 2
              ♡ A K 9 5
              ◊ A K Q J 4
              ♣ 7 6
```

As the cards lie, the contract can be made by ruffing and starting on diamonds immediately but that line could fail if the shortages in the two red suits are in the same hand.

Problem 2

We shall have to ruff this trick; otherwise we are staking everything on a 3–3 trump split and, in that case, it would be safe to ruff anyway. The danger now lies in a 4–2 trump split. If we are forced again, we shall be left shorter than the defender with the long trumps. Taking three top trumps and then switching to clubs is likely to fail. The defender with the fourth trump will ruff in on the third or fourth round of clubs, leaving dummy dead and our hand with at least one diamond loser. The trumps must be cleared before clubs are played and we should lose a trick immediately so that dummy can look after the next heart.

The deal:

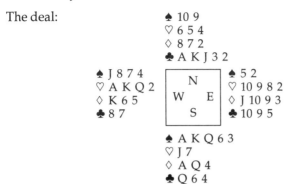

```
                        ♠ 10 9
                        ♡ 6 5 4
                        ◇ 8 7 2
                        ♣ A K J 3 2
    ♠ J 8 7 4          ┌─────────┐        ♠ 5 2
    ♡ A K Q 2          │    N    │        ♡ 10 9 8 2
    ◇ K 6 5            │ W     E │        ◇ J 10 9 3
    ♣ 8 7              │    S    │        ♣ 10 9 5
                       └─────────┘
                        ♠ A K Q 6 3
                        ♡ J 7
                        ◇ A Q 4
                        ♣ Q 6 4
```

We therefore ruff and play the ♣6. The ♠J will win but now the ♠10 will be able to ruff the next heart. We can subsequently draw the rest of the trumps to be sure of at least four trump tricks, five clubs and the ◇A.

Problem 3
Forced to ruff twice, our hand has been reduced to the same trump length as West's and now, if we try to clear trumps, we will be forced for a third time, leaving West in control. Notice East's un-block of the ◇Q. Once we have shown out, the position is clear and he now enables his partner to run diamonds uninterrupted. If we duck a spade now, or win and continue the suit, we will go down.

The deal:

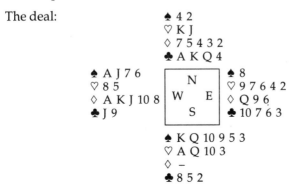

```
                        ♠ 4 2
                        ♡ K J
                        ◇ 7 5 4 3 2
                        ♣ A K Q 4
    ♠ A J 7 6          ┌─────────┐        ♠ 8
    ♡ 8 5              │    N    │        ♡ 9 7 6 4 2
    ◇ A K J 10 8       │ W     E │        ◇ Q 9 6
    ♣ J 9              │    S    │        ♣ 10 7 6 3
                       └─────────┘
                        ♠ K Q 10 9 5 3
                        ♡ A Q 10 3
                        ◇ –
                        ♣ 8 5 2
```

We must take the ♠Q but then abandon trumps to turn the forcing game on West. We cash our winners in hearts and clubs and allow him to take his two spade tricks whenever he feels like it.

The above exercises illustrated the importance of losing tricks at the right *time*. We have already spent considerable time on losing tricks to the right *hand* and will now look at more complex examples in connection with the ruffing finesse.

Hand No. 18
Dealer East
N–S vulnerable

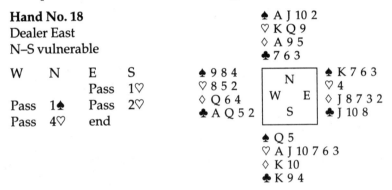

	♠ A J 10 2
	♡ K Q 9
	◇ A 9 5
	♣ 7 6 3

W	N	E	S
		Pass	1♡
Pass	1♠	Pass	2♡
Pass	4♡	end	

```
          ♠ A J 10 2
          ♡ K Q 9
          ◇ A 9 5
          ♣ 7 6 3
♠ 9 8 4          N          ♠ K 7 6 3
♡ 8 5 2      W       E      ♡ 4
◇ Q 6 4          S          ◇ J 8 7 3 2
♣ A Q 5 2                   ♣ J 10 8
          ♠ Q 5
          ♡ A J 10 7 6 3
          ◇ K 10
          ♣ K 9 4
```

As it happens, 3NT, played by South, is easy but that contract is difficult to reach.

West leads the ♡5 and South is lucky to have escaped the lethal spade lead. His problem now is to keep East off play so that the ♣K is protected. Let us look at the diamond position: we can insist on three rounds, winning two and losing none as the third round can be ruffed. But how about two winners and one loser, as long as the loser is conceded to West? We can then discard a spade on the third diamond, transposing

```
        A J 10 2                            A J 10 2
            N                                   N
  9 8 4  W     E  K 7 6 3      into    9 8 4  W     E  K 7 6 3
            S                                   S
          Q 5                                 Q
```

On the left, we have no hope but a finesse against West. That would lose to East and three club tricks would seal our fate. On the right, however, we can cash the ace and take a ruffing finesse through East, not worrying if West has the king as he cannot profitably attack clubs. We now make two spade tricks, two diamonds and six hearts for the contract. The play must therefore go as follows:

(i) The opening heart lead is won in dummy.
(ii) The ◊5 is led and, if East plays low, South's ◊10 loses to West's ◊Q.
(iii) A spade is won by dummy's ♠A.
(iv) A diamond to South's ◊K.
(v) A low trump, won in dummy.
(vi) The ◊A, South discarding ♠Q.
(vii) The ♠J from dummy, covered by East and ruffed high by South.
(viii) A low trump won in dummy.
(ix) The ♠10, South discarding a club.

South will now lose two clubs in addition to the early diamond at worst. Note the variations. If the ♠J loses to West, he cannot profitably attack clubs. A club will be thrown on the ♠10 later. If, at trick two, East puts in the ◊J, South wins with the ◊K and can, as the cards lie, take a finesse through West's ◊Q. In practice, he doesn't dare, for fear of letting East get the lead. He wins the second round with the ◊A and leads the ◊9, intending to discard a spade if East does not cover. If East does cover, i.e. he started with both diamond honours, South must ruff and hope that either the ♠K or ♣A is well placed for him. In that event, the diamond exercise has failed but trying it cost nothing.

Having seen the idea, can you do the next example under match conditions in under two minutes? Start your stop-watch.

Problem 4
Hand No. 19
Dealer West
E–W vulnerable

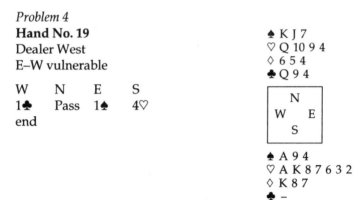

♠ K J 7
♡ Q 10 9 4
◇ 6 5 4
♣ Q 9 4

W	N	E	S
1♣	Pass	1♠	4♡
end			

♠ A 9 4
♡ A K 8 7 6 3 2
◇ K 8 7
♣ –

West leads the ♣A. How do you plan the play?

Solution
Again the object is to keep East off play to protect the ◇K, which is almost certainly badly placed. There are seven hearts and two spade tricks on top but, with the likelihood of West's holding the ♣K and ◇A, the bidding indicates that the spade finesse is prob-ably wrong. As before, tricks must be lost to West. We can start the ball rolling by trading our spade loser, which, considering the suit in isolation, would normally be lost to East, for a club loser to West. We therefore discard a spade on the ♣A. Say West switches to a spade.

The deal:

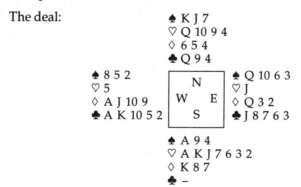

♠ K J 7
♡ Q 10 9 4
◇ 6 5 4
♣ Q 9 4

♠ 8 5 2
♡ 5
◇ A J 10 9
♣ A K 10 5 2

♠ Q 10 6 3
♡ J
◇ Q 3 2
♣ J 8 7 6 3

♠ A 9 4
♡ A K J 7 6 3 2
◇ K 8 7
♣ –

We can try the ♠J – it costs nothing – but, if East produces the ♠Q, we must win in hand and draw trumps, ending in dummy. We ruff a low club and follow with the ♠K and a spade ruff. Returning to dummy in trumps, we have this position:

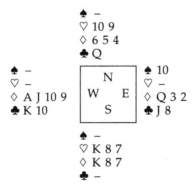

```
              ♠ –
              ♡ 10 9
              ◊ 6 5 4
              ♣ Q
♠ –                          ♠ 10
♡ –         ┌─────────┐      ♡ –
◊ A J 10 9  │    N    │      ◊ Q 3 2
♣ K 10      │ W     E │      ♣ J 8
            │    S    │
            └─────────┘
              ♠ –
              ♡ K 8 7
              ◊ K 8 7
              ♣ –
```

Now we trade losers again, this time leading the ♣Q and discarding a diamond on it, losing to West. He now has the choice of opening up the diamonds, giving us our tenth trick, or playing another club, giving us a ruff and discard. In the above position, West is *endplayed*, a concept I introduced in *The Expert Advancer*.

Let us now consider some more complex positions in this area. The endplay is often the only way out of a two- or three-card position in which, considered in isolation, we are booked to lose more tricks than we can afford. This is a typical example of the type studied in *The Expert Beginner*:

```
          Q 7 5
        ┌─────────┐
        │    N    │
A J 9   │ W     E │   8 6 3
        │    S    │
        └─────────┘
          K 10 4
```

West will win two tricks as long as he cannot be forced to lead the suit. But if he can, he will be held to one. Let us put this position into a complete deal:

Hand No. 20
Dealer West
E–W vulnerable

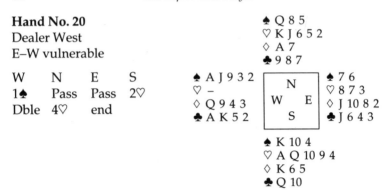

♠ Q 8 5
♡ K J 6 5 2
◇ A 7
♣ 9 8 7

W	N	E	S
1♠	Pass	Pass	2♡
Dble	4♡	end	

♠ A J 9 3 2
♡ –
◇ Q 9 4 3
♣ A K 5 2

♠ 7 6
♡ 8 7 3
◇ J 10 8 2
♣ J 6 4 3

♠ K 10 4
♡ A Q 10 9 4
◇ K 6 5
♣ Q 10

West starts with three rounds of clubs, South ruffing the third. He can only afford to lose one spade trick. He draws trumps and cashes the ◇A and ◇K before ruffing a diamond in dummy. That leaves:

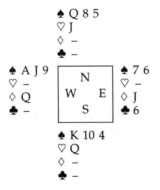

♠ Q 8 5
♡ J
◇ –
♣ –

♠ A J 9
♡ –
◇ Q
♣ –

♠ 7 6
♡ –
◇ J
♣ 6

♠ K 10 4
♡ Q
◇ –
♣ –

Even now, careful play is needed. The ♠Q would be fatal as West simply ducks it and waits for his two tricks. It must be a low spade to the ♠K (and, if South were in his hand at this point, he would have to *lead* the ♠K) and now West has no answer. If he ducks, South leads a low card towards the ♠Q, taking two tricks easily. So West must win but now must either concede a ruff and discard with the ◇Q or lead away from his ♠ J 9.

Having seen the idea, can you do this next example in match conditions in under two minutes? Start your stop-watch.

Problem 5
Hand No. 21
Dealer West
Both vulnerable

W	N	E	S
1NT	Pass	2◇	2♡
Pass	4♡	end	

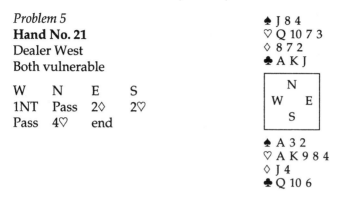

♠ J 8 4
♡ Q 10 7 3
◇ 8 7 2
♣ A K J

♠ A 3 2
♡ A K 9 8 4
◇ J 4
♣ Q 10 6

West leads the two top diamonds, East petering. On the ◇10, East produces the ◇Q and you ruff. On the ♡A, East drops the ♡J and, on the second round of trumps, he discards the ◇5. How do you continue?

Solution

We have 14 points and partner 11, leaving 15 unaccounted for and East has already shown up with the ◇Q and ♡J. That means West must have the remaining high cards, the king and queen of spades. Except in the most unlikely event of their being doubleton, we appear to be booked for two spade losers, unless he can be forced to lead the suit. Let us look at the three-card position, bearing in mind that we are on play at the moment and will have to lead the first round:

```
             J 8 4
          ┌─────────┐
          │    N    │
  K Q 10  │ W     E │  x x x
          │    S    │
          └─────────┘
             A 3 2
```

Leading the suit from dummy is hopeless: if we duck, West's ten (or nine) wins and his king and queen are solid against the ace. Playing the ace first is no good either – West plays low and takes his two honours. But try leading a low card towards the jack (effectively forgetting about the ace for the moment and leading from weakness through strength to strength). Now West is in trouble. He must win and play away from his other honour, allowing the jack to score.

The deal:

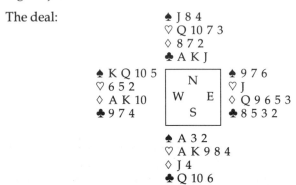

```
              ♠ J 8 4
              ♡ Q 10 7 3
              ◊ 8 7 2
              ♣ A K J
♠ K Q 10 5                    ♠ 9 7 6
♡ 6 5 2          N            ♡ J
◊ A K 10      W     E         ◊ Q 9 6 5 3
♣ 9 7 4          S            ♣ 8 5 3 2
              ♠ A 3 2
              ♡ A K 9 8 4
              ◊ J 4
              ♣ Q 10 6
```

To set the scene, we must draw trumps and eliminate the clubs, ending in hand. We then lead the ♠2 in this position:

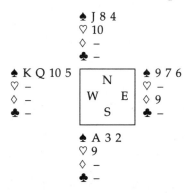

```
              ♠ J 8 4
              ♡ 10
              ◊ –
              ♣ –
♠ K Q 10 5                    ♠ 9 7 6
♡ –              N            ♡ –
◊ –           W     E         ◊ 9
♣ –              S            ♣ –
              ♠ A 3 2
              ♡ 9
              ◊ –
              ♣ –
```

West must win and continue the suit to our advantage. Note that it would not help him if he still had a minor-suit card in his hand. That would simply give him the option of giving us a ruff and discard instead!

In the earlier books, we learnt that ruffing can often give extra tricks, provided that the hand ruffing was, or would become, shorter in trumps than its partner. However, we also saw that opponents were not exempt from ruffing or overruffing either and, for that reason, ruffs often have to be very carefully timed. Let us look at this example:

Hand No. 22
Dealer South
N–S vulnerable

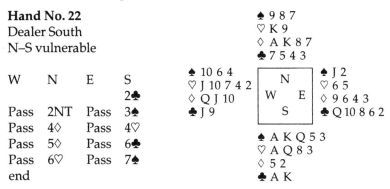

		♠ 9 8 7
		♡ K 9
		◊ A K 8 7
		♣ 7 5 4 3

♠ 10 6 4
♡ J 10 7 4 2
◊ Q J 10
♣ J 9

♠ J 2
♡ 6 5
◊ 9 6 4 3
♣ Q 10 8 6 2

♠ A K Q 5 3
♡ A Q 8 3
◊ 5 2
♣ A K

W	N	E	S
			2♣
Pass	2NT	Pass	3♠
Pass	4◊	Pass	4♡
Pass	5◊	Pass	6♣
Pass	6♡	Pass	7♠
end			

After South's 3♠ bid, a string of cue-bids followed, North showing his three big honours.

West leads the ◊Q and South sees the need for a 3–2 trump split. On that assumption, there are five tricks in spades, three in hearts and two each in the minors, giving twelve on top. The thirteenth must come from a heart ruff in dummy. This must be taken before all the trumps are drawn, otherwise there will be no trumps left there for the ruff. However, with only the one ruff required, he can afford to take two rounds of trumps. He therefore wins the first diamond, cashes the ace and king of trumps, the king and ace of hearts, and takes the ruff immediately. Note that there is no hurry to cash the ♡Q; it would be fatal to do so. She can wait until *after* trumps are drawn. After the ruff, South returns to hand with a club, draws the remaining trump and claims the rest.

This hand illustrates two important guides, first the need to draw as many trumps as possible while leaving just enough available for necessary ruffs; second, in the context of the suit to be ruffed, take the ruffs as early as possible to reduce the chance of winners being ruffed. Having seen the idea, try this next example under match conditions, aiming to get under one minute. Start your stop-watch.

Hand No. 23
Dealer North
Neither vulnerable

♠ J 6 2
♡ 10 4
◊ A 9 6 5 4
♣ 6 3 2

W	N	E	S
	Pass	Pass	1♣
1♠	Pass	Pass	2♡
Dble	3◊	Pass	4♣
Pass	5♣	end	

```
        N
    W       E
        S
```

♠ 9 8
♡ A K 8 3
◊ J
♣ A K Q 7 5 4

Let us first consider the bidding. South has reversed *on his own*, showing a stronger hand than a reverse following a bid from partner (which would promise 6 or more points). However, with all his points bar one in top cards in his two bid suits, he is entitled to value his hand up considerably. In practice, he will be unlucky not to make eight tricks on his own. Looking from North's viewpoint, for a hand which has passed twice, he is enormous in support of clubs for several reasons: the three trumps, the doubleton heart and the fact that his honour is an *ace*, which will only be wasted if South turns out to be void. For that reason, he shows his diamond feature with 3◊. With West having doubled for take-out, offering spades and diamonds, there is little point in bidding diamonds as a suit. South, who preferred to bid hearts instead of doubling 1♠ for take-out, offering *both* red suits as alternatives, is unlikely to be interested. The message is that, if South can stop spades (or show a half-stop with 3♠), the hand will be played in 3NT. When South cannot stop spades, North tries for game in clubs.

West leads the three top spades and you ruff the third round. How do you continue?

Barring an unlucky 4–0 club split (not impossible on the bidding), there are nine tricks on top and the other two must come from heart ruffs in dummy. With two needed, we can only afford to draw one round of trumps. After that, we must hope that the heart ruffs can be taken without disruption.

The deal:

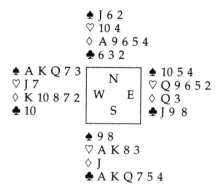

The three spades are followed by the ♣A, ♡A, ♡K, heart ruff, ◊A, diamond ruff to return to hand, heart ruff, diamond ruff and the other two high trumps to draw East's remaining two trumps. South's last card is a trump.

Where ruffs in dummy will not produce enough extra tricks, it may be possible to establish the long suit and we are now going to turn to more advanced work on this subject. In *The Expert Beginner*, we looked at large numbers of examples of how many tricks can be won and lost. However, to keep things simple there, I allowed unlimited trumps and access to both hands. We must now face reality and learn how to handle situations in which there may be problems in these areas. This was the sort of position we looked at:

A K x x x x

x x

Given no restrictions, we could play off the ace and king, ruff the third round, and return to dummy in a side suit to cash the remainder. Given a 3–2 split, that would mean five tricks without loss. But suppose I specified that:

1 There were no spare trumps available in the South hand. Now a trick would have to be lost, and that would mean five tricks

won for one lost. If I further specified that dummy had no outside entries, we could still arrange five tricks for one lost by ducking the first round.

2 There are spare trumps in the South hand but the suit breaks 4–1 and there is only one side entry to dummy. Now we could play the ace and king, ruff a third round, return to the entry and ruff the fourth round to set up the suit. But that would be no good as there would be no further entry to cash the winners. We cannot take five tricks for none lost in these circumstances but we can take four tricks for one lost if we duck the first round. Now provided that the side entry is not attacked prematurely, we can then play off the ace and king, ruff a fourth round and *then* use the side entry to cash the two established long cards.

3 There are no spare trumps in the South hand, the suit breaks 4–1 and there is only one entry to dummy. Now we can only take four tricks for two lost. We again duck the first round, play the ace, king and a fourth round, losing, and then use our side entry to reach the established cards.

We could go through this exercise with countless suit combinations and conditions, and many contracts depend on this type of reasoning. But having seen the idea, I should like you to try these three examples in match conditions aiming for well under ninety seconds each to complete the test in about four minutes.

Problem 6
Hand No. 24
Dealer East
Both vulnerable

♠ 7
♡ 9 6 4
◇ A Q 9 6 5 4
♣ 8 7 5

W	N	E	S
		Pass	2♣
Pass	2◇	Pass	3♠
Pass	4◇	Pass	4♡
Pass	4♠	Pass	5♣
Pass	5◇	Pass	6♠
end			

♠ A K Q J 10 4
♡ A Q
◇ 7 2
♣ A Q 6

After the game-forcing opening and negative response, South's 3♠

bid showed a solid suit and set it as trumps. North was now
expected to cue-bid and showed his ◊A. After South's 4♡, North
tried to sign off, having no further first or second-round controls
to show. South now optimistically made another try and North
could now show his third-round diamond control, at no cost,
below the level of 5♠. South, hoping for a heart or club lead, was
clearly carried away.

West leads the ♠3. It takes four rounds to draw the trumps,
West discarding the ♣3 and ♡5. How do you continue?

Problem 7
Hand No. 25
Dealer East
E–W vulnerable

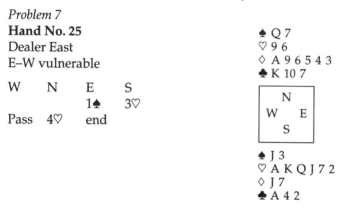

W	N	E	S
		1♠	3♡
Pass	4♡	end	

♠ Q 7
♡ 9 6
◊ A 9 6 5 4 3
♣ K 10 7

♠ J 3
♡ A K Q J 7 2
◊ J 7
♣ A 4 2

West leads the ♠5 and East cashes the ♠A and ♠K before switching to the ♣Q. How do you plan the play?

Problem 8
Hand No. 26
Dealer West
Both vulnerable

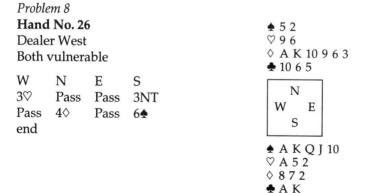

W	N	E	S
3♡	Pass	Pass	3NT
Pass	4◊	Pass	6♠
end			

♠ 5 2
♡ 9 6
◊ A K 10 9 6 3
♣ 10 6 5

♠ A K Q J 10
♡ A 5 2
◊ 8 7 2
♣ A K

South should, of course, have supported the diamonds but was carried away by those honours! As it was, he offered final contracts of 6♠ or 6NT.

West leads the ♡K, East following with the ♡3. On the second round of trumps, West discards the ♡4. How do you play, given that, on the first round of diamonds, West will play the ◊J?

Solutions

Problem 6

There are six top spade tricks and the contract will be made if all three side-suit finesses work. A better chance, however, lies in the possibility of a 3–2 diamond split. Now only the diamond finesse is needed.

The deal:

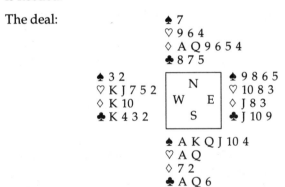

```
                        ♠ 7
                        ♡ 9 6 4
                        ◊ A Q 9 6 5 4
                        ♣ 8 7 5
        ♠ 3 2                           ♠ 9 8 6 5
        ♡ K J 7 5 2        N            ♡ 10 8 3
        ◊ K 10         W      E         ◊ J 8 3
        ♣ K 4 3 2          S            ♣ J 10 9
                        ♠ A K Q J 10 4
                        ♡ A Q
                        ◊ 7 2
                        ♣ A Q 6
```

With no entry to dummy, we must duck a diamond after trumps have been drawn (even if West puts on the king). Assume East wins and returns a club or heart. We win (refusing the finesse), take the diamond finesse and hope to run the rest of the suit; we shall have a trick to burn at the end.

Problem 7

This is good defence by East; he is trying to attack dummy's entry to the long diamonds. We have six trump tricks, two clubs and the ◊A on top and need to establish a long diamond for our tenth trick. Obviously the suit will have to break 3–2 but, even then, there could be entry problems. First, the ♣K must be kept intact as long as possible so we must win this trick with the ♣A and draw

trumps. At least three rounds will be needed – and did you specifically state what you intended to discard from dummy after the
second round? Let us look at the club position in detail:

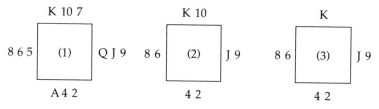

One of the defenders will have the thirteenth club but, as only
three rounds of the suit will be played, that is irrelevant. We
started with the three-card position in (1). After one round, we are
reduced to the two-card position in (2). In that position, we are safe
if East leads the suit (from strength) but not if West leads it (from
weakness). That will need to be taken into account when considering the diamonds in a moment. If we discard the ♣10 on a high
trump, we will have transposed to position (3) and now the ♣K
can be attacked by *either* defender. As we need to keep that card for
entry purposes, we must hold position (2) and therefore discard a
diamond on the third (and, if necessary, fourth) round of trumps.

We must now set up a long diamond and, with the shortage of
entries, must be able to play three rounds, before the ♣K is used.
We must therefore duck the first round and win the second to be
in dummy to ruff the suit high in the third. However, it is not only
that we duck the first round, it is the *way* we duck it that matters.
Let us look at a possible diamond position:

```
              A 9 6
            ┌───────┐
            │   N   │
     10 x   │ W   E │  K Q x
            │   S   │
            └───────┘
              J 7
```

We have agreed above that the first round must be lost to East, so
that the club entry cannot be attacked. If West has one of the big
honours and plays it on the first round, there is nothing we can do.
But if the position is as above, then our play is critical. If we play

the ◊7, West can put in the ◊10 and we are sunk, unable to duck without giving West the lead. We must play the ◊J, forcing East to win. Nothing can now prevent our setting up the suit and returning to the ♣K to cash a long winner, on which we discard our losing club.

The deal:

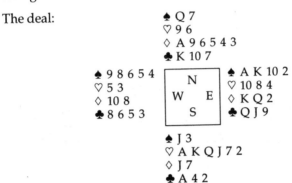

♠ Q 7
♡ 9 6
◊ A 9 6 5 4 3
♣ K 10 7

♠ 9 8 6 5 4
♡ 5 3
◊ 10 8
♣ 8 6 5 3

N
W E
S

♠ A K 10 2
♡ 10 8 4
◊ K Q 2
♣ Q J 9

♠ J 3
♡ A K Q J 7 2
◊ J 7
♣ A 4 2

Problem 8

We have five spades, two diamonds, the heart and two clubs, to total ten tricks on top so far, and we will have to establish two long diamonds. Obviously, we must win the first trick; the second round is going to be ruffed. There is no possibility of a heart ruff in dummy – East is bound to overruff. Once we have drawn five rounds of trumps (discarding one club, one heart and one diamond) we must see to it that, if a diamond trick is lost, it will be to East, who will be unable to lead back a heart for the setting trick. On the first diamond, with West playing the ◊J, we have to cater for a number of possible positions:

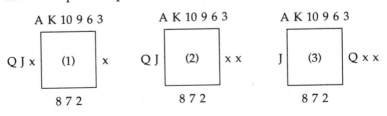

A K 10 9 6 3				A K 10 9 6 3		
J x	(4)	Q x	Q J x x	(5)	–
8 7 2				8 7 2		

In (2) and (4), we can cash out for an overtrick. However, winning the first round with the ace and then cashing the king risks defeat in (1), (3) and (5). In (5), the position will be marked when East shows out and we can return to hand twice in clubs to take two finesses against West. Where East follows to the first round, we could be in (1), (2), (3) or (4), requiring different handling. As so often applies, the rule of leading from weakness through strength to strength, i.e. commit ourselves as late as possible, is relevant. We return to hand in clubs and lead a diamond. Now:

1 If West plays the queen, we have (2) and cash out for an overtrick.
2 If West plays low, we play the ten, covering ourselves against (1) and merely foregoing the overtrick in (4).
3 If West shows out, we duck in dummy, allowing East to win but preserving our entry for the long cards.

The deal:

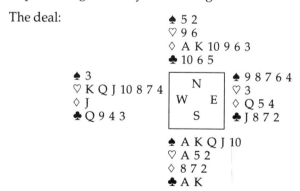

```
              ♠ 5 2
              ♡ 9 6
              ◊ A K 10 9 6 3
              ♣ 10 6 5
♠ 3                          ♠ 9 8 7 6 4
♡ K Q J 10 8 7 4    N        ♡ 3
◊ J              W     E      ◊ Q 5 4
♣ Q 9 4 3           S        ♣ J 8 7 2
              ♠ A K Q J 10
              ♡ A 5 2
              ◊ 8 7 2
              ♣ A K
```

We are going to conclude with a five-question miscellaneous test covering the work of this chapter. You should be aiming to do each example in just over a minute to complete the test in under six minutes. Start your stop-watch.

Problem 9
Hand No. 27
Dealer West
E–W vulnerable

W	N	E	S
3◊	Pass	Pass	3♡
Pass	4♡	end	

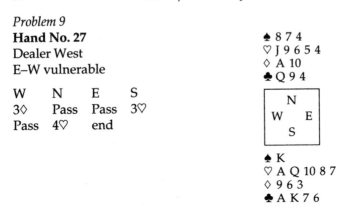

♠ 8 7 4
♡ J 9 6 5 4
◊ A 10
♣ Q 9 4

♠ K
♡ A Q 10 8 7
◊ 9 6 3
♣ A K 7 6

West leads the ◊K and East ruffs dummy's ◊A. He then cashes the ♠A and continues with the ♠J. How do you plan the play?

Problem 10
Hand No. 28
Dealer North
N–S vulnerable

W	N	E	S
	1♡	Pass	1♠
Pass	2NT	Pass	3♣
Pass	3♠	Pass	4NT
Pass	5♠	Pass	5NT
Pass	6♡	Pass	7♠
end			

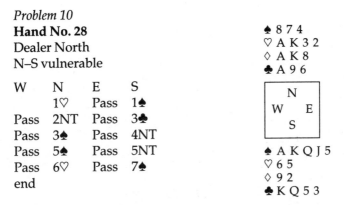

♠ 8 7 4
♡ A K 3 2
◊ A K 8
♣ A 9 6

♠ A K Q J 5
♡ 6 5
◊ 9 2
♣ K Q 5 3

West leads the ♡Q. If you start to draw trumps, both defenders will follow twice, the ♠10 remaining at large. On that assumption, how do you plan the play?

Problem 11
Hand No. 29
Dealer West
E–W vulnerable

W	N	E	S
4♡	Pass	Pass	5♢
end			

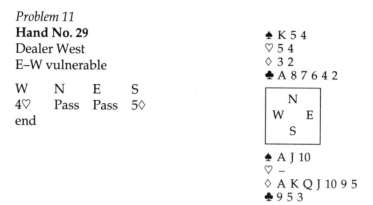

♠ K 5 4
♡ 5 4
♢ 3 2
♣ A 8 7 6 4 2

♠ A J 10
♡ –
♢ A K Q J 10 9 5
♣ 9 5 3

West leads the ♡A. You ruff and draw trumps in two rounds. When you lead a club, West discards the ♡8. How do you continue?

Problem 12
Hand No. 30
Dealer South
E–W vulnerable

W	N	E	S
			1♠
Pass	2♢	Pass	3♣
Pass	3♠	Pass	4♣
Pass	4♢	Pass	4♡
Pass	4NT	Pass	5♣
Pass	5♢	Pass	6♠
end			

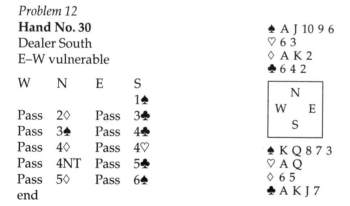

♠ A J 10 9 6
♡ 6 3
♢ A K 2
♣ 6 4 2

♠ K Q 8 7 3
♡ A Q
♢ 6 5
♣ A K J 7

After North agreed spades, cue-bidding started and now North's 4NT showed the ace of trumps.

West leads the ♢J. You win in dummy and both defenders follow to the first round of trumps. How do you continue?

Problem 13
Hand No. 31
Dealer West
Neither vulnerable

♠ Q 8 7
♡ K Q 10 8
◊ A 8 7 4 3
♣ 6

W	N	E	S
Pass	1◊	Pass	1♡
Pass	2♡	Pass	2♠
Pass	4♡	Pass	5♣
Pass	5◊	Pass	6♡
end			

```
      N
  W       E
      S
```

♠ A 5 2
♡ A J 6 3
◊ K 6 5
♣ A J 7

West leads the ♣10 to East's ♣Q. How do you plan the play?

Solutions

Problem 9
With the diamond ruff and ♠A already lost, it is a question of whether we can ensure the contract, irrespective of the position of the ♡K. There are two trumps left outstanding. In the unlikely event of West having both (i.e. East started with twelve black cards), there is nothing to be done as the heart and another diamond must be lost. But, if West has a singleton ♡K, we can win by playing for the drop, while, if East has both remaining hearts, we must cross to the ♣Q and take the finesse. Which is it to be?

In situations like this, it will pay to ask ourselves whether there is any possibility of recovery if we guess wrongly. Let us try both ways. If we take the finesse and West has the ♡K, he will cash another diamond for four tricks and immediate defeat. However, if we play for the drop and West shows out, all is not lost.

The deal:

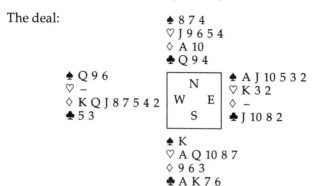

On ruffing the second spade, we cash the ♡A, cross to the ♣Q and ruff dummy's last spade to eliminate the suit. Now the ♣A and ♣K are followed by a club ruff, eliminating that suit too, leaving this position:

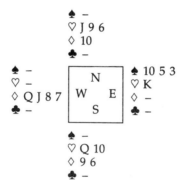

Now we exit with a trump and East, left with nothing but spades (a club would not help him anyway) must lead one, allowing us to ruff in hand and discard the ◊10 to save the diamond loser.

Problem 10
With five trumps, three clubs, and the two red ace-kings, there are twelve tricks on top. The thirteenth can only come from clubs, implying the need for a 3–3 break or the J 10 coming down as doubleton. There is also the chance that, if the clubs are 4–2, the hand with the doubleton also has a doubleton trump. In that case, we can take a ruff in dummy before the last trump is drawn.

We therefore take only two rounds of trumps and follow with three rounds of clubs. If they do break 3–3, nothing has been lost. But we can ruff our loser in dummy in this layout:

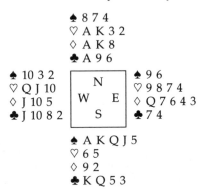

```
                    ♠ 8 7 4
                    ♡ A K 3 2
                    ◇ A K 8
                    ♣ A 9 6
   ♠ 10 3 2      ┌─────────┐    ♠ 9 6
   ♡ Q J 10      │    N    │    ♡ 9 8 7 4
   ◇ J 10 5      │ W     E │    ◇ Q 7 6 4 3
   ♣ J 10 8 2    │    S    │    ♣ 7 4
                 └─────────┘
                    ♠ A K Q J 5
                    ♡ 6 5
                    ◇ 9 2
                    ♣ K Q 5 3
```

We return to hand with a red suit, ruffed high, draw the remaining trump and claim the rest.

Problem 11
The problem is to make the contract without having to guess the position of the ♠Q. The clubs have broken badly but we can still set up the suit if we time the play correctly and keep the ♠K intact. We have to play four rounds without touching that king, so we must duck the first two rounds, and win the third with the ♣A so that we are in dummy for the fourth when South has run out. Having ruffed the suit high, we then return to the ♠K to cash a long card, discarding a potential spade loser from our hand.

The deal:

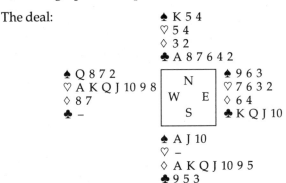

```
                    ♠ K 5 4
                    ♡ 5 4
                    ◇ 3 2
                    ♣ A 8 7 6 4 2
   ♠ Q 8 7 2         ┌─────────┐    ♠ 9 6 3
   ♡ A K Q J 10 9 8  │    N    │    ♡ 7 6 3 2
   ◇ 8 7             │ W     E │    ◇ 6 4
   ♣ –               │    S    │    ♣ K Q J 10
                     └─────────┘
                    ♠ A J 10
                    ♡ –
                    ◇ A K Q J 10 9 5
                    ♣ 9 5 3
```

Note that East cannot attack the spade entry without saving us the guess in that suit. Even if South had only A J 9 rather than A J 10, we would still be allowed two bites at the cherry if East attacked the suit, losing only if West had *both* the ten and queen, when we never had a chance anyway.

Problem 12

With a diamond ruff, we have six trump tricks, two top diamonds, two top clubs and the ♡A to total eleven so far. There are plenty of chances for the twelfth – the club finesse, the heart finesse, the club break or the ♣Q dropping early. As far as the hearts are concerned, there is little to discuss – it's the finesse or nothing. But the club position is worth looking at in great detail and we shall take the opportunity to add to our knowledge of suit combinations.

Considered in isolation, we could cash one top club (to cover a singleton queen with West) and then try the finesse. If that fails, we still have the chance of the 3–3 break or the heart finesse. Better, however, is to cash both top clubs (covering a singleton or doubleton queen with West) and then try a low club towards the jack. This only fails if West has queen to four.

However, in the context of the whole hand, we have the chance of an endplay against West, bearing in mind that he cannot profitably attack hearts from his side. The contract is, in fact, cold against any distribution. We play as follows, determined to lose a trick to West while the tenaces in clubs and hearts are kept intact. Suppose this is the layout, adverse on all counts:

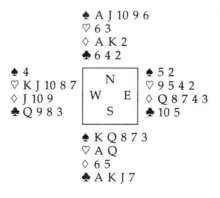

```
              ♠ A J 10 9 6
              ♡ 6 3
              ◊ A K 2
              ♣ 6 4 2
♠ 4                        ♠ 5 2
♡ K J 10 8 7    N          ♡ 9 5 4 2
◊ J 10 9     W     E       ◊ Q 8 7 4 3
♣ Q 9 8 3       S          ♣ 10 5
              ♠ K Q 8 7 3
              ♡ A Q
              ◊ 6 5
              ♣ A K J 7
```

On winning the opening diamond, we draw one round of trumps, cash the other top diamond and ruff the last diamond (high, to keep low trumps in hand) to eliminate the suit. Now we return to dummy in trumps and lead a low club. Now, if East fails to produce a card higher than the ♣7, we put in that card and lose the trick to West. With both club and heart tenaces intact, he is endplayed and must give a trick away in one of those suits or (if he had another diamond) a ruff and discard. So East must play the ♣8, ♣9 or ♣10. We win in hand with the ♣A, cross to dummy in trumps and lead another low club in this position:

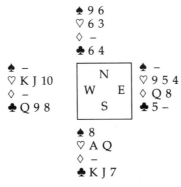

```
                    ♠ 9 6
                    ♡ 6 3
                    ◇ –
                    ♣ 6 4
      ♠ –                        ♠ –
      ♡ K J 10      N            ♡ 9 5 4
      ◇ –        W     E         ◇ Q 8
      ♣ Q 9 8       S            ♣ 5 –
                    ♠ 8
                    ♡ A Q
                    ◇ –
                    ♣ K J 7
```

Now, if East plays a card below the ♣7, we put in that card. West must win and is endplayed. So East again must play a higher card. This time, we cover with the ♣J. West wins with the ♣Q. Now:

1   If he has no more clubs, he is endplayed.
2   If he has one more club, the suit has broken 3–3.
3   If he has both remaining clubs, they will be the ♣10, ♣9 or ♣8 plus a low one. He is forced to play the suit round to our K 7.

This is a rather more advanced endplay position and I urge you to put the cards out in any combination you wish and satisfy yourself that this line (of leading clubs twice from dummy and arranging to lose a trick to West) always succeeds and therefore that the heart finesse is never needed.

Problem 13
We must first count our tricks carefully and then consider the

problem arising regarding the order of play. Assuming reasonable breaks, we have four top trump tricks, the two black aces and two club ruffs in dummy to total eight so far, which implies the need for four diamond tricks. These will materialize on a 3–2 split. At least three rounds will be needed to draw trumps and therefore the club ruffs will need to be taken *before* trumps are drawn. The long diamonds can only be cashed *after* trumps are drawn. So it looks as though the order of play should be: club ruffs, draw trumps, cash the diamonds.

So far so good, but the club ruffs will reduce dummy to two trumps and the drawing of trumps will reduce it to none. This means that the only entry available to cash the long diamonds will be the ◇A itself. Let us look at the three-card diamond position in that light:

A 8 7

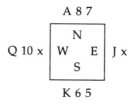

Q 10 x   W   E   J x

K 6 5

One trick will have to be lost but North–South can dictate which round. Playing the two tops and then losing the trick is out of the question as the entry will be removed too early. We must lose the trick on the first or second round – does it matter which? In the context of the diamond suit on its own, probably not; but, in the context of the whole hand, it does in that the ◇K may be needed as an entry to hand to draw trumps. Suppose this is the deal:

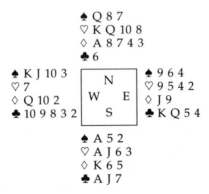

```
                    ♠ Q 8 7
                    ♡ K Q 10 8
                    ◇ A 8 7 4 3
                    ♣ 6
 ♠ K J 10 3                        ♠ 9 6 4
 ♡ 7              ┌─────────┐      ♡ 9 5 4 2
 ◇ Q 10 2        │    N    │      ◇ J 9
 ♣ 10 9 8 3 2    │ W     E │      ♣ K Q 5 4
                  │    S    │
                  └─────────┘
                    ♠ A 5 2
                    ♡ A J 6 3
                    ◇ K 6 5
                    ♣ A J 7
```

We win the first club and ruff a club. Now the best play is to give up the diamond at once. East wins and switches to a spade. We rise with the ♠A and ruff our last club. We cash the two trumps in dummy, cross back to the ◇K and draw two more trumps, discarding spades, before cashing the rest of the diamonds.

Try playing it again, intending to lose the second round of diamonds: ♣A, club ruff, ◇K, club ruff, two top trumps but then what? If we lose a diamond now to West, he will return a third round for East to ruff. If we cross back to the ♠A to draw the other trumps and then duck a diamond, they will be able to cash the ♠K and more clubs – several off now.

These last five hands have been tough ones and, as with the rest of this book, I strongly urge you play and replay them over and over again until they become second nature and – more important – you fully understand all the possible pitfalls. Do not begrudge the time; a little invested now will save you a great deal later on, particularly as we are now going to turn to defence, where we have to look at such positions from the other point of view.

Defence against No-trump Contracts

In this chapter, we are going to look at another measure to prevent declarer enjoying a long suit in dummy and add to our knowledge of defensive signalling.

In the trump declarer chapter just now, we discussed, at some length, the importance of keeping outside entries intact until needed. It is the defenders' duty to remove them as soon as possible. Let us look at an obvious example.

Hand No. 32
Dealer South
Neither vulnerable

W	N	E	S
			1NT
Pass	3NT	end	

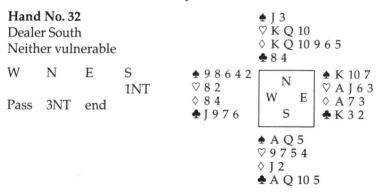

♠ J 3
♡ K Q 10
♢ K Q 10 9 6 5
♣ 8 4

♠ 9 8 6 4 2   ♠ K 10 7
♡ 8 2   ♡ A J 6 3
♢ 8 4   ♢ A 7 3
♣ J 9 7 6   ♣ K 3 2

♠ A Q 5
♡ 9 7 5 4
♢ J 2
♣ A Q 10 5

Let us look first at that diamond suit. When South leads the ♢J, West will peter (i.e. play the ♢8) to show an even number and East will hold up to the second round to exhaust South. Now a side-suit entry will be needed to reach the long diamonds, and that can only be in hearts. Unfortunately for declarer, West, on lead, realizes that with his total lack of entries there is little hope of establishing either of his black suits and aims to find his partner's long suit.

There is nothing to choose between the reds but, on the bidding, with no attempt by North–South to look for game in a major, it is usually better to lead a major suit. Therefore West starts with the ♡8 and, perhaps more by luck than judgment, has hit on the only lead to beat the contract.

If South tries the ♡10 on trick one, East will win with the ♡J and can now kill the entry by either cashing the ace and leading a third round or leading a low card, keeping the ace over dummy's remaining honour. If South plays an honour from dummy at trick one, East must duck. If he wins, he cannot play a second round from his side without giving a free finesse, after which South can keep an entry to dummy.

That is a simple example. Sometimes spectacular sacrifices have to be made to kill an entry. Let us look at this:

Hand No. 33
Dealer East
N–S vulnerable

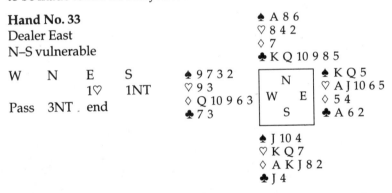

W	N	E	S
		1♡	1NT
Pass	3NT	end	

West dutifully leads his partner's suit, the ♡9, and East sees that, with at least 15 points and a double heart stop indicated in the South hand, the contract will be made easily if that club suit comes in. However, as long as South does not have all four outstanding clubs, he (East) will be able to hold up his ace until South is exhausted. Nevertheless, the ♣A is in the dummy as an entry and that must be removed from the scene immediately at all costs. Consequently, East wins the first heart and switches to the ♠K, West discouraging to deny possession of the jack. South, of course, does not want to play his ace, so he allows the king to hold and the jack becomes a second stopper in this two-card position:

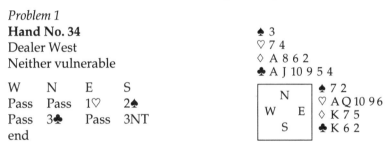

We see that it will cost a trick for East to lead a second round but, as the ♠A must be removed, East sacrifices that trick and leads the ♠Q. South now gains nothing by ducking although he might try it in case East started with ♠ K Q doubleton. East will then play a third round and the clubs are now dead. South will be allowed one trick in that suit but no more, although he can make life difficult for East by playing the second round from dummy and East has to judge whether his partner's ♣7 was a singleton or doubleton.

Having seen the idea, can you do this next example in match conditions in under one minute? Start your stop-watch.

Problem 1

Hand No. 34
Dealer West
Neither vulnerable

♠ 3
♡ 7 4
◇ A 8 6 2
♣ A J 10 9 5 4

W	N	E	S
Pass	Pass	1♡	2♠
Pass	3♣	Pass	3NT
end			

♠ 7 2
♡ A Q 10 9 6
◇ K 7 5
♣ K 6 2

South has made a jump overcall and, with his 3NT bid, is likely to have about 15 points. West leads the ♡8 and dummy plays low. How do you defend?

Solution

The lead is almost certainly singleton or top of a doubleton – South surely has the king and jack to form a double stop. Now let us consider the club position. If South has three or more cards in the suit, it can be brought in without an outside entry unless partner has a singleton queen. (Although, even then, South could bring it in by ducking twice.) However, with announced length in spades and probably four hearts, it is likely that South has only a doubleton club, in which case we are in a position to duck the first round and necessitate the use of the ◊A as entry.

Our aim, therefore, must be to remove that ace from the dummy prematurely. If partner has the ◊Q, the lead of the ◊K will do the trick without cost. Even if South has her, it will probably be worth giving up a trick. South is likely to be 5422 in this type of layout:

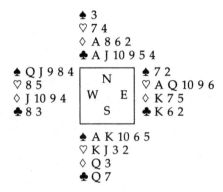

```
                ♠ 3
                ♡ 7 4
                ◊ A 8 6 2
                ♣ A J 10 9 5 4
 ♠ Q J 9 8 4    ┌─────────┐    ♠ 7 2
 ♡ 8 5          │    N    │    ♡ A Q 10 9 6
 ◊ J 10 9 4     │ W     E │    ◊ K 7 5
 ♣ 8 3          │    S    │    ♣ K 6 2
                └─────────┘
                ♠ A K 10 6 5
                ♡ K J 3 2
                ◊ Q 3
                ♣ Q 7
```

We win the first heart and switch to the ◊K. If South ducks, we simply continue the suit and the communication in it is cut. If the position in the entry suit looks like this:

```
            A x x
          ┌─────────┐
          │    N    │
  x x x   │ W     E │  K x x
          │    S    │
          └─────────┘
            Q x x
```

South can save himself by ducking the king and taking the second round with the queen, keeping the ace in dummy. Nevertheless, the defence may still be worthwhile because it gains a free trick without losing the lead – that could make all the difference. Let us alter that last hand slightly:

Hand No. 35
Dealer West
Neither vulnerable

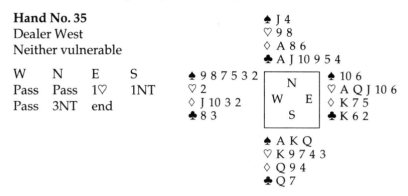

♠ J 4
♡ 9 8
◇ A 8 6
♣ A J 10 9 5 4

W	N	E	S
Pass	Pass	1♡	1NT
Pass	3NT	end	

♠ 9 8 7 5 3 2
♡ 2
◇ J 10 3 2
♣ 8 3

♠ 10 6
♡ A Q J 10 6
◇ K 7 5
♣ K 6 2

♠ A K Q
♡ K 9 7 4 3
◇ Q 9 4
♣ Q 7

West leads the ♡2 – obviously a singleton – so South has a double stop. If East wins and persists with the suit, he can make three heart tricks and the ♣K but no more. More urgent is to stop the club suit by removing the ◇A from the scene immediately. Unfortunately, considering the diamond suit in isolation, the play of the ◇K, known as the *Merrimac coup*, will not be effective. South simply ducks, intending to take the next round in hand with the ◇Q. In the context of the whole hand, however, it is still worth doing. If South takes the ◇K, the clubs are dead and he will be held to two tricks in each minor, three spades and one heart for eight tricks in total. (The defenders can set up a diamond trick, three hearts and the ♣K.) If South refuses the ◇K, then East reverts to hearts, ensuring three heart tricks, the stolen diamond and the ♣K to total five.

When there is a long suit in dummy which the defenders can stop once, it is often crucial for them to take their trick at the correct time – not too early, so that South is exhausted, but not too late so that he does not take more tricks than those to which he is entitled. We saw that the hand lacking the stop should signal his distribution (odd or even) to help his partner's timing. We are now going to turn to more work on suit preference which can be very important in respect of defenders' communications. This was the type of hand I showed in *Signal Success in Bridge* (Gollancz, 1989, reissued as a paperback in 1993) in which mishaps continually occur.

Hand No. 36
Dealer South
E–W vulnerable

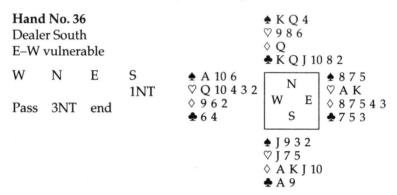

```
♠ K Q 4
♡ 9 8 6
◇ Q
♣ K Q J 10 8 2
```

W	N	E	S
			1NT
Pass	3NT	end	

```
♠ A 10 6              N          ♠ 8 7 5
♡ Q 10 4 3 2                     ♡ A K
◇ 9 6 2         W        E       ◇ 8 7 5 4 3
♣ 6 4                N           ♣ 7 5 3

              ♠ J 9 3 2
              ♡ J 7 5
              ◇ A K J 10
              ♣ A 9
```

West leads the ♡3 and East wins with the ace and then cashes the king. This is deliberately in the 'wrong' order to alert his partner that the two honours are doubleton. So East is still on play but how is he to continue? Looking at all four hands, it is easy to see that a spade switch leads to two off but, for all East knows, the hand could just easily have been:

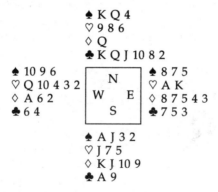

```
                ♠ K Q 4
                ♡ 9 8 6
                ◇ Q
                ♣ K Q J 10 8 2
♠ 10 9 6              N          ♠ 8 7 5
♡ Q 10 4 3 2                     ♡ A K
◇ A 6 2        W        E        ◇ 8 7 5 4 3
♣ 6 4                S           ♣ 7 5 3
                ♠ A J 3 2
                ♡ J 7 5
                ◇ K J 10 9
                ♣ A 9
```

and now East has to switch to a diamond or allow South to make an overtrick! How does he know? West has the opportunity to give suit preference with his second heart. In the first diagram, he will play the ♡10, a high card suggesting the higher-ranking of the two candidate suits. In the second, he will play the ♡2, a low card suggesting the lower-ranking suit, diamonds. Note that, with the long suit on the table, clubs are not in the reckoning. South will surely have to play the suit himself as the source of most of his tricks. Therefore, if West has the ♣A, it is most unlikely to run away. However, later on in the book I explain that, where all three non-heart suits are possible, a low card would ask for a club, a middle card for a diamond and a high card for a spade – so it is possible to cover that position.

Having seen the idea, try this next example in match conditions. You should be able to break the minute barrier. Start your stop-watch.

Problem 2
Hand No. 37
Dealer South
Both vulnerable

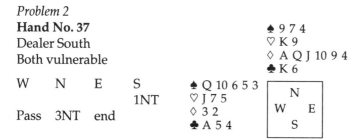

W	N	E	S
			1NT
Pass	3NT	end	

♠ 9 7 4
♡ K 9
◇ A Q J 10 9 4
♣ K 6

♠ Q 10 6 5 3
♡ J 7 5
◇ 3 2
♣ A 5 4

You lead the ♠5 to the ♣4, partner's ♠A and South's ♠8. Partner returns the ♠2 and declarer tries the ♠J, losing to your ♠Q. How do you continue and would it make any difference if your hand were: ♠Q 10 6 5 3 ♡ A 7 5 ◇ 3 2 ♣ J 5 4?

Solution
It is clear that South will play on diamonds and, if he has the king, there will probably be little to discuss – at any rate, we shall be able to signal for the ♣A by discarding the ♣5, followed by the ♣4, while the diamonds are being run. The critical case arises when partner has the ◇K and has to reach our hand early in the play. The choice of our third spade sends the message. Diamonds are obviously out of the reckoning – we cannot have an entry in that suit – so it is clubs or hearts and we play the ♠3 to show the ♣A, or the ♠10 to show the ♡A.

The deal:

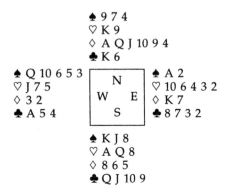

```
                    ♠ 9 7 4
                    ♡ K 9
                    ◇ A Q J 10 9 4
                    ♣ K 6
    ♠ Q 10 6 5 3  ┌─────────┐  ♠ A 2
    ♡ J 7 5       │    N    │  ♡ 10 6 4 3 2
    ◇ 3 2         │ W     E │  ◇ K 7
    ♣ A 5 4       │    S    │  ♣ 8 7 3 2
                  └─────────┘
                    ♠ K J 8
                    ♡ A Q 8
                    ◇ 8 6 5
                    ♣ Q J 10 9
```

We can extend this idea to situations where a defender, holding a trebleton in dummy's long suit, can choose the order of play to give a suit-preference message in addition to the count.

Hand No. 38
Dealer South
Both vulnerable

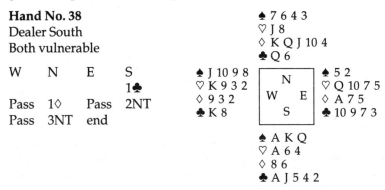

```
                              ♠ 7 6 4 3
                              ♡ J 8
                              ◇ K Q J 10 4
                              ♣ Q 6
  W    N    E    S
                 1♣          ♠ J 10 9 8  ┌─────────┐  ♠ 5 2
  Pass 1◇   Pass 2NT         ♡ K 9 3 2   │    N    │  ♡ Q 10 7 5
  Pass 3NT  end              ◇ 9 3 2     │ W     E │  ◇ A 7 5
                             ♣ K 8       │    S    │  ♣ 10 9 7 3
                                         └─────────┘
                              ♠ A K Q
                              ♡ A 6 4
                              ◇ 8 6
                              ♣ A J 5 4 2
```

West leads the ♠J, won by declarer's ♠Q. South starts on the diamonds and West plays the ◇2 on the first round to indicate an odd number, here almost certainly a trebleton. On the second round, East takes his ace and the spotlight turns on to West, who has a choice. Now the ♣Q will constitute a slow entry to the diamonds and, with South having bid the suit, clubs are not in the reckoning. West should tell his partner whether to continue spades (necessary if he started with ♠ A J 10 x x or ♠ K J 10 x x) or switch to hearts (necessary if the deal is as above). He follows the normal suit-preference principle of playing the ◇9 if he prefers the higher-ranking spades, the ◇3 if he prefers the lower-ranking hearts. Having seen the idea, can you do this next example in match conditions in under a minute? Start your stop-watch.

Problem 3
Hand No. 39
Dealer East
Both vulnerable

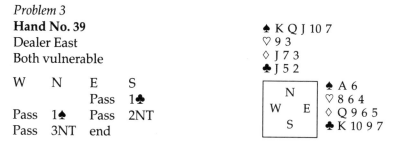

♠ K Q J 10 7
♡ 9 3
◇ J 7 3
♣ J 5 2

W	N	E	S
		Pass	1♣
Pass	1♠	Pass	2NT
Pass	3NT	end	

```
        N       ♠ A 6
   W        E   ♡ 8 6 4
        S       ◇ Q 9 6 5
                ♣ K 10 9 7
```

Partner leads the ♡J, won by declarer's ♡Q. South now follows with the ♠4 to partner's ♠8 and dummy's ♠10. If you win this trick, what do you lead next? If you refuse, another high spade is led and, when you win, West follows with the ♠9. Would it make any difference if West followed to the second round with the ♠2?

Solution
Here partner has tried to show an even number of spades, clearly four, leaving South with two, as is reasonable on the bidding. Therefore we must duck the first round to cut out the suit. South is likely to persist because, if he has ♣ A Q, the ♣J will be a possible slow entry to dummy if West has the ♣K. Also he might steal a second trick if the defenders err in holding up a second time. On the second round, we have to win, and now count is no longer relevant. The high spade asks for a continuation of hearts.

The deal:

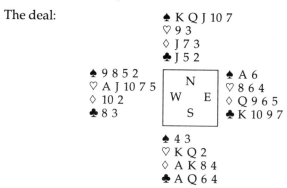

```
              ♠ K Q J 10 7
              ♡ 9 3
              ◇ J 7 3
              ♣ J 5 2
  ♠ 9 8 5 2                    ♠ A 6
  ♡ A J 10 7 5    N            ♡ 8 6 4
  ◇ 10 2       W     E         ◇ Q 9 6 5
  ♣ 8 3           S            ♣ K 10 9 7
              ♠ 4 3
              ♡ K Q 2
              ◇ A K 8 4
              ♣ A Q 6 4
```

Had West played a low spade second time, he would have indicated a diamond interest, South holding ♡ A K Q. So do we switch to a diamond now? No, no need! Before reading on, can you see why? The difference between this and Hand 38 is that, whereas there, South had a potential entry to the spades in the ♣Q, here he has no chance at all in either minor. There is therefore no need for desperation tactics and to lead a diamond would only help South. We *still* lead another heart but for a different reason. We are simply exiting passively rather than trying to build up tricks. If you got that right, you are doing extremely well. The point I was trying to illustrate is that defensive signalling is to be used for *information* only. Partner uses that information to plan his defence rather than respecting orders (positive or negative) like a machine.

Let us conclude this section with two more problems covering the new work. These should be relatively easy now, so see if you can do each in under half a minute to complete the test in under one minute. Start your stop-watch.

Problem 4
Hand No. 40
Dealer North
Neither vulnerable

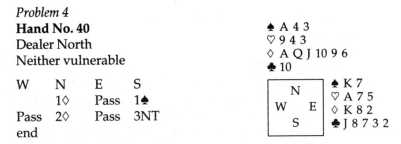

W	N	E	S
	1◊	Pass	1♠
Pass	2◊	Pass	3NT
end			

♠ A 4 3
♡ 9 4 3
◊ A Q J 10 9 6
♣ 10

        ♠ K 7
        ♡ A 7 5
        ◊ K 8 2
        ♣ J 8 7 3 2

West leads the ♡2 to dummy's ♡3. How do you defend?

Problem 5
Hand No. 41
Dealer South
N–S vulnerable

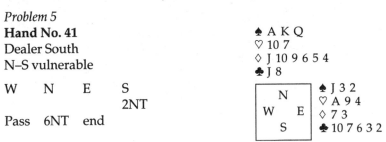

W	N	E	S
			2NT
Pass	6NT	end	

♠ A K Q
♡ 10 7
◊ J 10 9 6 5 4
♣ J 8

        ♠ J 3 2
        ♡ A 9 4
        ◊ 7 3
        ♣ 10 7 6 3 2

West leads the ♣9 to dummy's ♣A. How do you defend?

Solutions

Problem 4

South should have at least an opening bid and it is clear that, if those diamonds are cashed, the contract will be made easily. To prevent this, we must remove the ♠A from dummy with the intention of holding up our ◊K for one round. Our hope is that South has only two diamonds. Even this plan is unlikely to succeed. With South having bid spades, he will have at least four and we would need to find partner with the ♠Q to be able to drive out the ♠A. Before playing for this as our only hope, let us count our tricks. Partner appears to have four hearts, leaving South with three and, if they include the ♡K, we can set up three tricks in the suit in addition to the ◊K.

The deal:

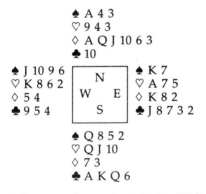

```
                      ♠ A 4 3
                      ♡ 9 4 3
                      ◊ A Q J 10 6 3
                      ♣ 10
        ♠ J 10 9 6          ┌───────┐          ♠ K 7
        ♡ K 8 6 2          │   N   │          ♡ A 7 5
        ◊ 5 4              │ W   E │          ◊ K 8 2
        ♣ 9 5 4            │   S   │          ♣ J 8 7 3 2
                           └───────┘
                      ♠ Q 8 5 2
                      ♡ Q J 10
                      ◊ 7 3
                      ♣ A K Q 6
```

Therefore, provided we pinch a trick with the ♠K first (South must let him hold) we can revert to hearts, West ducking the second round to maintain communication, and can defeat the contract before the diamonds are cashed. We therefore take the ♡A and switch to the ♠K. West should encourage spades if he has the queen but discourage without her. With the strong spades in the above diagram, he may even be able to afford to clarify the position by playing the ♠J, playing as close to the card led as possible, clearly denying the ♠Q.

Problem 5

It is clear that, with 20 plus points in the South hand, the contract will be easily made if those diamonds can be cashed. It is possible, however, that partner has a stop and in that case, our ♡A will take the setting trick – provided that partner knows what to do when he gets in. On trick one, we have the opportunity to tell him. It is clear that we are not going to get rich on spades and giving partner the count is hardly relevant. What *is* important is the choice of switch.

The deal:

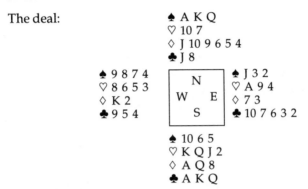

```
              ♠ A K Q
              ♡ 10 7
              ◇ J 10 9 6 5 4
              ♣ J 8
♠ 9 8 7 4              ♠ J 3 2
♡ 8 6 5 3       N      ♡ A 9 4
◇ K 2        W     E   ◇ 7 3
♣ 9 5 4         S      ♣ 10 7 6 3 2
              ♠ 10 6 5
              ♡ K Q J 2
              ◇ A Q 8
              ♣ A K Q
```

With the hand above, we want the higher-ranking of the two candidate suits (clubs and hearts) and therefore we play the high card, the ♠J. Had our ♡A been the ♣A, the ♠2 would have sent the message. It is a good habit to be on the look-out for situations like this. Where partner has found an obviously hopeless lead, encouragement/discouragement is clear and count irrelevant, a suit-preference signal (which usually costs nothing) is often crucial.

Defence against Trump Contracts

In this chapter, we shall concentrate on three main topics:

1 Gleaning information from opponents' bidding and declarer's play;
2 Communications in respect of defenders' ruffs;
3 Discarding – we discussed this briefly under no-trump contracts in *The Expert Advancer*. With the availability of ruffing, it is bound to be more complicated and has therefore been left to this stage.

In the beginners' book, we spent considerable time on the one-closed-hand exercise, looking at thirty-nine cards and trying to read out the other thirteen against the stop-watch. This was the first step towards the two-closed-hand exercise, looking at twenty-six cards and trying to place the other twenty-six. This is what we have to do as soon as the dummy goes down and, from there, we must complete our seven roll-calls (spades, hearts diamonds, clubs, points, tricks available to declarer and tricks available to defenders) to work out the necessary line of defence.

The opponents' bidding (even if it is less than perfect) and the way in which declarer plays a hand are very often mines of information in respect of their holdings. Let us look at a simple example:

Problem 1
Hand No. 42
Dealer East
E–W vulnerable

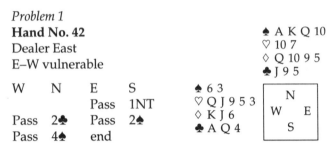

♠ A K Q 10
♡ 10 7
◇ Q 10 9 5
♣ J 9 5

W	N	E	S
		Pass	1NT
Pass	2♣	Pass	2♠
Pass	4♠	end	

♠ 6 3
♡ Q J 9 5 3
◇ K J 6
♣ A Q 4

You lead the ♡Q to the ♡7, partner's ♡2 and declarer's ♡A. Trumps are drawn in three rounds, partner following with the ♠2, ♠4 and ♠9. Now follows the ◇5 to partner's ◇7, South's ◇A and your ◇6. South follows with the ◇4, which you take with the ◇K, partner following with the ◇2 to complete a peter, showing an even number. How do you continue?

Solution
This problem is a beautiful example of how to dissect a hand into its component parts and then play as if you can see all four hands. Let us go through our roll-calls in detail:

Spades: South showed exactly four cards in the bidding; with five, he probably would have opened 1♠ and partner's following suit three times confirms the count of four beyond all doubt.

Hearts: In response to Stayman, South failed to show a four-card heart suit but, as he opened 1NT, he must have two or three.

Diamonds: Partner showed an even number, so either he has four and declarer two or vice versa.

Clubs: At the moment, we know little.

Points: Declarer, although he has not yet played it, must have the ♠J. In hearts, he has shown the ace and must also have the king as partner discouraged. No, partner cannot have the king and two alone, that would leave South with four, which he would have bid. In diamonds, he has shown the ace. That gives 12 points in total and the ♣K would take him to 15, out of range for a 12–14 point 1NT. Therefore partner has the ♣K.

Tricks: Declarer has four top trumps and is likely (though not certain) to have a heart ruff. The diamonds have proved to be well placed for him and he will make three tricks there. He also has the two top hearts.

The deal:

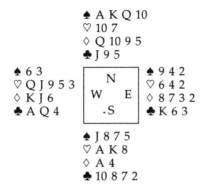

```
                    ♠ A K Q 10
                    ♡ 10 7
                    ◊ Q 10 9 5
                    ♣ J 9 5
   ♠ 6 3              N          ♠ 9 4 2
   ♡ Q J 9 5 3   W       E       ♡ 6 4 2
   ◊ K J 6          ·S           ◊ 8 7 3 2
   ♣ A Q 4                       ♣ K 6 3
                    ♠ J 8 7 5
                    ♡ A K 8
                    ◊ A 4
                    ♣ 10 8 7 2
```

That gives him ten tricks unless we cash four first and it is clear that we must switch to clubs immediately to guard against the above layout in which South is threatening to discard two losing clubs on the diamonds. Note that, if South has the same shape as North, i.e. there is no heart ruff, we cannot defeat the contract by passive defence (getting off play now with a diamond or heart) if South has, after all, got the ♣K. The three-card club position is:

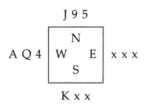

```
            J 9 5
              N
   A Q 4   W     E   x x x
              S
            K x x
```

South can play a low card towards the king or a low card towards the jack. Either way, we cannot prevent him from taking one trick.

You should also have remarked on the way partner followed to the trumps. He had three (all losers) and there were therefore no less than six different orders in which he could have played them. In *Signal Success in Bridge*, I explained at length the various meanings the order of play could give. For the time being, it will suffice to say that he followed with low cards first, indicating, if anything, the lower-ranking suit, clubs.

This was a very detailed analysis but really it was no more than counting up to thirteen in several disciplines (suits and tricks) and to forty in points. I explained in the beginners' book that you need little more than kindergarten arithmetic to do it and yet it seems to be beyond most people, including many at the top of some very high-powered professions. All it needs is practice and that is why we worked so hard on this from the start.

Having seen the idea, I should like you to do a similar analysis on this next example in match conditions. Write down all the relevant information and state your line of defence, with good reasons, in under two minutes. Start your stop-watch.

Problem 2

Hand No. 43
Dealer North
E–W vulnerable

♠ J 9
♡ J 10 8 6 5
◊ Q 10 9 6
♣ K 7

W	N	E	S
	Pass	Pass	1♡
Dble	3♡	Pass	4♡
end			

♠ A Q 10 8
♡ K 2
◊ A J
♣ Q J 10 9 2

```
        N
   W         E
        S
```

You lead the ♣Q to dummy's ♣K, partner's ♣4 and declarer's ♣5. The ♡J is run round to your ♡K and you return the ♣J to South's ♣A, partner following with the ♣3. Declarer crosses to dummy with the ♡10; partner discards the ♠2 and leads the ◊6 to partner's ◊4 and his own ◊K. Again you can see that dummy's diamonds are going to be set up. How do you defend?

There are similarities with Problem 1, but appearances may be deceptive. To make sure, let us do our seven roll-calls again.

Spades: We know little about distribution but, as partner has discarded the two, declarer should have the king.

Hearts: Open book – South has five and partner one.

Diamonds: The honours have all been seen but distribution is as yet uncertain.

Clubs: Partner has shown an even number, two or four.

Points: We have 17 and the opponents are in game. Partner cannot have anything – confirmed by his ♠2 discard.

The deal:

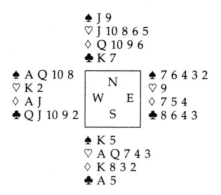

```
            ♠ J 9
            ♡ J 10 8 6 5
            ◊ Q 10 9 6
            ♣ K 7
♠ A Q 10 8              ♠ 7 6 4 3 2
♡ K 2        N         ♡ 9
◊ A J     W     E      ◊ 7 5 4
♣ Q J 10 9 2   S       ♣ 8 6 4 3
            ♠ K 5
            ♡ A Q 7 4 3
            ◊ K 8 3 2
            ♣ A 5
```

Declarer has four trumps for one lost, two top clubs and three diamonds to total nine tricks so far. Therefore, if he has four clubs, rather than two, he can take two ruffs on the table to make the contract in comfort. We must therefore consider the position where he has only two and now, irrespective of his distribution in diamonds and spades, he only has nine tricks as above. Last time, we needed panic measures and had to attack clubs, even if it meant leading from ace-queen. This time, we have worked out that we can afford to play passively. To play a club would give away a ruff and discard. To play a spade would give a free finesse and is also ruled out. The only defence is to win the diamond now and return the ◊J, leaving South to play the hand.

So it would appear that, in the two hands where we had to discuss the wisdom of leading away from an ace-queen combination, it was a question of working out whether partner or declarer had the king and play accordingly. Is that the last word on the subject? See if you can work this one out in under two minutes. Start your stop-watch.

Problem 3   ♠ J 10 9 8 3
Hand No. 44   ♡ Q J 9
Dealer North   ◇ A 6
Both vulnerable   ♣ 9 5 3

                        ♠ A Q 2

W	N	E	S	♡ 6 3	N
	Pass	Pass	1♡	◇ Q J 10 4	W E
Dble	2♡	Pass	4♡	♣ A Q 10 4	S
end					

You lead the ◇Q to the ◇6, partner's ◇2 and declarer's ◇K. South draws trumps in two rounds, ending in dummy, partner following with the ♡8 and ♡10. Now comes the ♣3 to the ♣5, ♣K and your ♣A. How do you continue?

Solution

The honour positions in the major suits are an open book and it is clear that, with a stiff ace on the table, we have no hope in diamonds. However, if South has another spade, it would appear that we shall make two tricks in that suit plus two clubs, our tenace being well placed over declarer's king. Sadly, the second club trick may never materialize. Unlike the last hand, where we worked out that we could sit back and wait, here South is threatening to set up and cash dummy's long suit, giving him three spade tricks, the two top diamonds and six trumps – making the contract with a trick to spare. It is clear that we cannot get partner in to lead a club through, so is there any solution?

With 15 points in our hand and opponents in game, partner is left with virtually nothing but he could have the ♣J. Crediting that card to him, let us look at the three-card position:

                    9 5 3

                    N

A Q 10   W   E   J x x

                    S

                    K x x

In dreamland, of course, if East were on lead, he could start with the jack, giving East–West three tricks for none lost but, in real life, West is on lead. Nevertheless, the defenders can still take two tricks for one lost, good enough to defeat the contract if it is done before the spades are set up. We should therefore switch to a club immediately.

The deal:

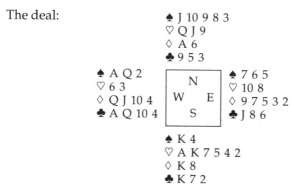

```
              ♠ J 10 9 8 3
              ♡ Q J 9
              ◇ A 6
              ♣ 9 5 3
♠ A Q 2                        ♠ 7 6 5
♡ 6 3         ┌─────────┐      ♡ 10 8
◇ Q J 10 4    │    N    │      ◇ 9 7 5 3 2
♣ A Q 10 4    │ W     E │      ♣ J 8 6
              │    S    │
              └─────────┘
              ♠ K 4
              ♡ A K 7 5 4 2
              ◇ K 8
              ♣ K 7 2
```

Very often, tricks have to be sacrificed when a race is on and one defender is desperately short of entries and this is an excellent lead into closer study of the subject of defensive communications. Let us look at another hand, altering the club position only slightly but utilising partner's sole asset, the ♣J, for another purpose.

Hand No. 45
Dealer West
Both vulnerable

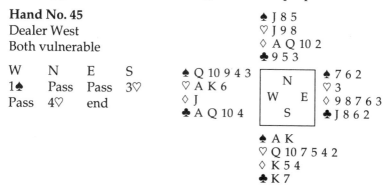

W	N	E	S
1♠	Pass	Pass	3♡
Pass	4♡	end	

```
              ♠ J 8 5
              ♡ J 9 8
              ◇ A Q 10 2
              ♣ 9 5 3
♠ Q 10 9 4 3                   ♠ 7 6 2
♡ A K 6       ┌─────────┐      ♡ 3
◇ J           │    N    │      ◇ 9 8 7 6 3
♣ A Q 10 4    │ W     E │      ♣ J 8 6 2
              │    S    │
              └─────────┘
              ♠ A K
              ♡ Q 10 7 5 4 2
              ◇ K 5 4
              ♣ K 7
```

West leads the ◇J, won by South's ◇K. Declarer leads a trump and West wins. Where are the four defensive tricks to come from? There are two top hearts and two clubs, but declarer is threatening to cash four diamonds, discarding a club, and complete the contract with four trumps and two top spades. The only hope is a diamond ruff, but that means getting partner in and the ♣J is the lifeline. Let us look at that club position in isolation:

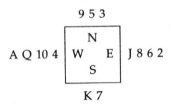

9 5 3

A Q 10 4 | W   E | J 8 6 2

K 7

With South having a doubleton, the first two rounds only are important and the best way to a solution is trial and error. Leading the ace is hopeless. South plays low and the king controls the second round. But try the queen or ten and now South is sunk. If he wins and plays a second trump, West wins and plays a low club to East's jack, after which a diamond ruff defeats the contract. If South ducks the first club, West cashes the ace and takes two tricks in the suit after all.

Problems of this kind crop up quite often when West has most of the defenders' forces and needs to get his partner in – either for a ruff or for a lead through to a tenace. Having seen the idea, can you do this next example in match conditions in under ninety seconds? Start your stop-watch.

Problem 4
Hand No. 46
Dealer East
E–W vulnerable

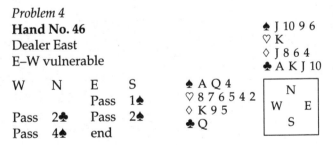

♠ J 10 9 6
♡ K
◇ J 8 6 4
♣ A K J 10

W	N	E	S
		Pass	1♠
Pass	2♣	Pass	2♠
Pass	4♠	end	

♠ A Q 4
♡ 8 7 6 5 4 2
◇ K 9 5
♣ Q

Your lead of the ♣Q is won in dummy. South calls for the ♠J, on which partner discards the ♡3. South plays low and you win with the ♠Q. How do you continue?

Solution
Partner has signalled no interest in hearts and therefore the ♡A must be credited to South. This means that South is threatening to take four spade tricks for two lost, four clubs and presumably the

◇A (partner would surely have thrown a high diamond if he had that card). That totals nine tricks so far and, except in the most unlikely event of his heart being singleton, there will be at least one heart ruff in dummy for the tenth. Meanwhile, where are our four tricks to come from? The only hope is in diamonds, which means that partner will need the ◇ Q 10. In that case, we may be able to establish two tricks by force if South can follow three times. The question arises whether there is anything we can do in the critical case where South only has a doubleton:

The deal:

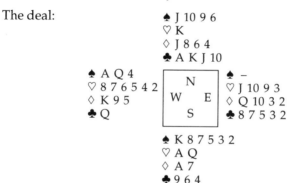

```
                 ♠ J 10 9 6
                 ♡ K
                 ◇ J 8 6 4
                 ♣ A K J 10
  ♠ A Q 4            N          ♠ —
  ♡ 8 7 6 5 4 2   W     E       ♡ J 10 9 3
  ◇ K 9 5            S          ◇ Q 10 3 2
  ♣ Q                           ♣ 8 7 5 3 2
                 ♠ K 8 7 5 3 2
                 ♡ A Q
                 ◇ A 7
                 ♣ 9 6 4
```

Now we must aim for a diamond trick and a club ruff in addition to our two trump tricks. Therefore we have to get partner in. Let us look at the diamond position in isolation:

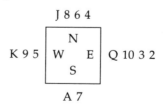

```
              J 8 6 4
                 N
     K 9 5    W     E    Q 10 3 2
                 S
              A 7
```

Clearly, it is one trick each and the enemy trick will be won by South. But can we insist that our trick is won by East? Again, trial and error will point the way. Leading the king is hopeless: South just ducks, losing to us. The nine or five is better. If dummy plays low, East puts in the ten, forcing South's ace. On regaining the lead in trumps, we underlead again to partner's queen and receive the club ruff.

So far, we have considered examples in which a defensive ruff was sufficient to defeat the contract and the problem was how to organize the entry. Often, however, hands turn up in which such a ruff is available but, on its own, is insufficient. In such cases, it is a good habit to consider the aftermath. This is a common example in which declarers are frequently let off the hook:

Hand No. 47
Dealer East
E–W vulnerable

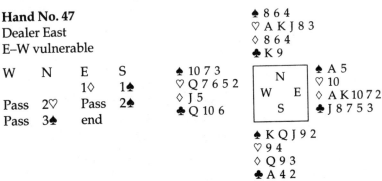

```
                              ♠ 8 6 4
                              ♡ A K J 8 3
                              ◇ 8 6 4
                              ♣ K 9
W    N    E    S    ♠ 10 7 3   ┌──────────┐   ♠ A 5
          1◇   1♠   ♡ Q 7 6 5 2│   N      │   ♡ 10
                    ◇ J 5      │ W     E  │   ◇ A K 10 7 2
Pass 2♡   Pass 2♠   ♣ Q 10 6   │   S      │   ♣ J 8 7 5 3
Pass 3♠   end                  └──────────┘
                              ♠ K Q J 9 2
                              ♡ 9 4
                              ◇ Q 9 3
                              ♣ A 4 2
```

West leads the ◇J and the position is revealed when East cashes his ace and king. How exciting – a ruff! Without further thought, East leads a third round, ruffed by West, but the last laugh belongs to South. He wins the club or heart return, takes the ♣K, ♣A and club ruff before conceding the ♠A and claiming the remainder. Returning a trump after the diamond ruff is no better. South can afford to ruff the fourth round of diamonds high.

East was at fault for failing to work out the whole hand. The two top diamonds, the ruff and trump ace total four tricks, but how about the fifth? No thought given! Less rush and a little more planning would have saved the day. Partner is unlikely to have a top trick in either black suit and the only realistic hope is a heart ruff. As East has early trump control, this can be organized. At trick three, he leads the ♡10. South wins and attacks trumps. East wins the first round and only *now* gives the diamond ruff, choosing the ◇10 to indicate the preference for higher-ranking heart return (which should be obvious anyway).

Having seen the idea, can you do this next example in match conditions in under one minute? Start your stop-watch.

Problem 5
Hand No. 48
Dealer West
Both vulnerable

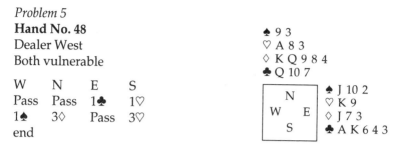

♠ 9 3
♡ A 8 3
◇ K Q 9 8 4
♣ Q 10 7

W	N	E	S
Pass	Pass	1♣	1♡
1♠	3◇	Pass	3♡
end			

N
W   E
S

♠ J 10 2
♡ K 9
◇ J 7 3
♣ A K 6 4 3

After his initial pass, North's 3◇ bid described his hand beautifully – showing just under opening strength with a good diamond suit and heart support, although the hand is devalued a little because of the poor position of the ♣Q under East's bid.

West leads the ♣J and dummy covers. You take the ♣K and ♣A, West following with the ♣9. How do you continue?

Solution

We have two top clubs and and a ruff is available. Add the well-placed ♡K and we have four tricks so far but how about the fifth? Partner is likely to have one top card for his bid. If it is the ◇A, ◇K or ♣A, that will not run away. Equally the ♠K is well placed over South's presumed ace but he may not be able to attack the suit effectively from his side if the deal looks like this:

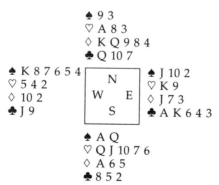

♠ 9 3
♡ A 8 3
◇ K Q 9 8 4
♣ Q 10 7

♠ K 8 7 6 5 4
♡ 5 4 2
◇ 10 2
♣ J 9

N
W   E
S

♠ J 10 2
♡ K 9
◇ J 7 3
♣ A K 6 4 3

♠ A Q
♡ Q J 10 7 6
◇ A 6 5
♣ 8 5 2

With South having rejected the game try, it is unlikely that he has more than five hearts (and he may well have been put off by the badly-placed spade tenace as above). Therefore there is no hurry for the club ruff. We must use this opportunity to establish the spade trick first. Later, on regaining the lead with the ♡K, we then give the ruff and partner will be ready to cash the ♠K for the fifth trick.

The anticipation of the *entire play* of a hand, rather than merely the next trick or two, is of utmost importance when considering discards. Poor discarding allows declarers to get away with bidding that could be described as outrageous (or worse) and this is one of the main reasons why persistent overbidders are still flourishing and becoming more daring, notably against weak opposition. I explained in an earlier book that the most common offenders are defenders, holding very poor cards, tending to lose interest in the proceedings, unaware that a relatively low card could make all the difference.

The basic guide – but remember it is no more than a guide – is that, if it is clear that a certain number of rounds of a particular suit will be played, it usually pays to keep that number of cards even if your holding is completely useless. Let us start with a very extreme example to press this point home.

Problem 6
Hand No. 49
Dealer South
Both vulnerable

♠ Q 7 5 2
♡ 9 5
◇ 8 5 4 3 2
♣ A K

				N
				♠ 3
				♡ J 10 7 4 3
W		E		◇ J 10 9 7 6
				♣ 3 2
			S	

W	N	E	S
			2♣
Pass	3♠	Pass	4◇
Pass	5♣	Pass	5♡
Pass	6♣	Pass	7♠
end			

West leads the ◇K won by South's ◇A. All follow to the ♠A and West follows again when South plays a low spade to the ♠Q. What do you discard?

Solution
Well a fat lot of hope there is for the ♣3 and ♣2 with the ♣A and ♣K in the dummy, not to mention any further clubs in the South hand which must be higher than ours! So is it safe to discard a

club? In fact, it is fatal. Let us look at the deal:

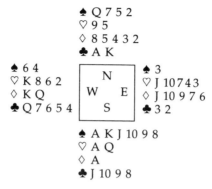

```
              ♠ Q 7 5 2
              ♡ 9 5
              ◇ 8 5 4 3 2
              ♣ A K
  ♠ 6 4                        ♠ 3
  ♡ K 8 6 2        N           ♡ J 10 7 4 3
  ◇ K Q        W     E         ◇ J 10 9 7 6
  ♣ Q 7 6 5 4      S           ♣ 3 2
              ♠ A K J 10 9 8
              ♡ A Q
              ◇ A
              ♣ J 10 9 8
```

Partner's lead was clearly from ◇ K Q doubleton, leaving South with a singleton ace. He should have six spades for his opening bid, leaving six other cards for clubs and hearts. There is no club trick for us, as any losers can be ruffed in dummy, so the only hope is in hearts. South has announced the ♡A so partner will probably need to have the king. If South has the ♣Q, a heart loser can be discarded from dummy so she must be credited to partner. The critical case arises where the heart finesse is going to fail. However, South can try his luck in clubs first.

Observe what happens if we discard a club. When the ace and king are cashed, we shall show out, revealing the position. South can now return to hand, take a ruffing finesse against partner's queen and claim the contract. As we can see that two rounds of clubs cannot be avoided, we should keep our two clubs. Did you realize that the same principle applies in diamonds? Were we to discard one carelessly, South can arrange for five rounds, setting up a crucial winner. Let us play it.

   (i) ◇A
  (ii) ♠A
 (iii) ♠Q (we discard a diamond)
 (iv) Diamond ruff
  (v) ♣K
 (vi) Diamond ruff
(vii) ♣A

(viii) Diamond ruff

  (ix) Club ruff

   (x) Winning diamond (thanks to our poor discarding) on which
       South discards the ♡Q.

 (xi) ♡A

 (xii) Club ruff

(xiii) South's last trump.

As long as we keep both clubs and diamonds intact, South is likely
to go down. It could be argued that, once diamonds fail to break,
the ruffing finesse in clubs is a better chance than trying to drop
the ♣Q by ruffing. This is true, but only in the context of the club
suit considered in isolation. If South takes the ruffing finesse in
clubs, he is staking the whole contract on that finesse – a 50%
chance. But the principle of 'drop first; then finesse' applies here.
He should try to drop the ♣Q by ruffing, holding the lead if it fails.
He now has the heart finesse to fall back on. With that finesse
being a 50% chance on its own, the total probability of the two
chances is way over 50% and is therefore the superior line.

The mathematically inclined can work out that, once both
defenders have followed two rounds of clubs and West has played
low on the third round, the chance of dropping the queen by
ruffing is about 26% The total chance of the line of play succeeding
is 100% − (74% x 50%) = 63%, a considerable improvement on the
50% for the ruffing finesse alone.

I have gone to town on this hand because it is typical of the type
of situation in which a player holding a poor hand (with the 2
points above hardly arousing interest in the proceedings) discards
carelessly; and look at the cost in a grand slam contract! Having
seen the idea, I should like you to do the following two simple
examples under match conditions in well under sixty seconds
each, to complete the test in under two minutes. Start your stop-
watch.

Problem 7
Hand No. 50
Dealer West
Neither vulnerable

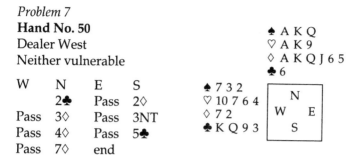

	♠ A K Q
	♡ A K 9
	◇ A K Q J 6 5
	♣ 6

W	N	E	S
	2♣	Pass	2◇
Pass	3◇	Pass	3NT
Pass	4◇	Pass	5♣
Pass	7◇	end	

♠ 7 3 2
♡ 10 7 6 4
◇ 7 2
♣ K Q 9 3

South's 5♣ was a cue-bid.

You lead the ♣K and South wins with the ♣A, East follows with
the ♣2, so South obviously has the ♣J. South reels off six rounds of
diamonds, partner following three times and discarding three
small clubs. Now follow three top spades, partner following. On
the last one, you can see:

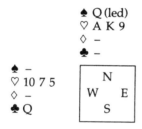

```
              ♠ Q (led)
              ♡ A K 9
              ◇ –
              ♣ –
   ♠ –
   ♡ 10 7 5        N
   ◇ –          W     E
   ♣ Q             S
```

and something has to go. What do you discard?

Problem 8
Hand No. 51
Dealer East
N – S vulnerable

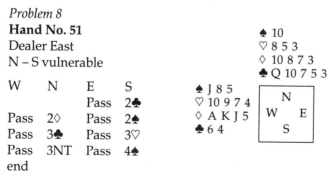

	♠ 10
	♡ 8 5 3
	◇ 10 8 7 3
	♣ Q 10 7 5 3

W	N	E	S
		Pass	2♣
Pass	2◇	Pass	2♠
Pass	3♣	Pass	3♡
Pass	3NT	Pass	4♠
end			

♠ J 8 5
♡ 10 9 7 4
◇ A K J 5
♣ 6 4

You lead the two top diamonds, partner following with the ◊2 and ◊4 and declarer with the ◊9 and ◊Q. You switch to the ♣6 and partner's ace wins, South dropping the ♣K. Partner now leads the ◊6 and South ruffs. He draws trumps in three rounds, partner following with ♠2, ♠4 and ♠6, and plays out two more trumps. You can afford to throw your ♣4 on the first one but on the second, you can see:

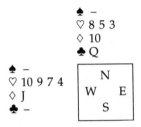

```
            ♠ –
            ♡ 8 5 3
            ◊ 10
            ♣ Q
♠ –
♡ 10 9 7 4    ┌─────────┐
◊ J           │   N     │
♣ –           │ W     E │
              │   S     │
              └─────────┘
```

What do you discard now?

Solutions

Problem 7
This is really an insult to your intelligence, but it is amazing how many people would go wrong in this position. It is clear that South is stuck on the table and that the last three tricks will be played in hearts. Therefore, we must keep three hearts, especially as our ten can beat dummy's lowest card.

The deal:

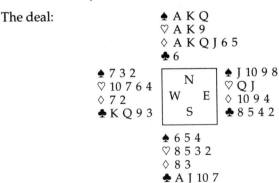

```
                  ♠ A K Q
                  ♡ A K 9
                  ◊ A K Q J 6 5
                  ♣ 6
   ♠ 7 3 2                      ♠ J 10 9 8
   ♡ 10 7 6 4   ┌─────────┐     ♡ Q J
   ◊ 7 2        │   N     │     ◊ 10 9 4
   ♣ K Q 9 3    │ W     E │     ♣ 8 5 4 2
                │   S     │
                └─────────┘
                  ♠ 6 5 4
                  ♡ 8 5 3 2
                  ◊ 8 3
                  ♣ A J 10 7
```

The fact that discarding the ♣Q sets up South's ♣J is purely of academic interest. He can never reach his hand to enjoy it.

Problem 8

Discarding the ♢J now will set up dummy's ♢10 but the bidding and early play indicates that this does not matter. South cannot reach the dummy. He has shown six spades and four hearts and has already followed to two rounds of diamonds and one club. He is therefore left with nothing but his four hearts and the minor suits are out of the game. We must hope that partner has one honour and keep our heart holding intact: we expect four rounds of hearts to be played and must keep the appropriate number of cards.

The deal:

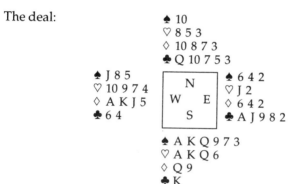

```
              ♠ 10
              ♡ 8 5 3
              ♢ 10 8 7 3
              ♣ Q 10 7 5 3
♠ J 8 5                    ♠ 6 4 2
♡ 10 9 7 4      N          ♡ J 2
♢ A K J 5    W   E         ♢ 6 4 2
♣ 6 4           S          ♣ A J 9 8 2
              ♠ A K Q 9 7 3
              ♡ A K Q 6
              ♢ Q 9
              ♣ K
```

This is the kind of situation, where declarer's or dummy's hand is dead, in which totally unnecessary mistakes are made by the hundred – and experts are certainly not exempt from criticism! Of course, 3NT is cold, but we are not here to criticize opponents' bidding!

We are going to conclude with a miscellaneous test covering the three topics studied in this chapter. You should be speeding up by now and be able do each example in under one minute, to complete the test in under six minutes.

Problem 9
Hand No. 52
Dealer East
E–W vulnerable

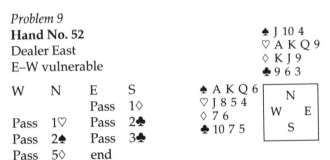

♠ J 10 4
♡ A K Q 9
◊ K J 9
♣ 9 6 3

♠ A K Q 6
♡ J 8 5 4
◊ 7 6
♣ 10 7 5

W	N	E	S
		Pass	1◊
Pass	1♡	Pass	2♣
Pass	2♠	Pass	3♣
Pass	5◊	end	

North's 2♠ bid was fourth-suit forcing, suggesting no-trumps if South had a stop in that suit. South showed at least 5–5 in the minors. You cash two top spades but South ruffs the third round. He then draws trumps in three rounds, partner following low, and then plays his last trump. You can easily afford to discard your last spade on the third diamond but, on the last round, you are down to your four hearts and three clubs. What do you discard this time?

Problem 10
Hand No. 53
Dealer North
Neither vulnerable

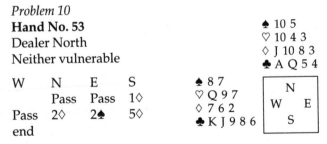

♠ 10 5
♡ 10 4 3
◊ J 10 8 3
♣ A Q 5 4

♠ 8 7
♡ Q 9 7
◊ 7 6 2
♣ K J 9 8 6

W	N	E	S
	Pass	Pass	1◊
Pass	2◊	2♠	5◊
end			

You lead the ♠8 and partner cashes the ♠J and ♠Q before switching to the ♡5. Declarer wins with the ♡A and ruffs a spade in dummy, partner following with the ♠6 while you discard a club. Returning to hand with the ◊A, partner following, declarer ruffs another spade in dummy, partner following with the ♠K while you discard another club. Four more trumps follow, partner discarding the ♡6, ♣7 and ♣2. You follow three times but, on the last one, this is what you can see:

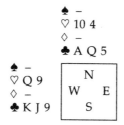

```
        ♠ –
        ♡ 10 4
        ◊ –
        ♣ A Q 5
♠ –
♡ Q 9         ┌─────────┐
◊ –           │    N    │
♣ K J 9       │  W   E  │
              │    S    │
              └─────────┘
```

What do you discard this time?

Problem 11
Hand No. 54
Dealer West
Neither vulnerable

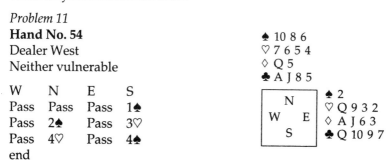

W	N	E	S
Pass	Pass	Pass	1♠
Pass	2♠	Pass	3♡
Pass	4♡	Pass	4♠
end			

```
        ♠ 10 8 6
        ♡ 7 6 5 4
        ◊ Q 5
        ♣ A J 8 5
              ┌─────────┐ ♠ 2
              │    N    │ ♡ Q 9 3 2
              │  W   E  │ ◊ A J 6 3
              │    S    │ ♣ Q 10 9 7
              └─────────┘
```

South's 3♡ bid was a long-suit trial and you marvel at North's optimism. Was it the rock-solid nature of the heart suit or those fabulous spades that prompted him to raise to game with every single point in the wrong place?

West leads the ◊10 and dummy plays low. How do you defend?

Problem 12
Hand No. 55
Dealer West
Both vulnerable

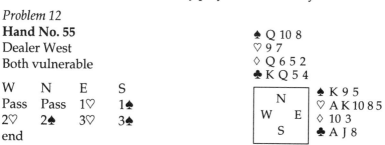

W	N	E	S
Pass	Pass	1♡	1♠
2♡	2♠	3♡	3♠
end			

```
        ♠ Q 10 8
        ♡ 9 7
        ◊ Q 6 5 2
        ♣ K Q 5 4
              ┌─────────┐ ♠ K 9 5
              │    N    │ ♡ A K 10 8 5
              │  W   E  │ ◊ 10 3
              │    S    │ ♣ A J 8
              └─────────┘
```

West leads the ♡2 to the ♡7, ♡K and ♡3. How do you continue?

Problem 13
Hand No. 56
Dealer East
Both vulnerable

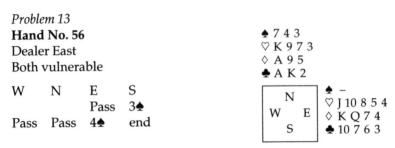

W	N	E	S
		Pass	3♠
Pass	Pass	4♠	end

♠ 7 4 3
♡ K 9 7 3
◇ A 9 5
♣ A K 2

♠ –
♡ J 10 8 5 4
◇ K Q 7 4
♣ 10 7 6 3

West leads the ◇J and it holds. He continues with the ◇3, dummy's ◇A winning. On the first round of trumps, you discard a diamond and South's ♠Q loses to West's ♠K. West persists with a third diamond, South ruffing. On the second round of trumps, you can easily spare a heart. On the third, partner follows with the ♠10 and you are down to four hearts and four clubs. Bearing in mind that South has three more trumps, what do you discard this time?

Problem 14
Hand No. 57
Dealer East
Both vulnerable

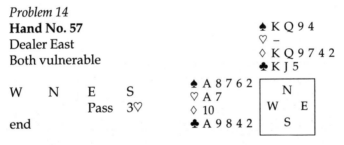

W	N	E	S
		Pass	3♡
end			

♠ K Q 9 4
♡ –
◇ K Q 9 7 4 2
♣ K J 5

♠ A 8 7 6 2
♡ A 7
◇ 10
♣ A 9 8 4 2

You lead the ♣A and strike oil when partner produces the ♣Q. How do you continue?

Solutions

Problem 9
The bidding and play so far have marked South with a singleton heart (note that, with a void, he would not have cut himself off from dummy's hearts but would have cashed them while he was in dummy with a high trump). He has five tricks in trumps and three in hearts. A roll-call of the clubs should keep you on the right track. South is known to have five and, with eleven on view,

partner is left with two. If he has the ace or king-queen, declarer has no chance. If declarer has three honours including the ace, the defenders have no chance. The critical case arises when partner has the king-jack or queen-jack. Now our ten will come into the reckoning as long as we keep the trebleton intact. We must hope that partner has the ♡10 (and thus controls the fourth round of the suit), and discard a heart.

The deal:

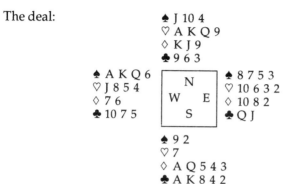

```
                    ♠ J 10 4
                    ♡ A K Q 9
                    ◇ K J 9
                    ♣ 9 6 3
  ♠ A K Q 6                          ♠ 8 7 5 3
  ♡ J 8 5 4        N                 ♡ 10 6 3 2
  ◇ 7 6         W     E              ◇ 10 8 2
  ♣ 10 7 5          S                ♣ Q J
                    ♠ 9 2
                    ♡ 7
                    ◇ A Q 5 4 3
                    ♣ A K 8 4 2
```

You should satisfy yourself that there is no lie of the clubs for which the discard of a heart could make a difference to the fate of the contract.

Problem 10

There are a large number of instructive points in this hand so it is worth going into it in great detail. First, the bidding: partner passed originally and then overcalled with 2♠. He has shown up with a five-card suit to the top four honours and therefore cannot have any more honours. You know that and, far more important, *so does declarer*. He therefore realizes that the heart finesse is wrong for him but the club finesse is right – there is no guessing involved. In situations like this, it is partner's duty to give count and he has clearly indicated three hearts and an even number of clubs.

Now let us count tricks. South has five top diamonds and has taken two spade ruffs in dummy and a top heart – eight in total so far. There is still the ♡K to come to make nine and therefore we can see that, if he has a club in his hand, the finesse will give him eleven. However, with the count given, South appears to be 4450 and we can throw a club with impunity.

The deal:

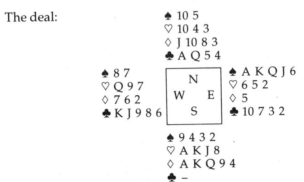

```
                        ♠ 10 5
                        ♡ 10 4 3
                        ◇ J 10 8 3
                        ♣ A Q 5 4
        ♠ 8 7            ┌─────────┐        ♠ A K Q J 6
        ♡ Q 9 7         │    N    │        ♡ 6 5 2
        ◇ 7 6 2         │ W     E │        ◇ 5
        ♣ K J 9 8 6     │    S    │        ♣ 10 7 3 2
                        └─────────┘
                        ♠ 9 4 3 2
                        ♡ A K J 8
                        ◇ A K Q 9 4
                        ♣ –
```

Note the brilliant play by declarer. Realizing that a discard on the ♣A would not help him, he decided to go for what is known as a *pseudo-squeeze* or *Dutch squeeze* – an attempted squeeze on our hand in which the club threat was no more than a toy gun.

If you got this one right, I have some good news for you; you have outperformed a certain gentleman, who, on one occasion in my presence, described himself as the 'best player in the world'. It was only unbelievable self-restraint and courtesy that prevented me from politely pointing out that this shows how bad everybody else is!

Problem 11
With South known to have started with length in both majors, it cannot possibly gain to play low. Even if South started with ◇ K x x, there is nothing he could profitably discard on his extra diamond trick. Indeed, ducking could be very costly. We must take the ◇A and switch to hearts, the area of South's announced losers.

The deal:

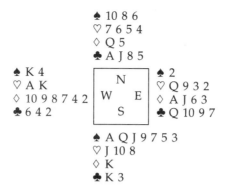

It is really an insult to your intelligence but this hand came up in an international trial and a household name played low at trick one. South now had the chance to roll-call the hand before committing himself to the finesse chances in the black suits.

East was clearly marked with the ace and jack of diamonds: 5 points. If he also had the ♠K, that would make 8, and West's failure to lead a heart surely ruled him out of holding all the honours in the suit. East was likely to hold at least one. That would be getting very near an opening bid and, as East had failed to open in third position, non-vulnerable, South correctly decided that the spade finesse was a non-starter and that the drop was a better chance.

Winning with the ◊K, he could play the ♣K and ♣A and ruff a third round in hand. Now he could exit with a heart, losing to West. West could do no more than cash his other heart and exit in diamonds, South ruffing East's ace. South would then cash the ♠A and continue spades. West would win and, left with only diamonds, would have to concede a ruff and discard, allowing South to get rid of his third heart loser to make the contract.

That, however, is not what happened in practice. South was confident that one defensive blunder would lead to another and played two rounds of spades immediately. West won and duly led a second diamond (he should have cashed his hearts first). South ruffed, took three rounds of clubs and then exited in hearts to endplay West. West had not led hearts originally because he did not want to ruff, still less help to set up the ♡Q, which was 'marked' in dummy by North's bidding.

Problem 12

We have two heart tricks and the ♣A to total three so far. There is a possibility of a trump trick but it is not guaranteed so it appears that we shall have to credit partner with one of the top diamonds. It is most unlikely that we shall be able to enjoy a second club trick. South would need a trebleton, excluding the ♣10. A better chance lies in a diamond ruff and the question is whether we can arrange it before trumps are drawn.

The crucial point here is that South cannot draw trumps without loss unless he leads them from dummy. He can get there in either minor but it will take time and this factor gives us our chance. We shall have to credit South with three hearts to the jack only so that he cannot draw trumps without depriving himself of a heart ruff:

The deal:

```
                    ♠ Q 10 8
                    ♡ 9 7
                    ◊ Q 6 5 2
                    ♣ K Q 5 4
      ♠ 6                          ♠ K 9 5
      ♡ Q 6 2          N           ♡ A K 10 8 5
      ◊ K 9 7 4    W       E       ◊ 10 3
      ♣ 10 7 6 3 2     S           ♣ A J 8
                    ♠ A J 7 4 3 2
                    ♡ J 4 3
                    ◊ A J 8
                    ♣ 9
```

Try the effect of an immediate diamond switch. If South wins, he will be defeated easily. He will have to play a heart or club to reach dummy for the spade finesse. Partner wins, cashes the ◊K and gives us a ruff for our fifth trick. So South must play low, allowing partner's ◊K to win, and West returns the suit. Say South wins in dummy. He can now draw trumps without loss but is left with two more heart losers. If he plays a heart, we must allow West to win so that he can give us our diamond ruff.

Note the crucial point of this hand – we must *not* cash the second heart winner at trick two. If we do, we lose the communication with partner and allow South to ruff his third losing heart *before* drawing trumps.

Problem 13

A simple count of tricks will keep us on the right track and yet, when this hand came up in a major tournament, a well-known player went wrong. It is clear that South will make six spade tricks out of seven and we can see three top winners in the minors in dummy, to total nine so far. Now we consider the heart position in that light. With the ace well placed for declarer (in partner's hand), South only needs to have a small singleton in his own hand to be sure of the contract. We must therefore play for the only hope – a void. Now the ♡K is of no benefit and we can count South's hand as 7024.

The deal:

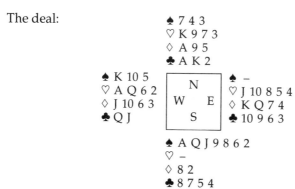

```
                    ♠ 7 4 3
                    ♡ K 9 7 3
                    ◊ A 9 5
                    ♣ A K 2
  ♠ K 10 5      ┌─────────┐   ♠ –
  ♡ A Q 6 2     │    N    │   ♡ J 10 8 5 4
  ◊ J 10 6 3    │ W     E │   ◊ K Q 7 4
  ♣ Q J         │    S    │   ♣ 10 9 6 3
                └─────────┘
                    ♠ A Q J 9 8 6 2
                    ♡ –
                    ◊ 8 2
                    ♣ 8 7 5 4
```

The only hope for South now is in clubs. We must hang on to our holding to restrict him to two tricks. Our hearts are of no value. At the time, East, obsessed with the dictum 'Never discard from jack to four', hung on to his hearts, allowing South to play three rounds of clubs to set up a long card for his tenth trick.

Problem 14

It looks as though this contract is going to be heavily defeated and it is therefore easy to miss the danger. A roll-call will indicate South's chance. He is marked with at least seven hearts for his vulnerable preempt and the play on trick one gives him four clubs. All of a sudden, a void of spades is a strong possibility. If he also has the ◊A (absolute maximum for the preempt and some would consider that too good), we shall only have the ♣A, ♡A and two club ruffs. The fifth trick can only come from a diamond ruff.

The deal:

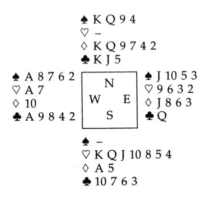

```
                    ♠ K Q 9 4
                    ♡ –
                    ♢ K Q 9 7 4 2
                    ♣ K J 5
     ♠ A 8 7 6 2         N          ♠ J 10 5 3
     ♡ A 7                          ♡ 9 6 3 2
     ♢ 10            W       E      ♢ J 8 6 3
     ♣ A 9 8 4 2         S          ♣ Q
                    ♠ –
                    ♡ K Q J 10 8 5 4
                    ♢ A 5
                    ♣ 10 7 6 3
```

We should lead the ♣2, indicating the wish for the lower-ranking suit, diamonds. We could also lead a diamond at trick two. Now after the ♡A and a club ruff, East will return a diamond if he has four or fewer diamonds but a spade if he has five diamonds.

That is as far as I intend to go in play and defence but, as always, I urge you to play and replay all the examples throughout the book until they become second nature in the recommended times, or preferably considerably less. You will then be far better prepared for similar situations which constantly recur at the table.

SECTION 2:

Duplicate Bridge

Introducing Duplicate Bridge

When I first introduced the game in the beginners' book, the procedure and scoring referred to the original format of contract bridge, known as *rubber bridge*. During the years following the Second World War, *duplicate bridge* although first introduced decades earlier, became increasingly popular.

Bridge has earned its popularity as a perfect blend of skill and luck in that, while in the long run, the better players should come out on top, the weaker participants still have a chance. The luck element has various components, of which one of the biggest is whether a player picks up his fair share of the high cards. Over a long period, one should average 10 points per hand and pick up a reasonable cross-section of distributions. But the word to underline there is *long*. In the short term, say an evening's bridge, anything can happen and the luck element is therefore arguably too big.

Duplicate bridge eliminates this element by insisting that, instead of playing a series of deals at one table and measuring *absolute* scores, the same deal will be played at two or more tables and the *relative* scores will be taken into account. This is best illustrated by an example. Suppose at rubber bridge, we sit North–South and play a hand in 4♠, just making it. We would write down 120 under the line and, feeling very satisfied, go on to the next hand. But now let us suppose that this same hand is passed on to another table. Again 4♠ is bid but made with an overtrick, scoring 120 as before + 30 over the line for the extra trick. Previously, we were very happy to win our game. Now the picture is not so bright. Whereas before, we were comparing our performance with the East–West pair at *our* table, now it is compared with that of the pair sitting North–South at the *other* table.

This is much fairer as we are considering how players perform in *identical* circumstances. The North–South pair at the other table have outperformed us by one trick and will be rewarded accordingly. Similarly, looking from the point of view of the East–West pair sitting at our table, they have performed 'well' in that they conceded 4♠ exactly, whereas their counterparts at the other table conceded 4♠ + 1. Again, they will be rewarded accordingly.

Although there are a number of clubs where you can still play rubber bridge for widely varying stakes, this form of the game is on the way out and – if you want to make any sort of name for yourself, rather than just money – you should play duplicate in clubs and/or tournaments.

In this chapter, we are going to learn about club and tournament bridge and the various scoring systems for duplicate so that, when you arrive, you will know and fully understand exactly what is going on and how to vary your tactics to suit the form of scoring.

First of all, as a deal or, as it is known, *board*, needs to be played at least twice and possibly several times, it must be kept intact. When we learnt rubber bridge, cards were played by placing them in the middle of the table. The winner of the trick gathered it up and placed it beside him. At the end of the hand, the tricks were all gathered and the cards shuffled for a later deal. In duplicate, this not the case. When you play a card, you place it face up *just in front of you*. When all four players have contributed to the trick, the cards are turned over, i.e. face down. If you have won the trick, you place it vertically; if you have lost it, you place it horizontally. The way to remember this is to think of the alphabet: tricks Won go Vertically; tricks Lost go Horizontally. W and V are near each other in the alphabet as are L and H. At the end of the hand, you will have all your cards face down in front of you and you will be able to count how many tricks you have won by counting the verticals, and vice versa.

For ease of passage of a deal to the next table, a *duplicate board* is used which looks like this:

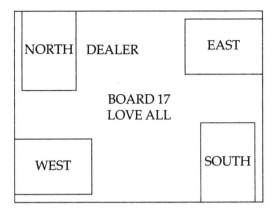

Each player has a little 'pocket' which will accommodate thirteen cards and, at the end of play, each player replaces his cards into his respective pocket and the whole board is passed to another table to be replayed. You will notice that the board is printed with a certain amount of information. Above, we have the number of the board (here 17), dealer (here North) and the vulnerability (here Love All – i.e. neither side vulnerable).

This brings us to our second important point about duplicate – namely that each board is a separate entity and has no relation to other boards. When we learnt the scoring, we had a section on 'the unfinished rubber' and we learnt that a part-score carries a bonus of 50 and a game 300. In duplicate, this is effectively happening all the time – each board is one of an unfinished rubber. We are given the vulnerability and have to imagine that this is a hand played when a rubber has reached this stage. Both sides are assumed to have a part-score of *nil* at all times in duplicate, irrespective of scores on previous boards.

Therefore in the above case, we can assume that this is the first board of a rubber. If we move on to board 18, it will look like this:

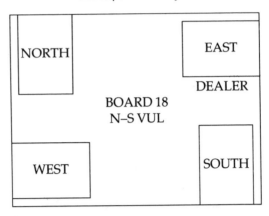

This time, East is the dealer and North–South are deemed to be vulnerable. Therefore, if a contract fails, North–South will be penalized at vulnerable rates, while East–West will be penalized at non-vulnerable rates. On board 19, the picture changes again:

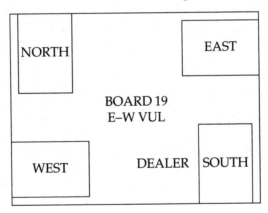

Now South is the dealer and East–West are vulnerable. East–West will be penalized at vulnerable rates if they fail to make a contract while North–South will be penalized at non-vulnerable rates.

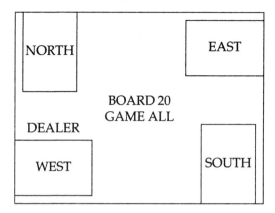

```
NORTH          EAST

        BOARD 20
        GAME ALL
DEALER

WEST           SOUTH
```

Finally, on board 20, West is the dealer and *both sides* are deemed to be vulnerable and will be penalized accordingly if they fail to make a contract.

In addition, game and slam bonuses differ slightly in duplicate bridge, according to vulnerability:

A part-score earns a bonus of 50 as before.

A non-vulnerable game earns a bonus of 300 as before.

A vulnerable game earns a bonus of 500, *irrespective* of opponents' vulnerability. The 700 bonus for winning a rubber against non-vulnerable opponents does not apply in duplicate.

Slam bonuses as before:

small: 500 (non-vulnerable) 750 vulnerable

grand: 1000 (non-vulnerable) 1500 (vulnerable)

Although there are one or two very rare exceptions, honours, in principle, do not count in duplicate.

So our first job is to relearn the scoring table, duplicate style. In the beginner's book, we learnt that tricks bid and made were scored under the line, while overtricks and penalties were scored over it. In duplicate, as we are effectively playing a one-deal rubber, the line is not needed and there is one score only. When learning the scoring for rubber bridge, we divided the table into part-scores, games, small slams and grand slams:

1♣	1◇	1♡	1♠	1NT
2♣	2◇	2♡	2♠	2NT
3♣	3◇	3♡	3♠	3NT
4♣	4◇	4♡	4♠	4NT
5♣	5◇	5♡	5♠	5NT
6♣	6◇	6♡	6♠	6NT
7♣	7◇	7♡	7♠	7NT

and we listed the respective scores as below:

1♣ or 1◇:	20	1♡ or 1♠:	30	1NT:	40
2♣ or 2◇:	40	2♡ or 2♠:	60	2NT:	70
3♣ or 3◇:	60	3♡ or 3♠:	90	3NT:	100
4♣ or 4◇:	80	4♡ or 4♠:	120	4NT:	130
5♣ or 5◇:	100	5♡ or 5♠:	150	5NT:	160
6♣ or 6◇:	120	6♡ or 6♠:	180	6NT:	190
7♣ or 7◇:	140	7♡ or 7♠:	210	7NT:	220

Now, for duplicate, we shall have to add:

50 to all the part-scores, irrespective of vulnerability
300 to all the games (non-vulnerable)
500 to all the games (vulnerable)
300 + 500 = 800 to all the small slams (non-vulnerable)
500 + 750 = 1250 to all the small slams (vulnerable)
300 + 1000 = 1300 to all the grand slams (non-vulnerable)
500 + 1500 = 2000 to all the grand slams (vulnerable)

So our new table will look like this (with vulnerable scores in brackets):

1♣ or 1◇:	70		1♡ or 1♠:	80		1NT:	90	
2♣ or 2◇:	90		2♡ or 2♠:	110		2NT:	120	
3♣ or 3◇:	110		3♡ or 3♠:	140		3NT:	400	(600)
4♣ or 4◇:	130		4♡ or 4♠:	420	(620)	4NT:	430	(630)
5♣ or 5◇:	400	(600)	5♡ or 5♠:	450	(650)	5NT:	460	(660)
6♣ or 6◇:	920	(1370)	6♡ or 6♠:	980	(1430)	6NT:	990	(1440)
7♣ or 7◇:	1440	(2140)	7♡ or 7♠:	1510	(2210)	7NT:	1520	(2220)

Once again, this should be at your fingertips. As a tournament director, I lose count of the number of times each week I have to ask slow players to 'score up quickly' so that they can move for the next round promptly. So we are now going repeat the test we did in the beginners' book. These were the three model examples I gave with the calculations at rubber bridge.

Contract	Tricks taken	Result	Calculations	Scoresheet
2♡	8	=	2 x 30	
				60
4♠	11	+1	4 x 30 + 30	30
				120
6♣ (V)	9	–3	3 x 100	300

At duplicate, the calculations will look like this:

Contract	Tricks taken	Result	Calculations	Scoresheet
2♡	8	=	2 x 30 + 50	110
4♠	11	+1	4 x 30 + 30 + 300	450
6♣ (V)	9	–3	3 x 100	300

Now start your stop-watch and fill in the answers for the following. You should take no more than ten seconds for each, to complete the test in about six minutes.

(1) 1♡ 7	(2) 2◇ 8	(3) 6NT 12	(4) 3♡ 8
(5) 5♣ 12	(6) 1♣ 9	(7) 5♠ 13	(8) 3◇ 4
(9) 2♣ 10	(10) 4◇(V) 9	(11) 3♣ 11	(12) 1◇ 11
(13) 3NTx 6	(14) 6♣ 12	(15) 4NT 11	(16) 5♡x 8
(17) 1♡x(V) 4	(18) 1NTxx(V) 4	(19) 6♣xx 9	(20) 4♠x(V) 11
(21) 2◇(V) 5	(22) 5NT 11	(23) 7♠ 13	(24) 1NT 7
(25) 4♡x 8	(26) 4♠x(V) 12	(27) 7♠(V) 13	(28) 6NT(V) 13
(29) 6◇x 11	(30) 7NT(V) 13	(31) 6♣(V) 12	(32) 6♠(V) 13
(33) 6♡(V) 12	(34) 5♣xx 10	(35) 3NTxx 7	(36) 1♠xx(V) 8
(37) 7♠x 7	(38) 2♡ 8	(39) 4♣ 8	(40) 2♣x 9
(41) 6◇ 12	(42) 1♣xx 11	(43) 4♡ 12	(44) 2♠ 10

(45) 5◇ 13   (46) 2◇xx 12   (47) 1NT 10   (48) 7♣x 13
(49) 6♠xx 13   (50) 3♣ 6

Let us work through the answers:

(1)	1♡	7	=	30 + 50	80
(2)	2◇	8	=	2 x 20 + 50	90
(3)	6NT	12	=	6 x 30 + 10 + 300 + 500	990
(4)	3♡	8	-1	50	50
(5)	5♣	12	+1	5 x 20 + 20 + 300	420
(6)	1♣	9	+2	20 + 2 x 20 + 50	90
(7)	5♠	13	+2	5 x 30 + 2 x 30 + 300	510
(8)	3◇	4	-5	5 x 50	250
(9)	2♣	10	+2	2 x 20 + 2 x 20 + 50	130
(10)	4◇(V)	9	-1	100	100
(11)	3♣	11	+2	3 x 20 + 2 x 20 + 50	150
(12)	1◇	11	+4	20 + 4 x 20 + 50	150
(13)	3NTx	6	-3	(3 x 2 – 1) x 100	500
(14)	6♣	12	=	6 x 20 + 300 + 500	920
(15)	4NT	11	+1	4 x 30 + 10 + 30 + 300	460
(16)	5♡x	8	-3	(3 x 2 – 1) x 100	500
(17)	1♡x(V)	4	-3	(3 x 3 – 1) x 100	800
(18)	1NTxx(V)	4	-3	(3 x 3 – 1) x 100 x 2	1600
(19)	6♣xx	9	-3	(3 x 2 – 1) x 100 x 2	1000
(20)	4♠x(V)	11	+1	(4 x 30) x 2 + 50 + 200 + 500	990
(21)	2◇(V)	5	-3	3 x 100	300
(22)	5NT	11	=	5 x 30 + 10 + 300	460
(23)	7♠	13	=	7 x 30 + 300 + 1000	1510
(24)	1NT	7	=	40 + 50	90
(25)	4♡x	8	-2	(2 x 2 – 1) x 100	300
(26)	4♠x(V)	12	+2	4 x 30 x 2 + 50 + 2 x 200 + 500	1190
(27)	7♠(V)	13	=	7 x 30 + 500 + 1500	2210
(28)	6NT (V)	13	+1	(6 x 30 + 10) + 30 + 500 + 750	1470
(29)	6◇x	11	-1	100	100
(30)	7NT(V)	13	=	7 x 30 + 10 + 300 + 1500	2220
(31)	6♣(V)	12	=	6 x 20 + 500 + 750	1370
(32)	6♠(V)	13	+1	6 x 30 + 30 + 500 + 750	1460
(33)	6♡(V)	12	=	6 x 30 + 500 + 750	1430
(34)	5♣xx	10	-1	100 x 2	200

(35)	3NTxx	7	-2	$(2 \times 2 - 1) \times 100 \times 2$	600
(36)	1♠xx(V)	8	+1	$30 \times 4 + 100 + 400 + 500$	1120
(37)	7♠x	7	-6	$(6 \times 3 - 4) \times 100$	1400
(38)	2♡	8	=	$2 \times 30 + 50$	110
(39)	4♣	8	-2	2×50	100
(40)	2♣x	9	+1	$(2 \times 20) \times 2 + 50 + 100 + 50$	280
(41)	6◇	12	=	$6 \times 20 + 500 + 300$	920
(42)	1♣xx	11	+4	$20 \times 4 + 100 + 4 \times 200 + 50$	1030
(43)	4♡	12	+2	$4 \times 30 + 2 \times 30 + 300$	480
(44)	2♠	10	+2	$2 \times 30 + 2 \times 30 + 50$	170
(45)	5◇	13	+2	$5 \times 20 + 2 \times 20 + 300$	440
(46)	2◇xx	12	+4	$(2 \times 20) \times 4 + 100 + 4 \times 200 + 300$	1360
(47)	1NT	10	+3	$40 + 3 \times 30 + 50$	180
(48)	7♣x	13	=	$(7 \times 20) \times 2 + 50 + 1000 + 300$	1630
(49)	6♠xx	13	+1	$(6 \times 30) \times 4 + 100 + 200 + 500 + 300$	1820
(50)	3♣	6	-3	150	150

Of course, as you surely will have seen in your playing experience so far, many of these results would occur rarely, if ever, in practice but the important thing is to know how to calculate the score in any eventuality.

There are a number of ways of comparing results for duplicate scoring, and these will be discussed in the following chapters. But before we go on to those, there are a few practical points of which new duplicate players should be aware.

First, very occasionally, you will meet a blind player and cards with Braille markings will be used. In that case, his partner will tell him the dealer and vulnerability, after which bidding will proceed as usual. During the play, however, you announce which card you play as you play it.

Second, and far more important, you will also meet elderly people who are hard-of-hearing. They might use a silent bidder which will look something like the example over the page.

When it is your turn, you should point to the bid you wish to make in addition to announcing it. You will notice the two words 'Stop' and 'Alert' on the above diagram and these two procedures must now be explained.

The 'Stop' procedure was introduced some years ago to protect

PASS		DOUBLE		REDOUBLE		STOP	
♠	1	2	3	4	5	6	7
♡	1	2	3	4	5	6	7
◇	1	2	3	4	5	6	7
♣	1	2	3	4	5	6	7
			ALERT				

players against being accused of unethically taking advantage of partner's hesitations. If a player hesitates for a long time and then passes, it may be obvious that he was close to a bid and therefore it may be difficult for his partner to erase that information from his mind if he too is close to bidding. This particularly applies after a preemptive bid. Therefore, if South deals and wishes to open 3◇, he says: 'Stop! Three diamonds.' West must now pause for ten seconds before making his bid, be it a positive bid, double or pass, so that his partner remains ignorant as to whether he had a problem. The laws now state that all jump bids must preceded by a 'Stop'. Therefore, if 1◇ is bid against you or by your partner, and you wish to bid 2♡ or more (even if there have been passes, doubles and redoubles in between) you must say 'Stop' before announcing your bid. If a player hesitates beyond the ten seconds, that is not unethical in itself, but his partner must be careful not to take the obvious problem into account when deciding his bid.

The 'Alert' procedure applies to conventional bids. So far, we have only learnt Stayman, Blackwood, directional-asking and cue-bids. However, in the bidding section we shall be learning many more. The basic rule is that any bid which does not mean exactly what it says must be alerted by the partner of the player who makes it. To give an example, suppose South deals and opens 1NT. That means what it says and should not be alerted. West passes and North bids a Stayman 2♣. That does not mean what it says and must be alerted by South. He does so by gently but firmly knocking on the table (and pointing to the alert sign if the silent bidder is used). The player whose turn it is to bid (here East) is *then entitled* to ask South what he *understands* by the bid. He is not allowed to ask North what he *means* by the bid. He should, however, only ask questions if he intends to enter the auction and the meaning of the bid is likely to affect his judgment in this respect; it is unethical to do so otherwise. Suppose East decides to pass and South bids 2◊. Again, although South is likely to have diamonds, this does not specifically mean what it says and North should alert. It is now West's turn and he is entitled to ask the meaning of either or both alerted bids.

Remember you should only ask for an explanation:

1 When it is your turn to bid.
2 The question should be addressed to the partner of the conventional bidder, i.e. the player who made the alert.
3 Only ask questions if you are likely to want to enter the auction.

At the end of the auction, the player on lead may ask for a review of the auction (and indeed may do so during the auction *when it is his turn to bid*) and explanations of all alerted bids. When he has decided what to lead, he places his card, *face downwards*, on the table. At this point, the partner of the opening leader is entitled to ask questions regarding alerted bids. Note that he does not do so before the lead is chosen as a question could (intentionally or otherwise) indicate a specific lead to his partner. Once questions

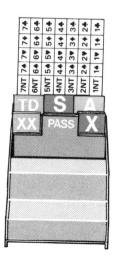

are completed, the lead is turned upwards, the dummy is exposed and play continues normally.

Another device to help the deaf is the bidding box. This is now standard in important competitions. When it is your turn to bid and you wish to make a contract bid, you put your thumb on that bid and your fingers to the back of the box and pull out all the cards between the two. Then place them upside-down as you look at it so that your bid is easily seen by the other three players.

Therefore, if your first bid in the auction were 2♣, you would put the 2♣ card and all those behind it down in front of you like this:

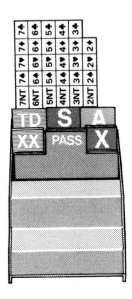

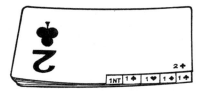

If you wish to pass, put down one green card so that, if your second bid in the auction were a pass, your bidding cards would look like this:

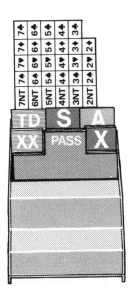

and if your third bid were 4♡,
the cards would look like this:

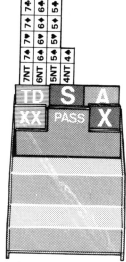

There are red cards (with D or X) for double and a blue cards (with R or XX) for redouble. For a Stop bid, put down your bid with the Stop card and then remove the Stop card after ten seconds. Your left-hand opponent may then make his bid. If partner makes a conventional bid, *immediately* put down the Alert card for a second or two and then remove it. However note that, if you make a conventional bid and partner *fails* to alert, you must *remain silent* until the end of the auction and only then point out the infringement. If your opponents feel they have been disrupted or *damaged*, they are entitled to call the tournament director, who will then give a ruling on what is to be done. This you will have to accept.

Once explanations are completed and the opening lead is made, the bidding cards are all removed and replaced in their boxes. You can see that, apart from helping the deaf, there are a number of additional advantages:

1 There is never a need for a review of the bidding.
2 The voice is not used, so that a player can never be accused of making a bid with intonation, e.g. a very loud or dubiously quiet double could have different interpretations!
3 The whole tournament atmosphere is much quieter.

Match-pointed Pairs

As the name implies, this is a contest between pairs, i.e. each player plays with the same partner throughout. This is the commonest form of the game in local clubs and tournaments. The best way to illustrate the form of scoring and the considerable difference between this type of game and rubber bridge is to pay an imaginary visit to a local club.

Starting times vary from about 7.15–8.00 pm and it is wise to be in your place a few minutes beforehand. When you arrive, you will find a large number of tables spread around the room. There may be a large letter N pinned on to one wall to indicate the North direction. Few things irritate a director more than having to move people around to fill up tables because too many pairs have sat North–South and not enough East–West (or vice versa) – so do try to complete a table rather than choosing an empty one.

Sometimes table money – the charge for the evening's play – is taken at the door. Otherwise you will find on your table a small bag or wallet with a name slip inside, on which you should fill in your name and pair number. The completed slip and table money will be collected during the early part of the evening. Most clubs have an arrangement by which you can become a member. Once you join, you pay a lower members' rate, while those who are not members pay at the guest rate. Some clubs (though not all) have a special rate for elderly and student members.

Generally, players are expected to turn up with a partner for pairs' evenings but, if you turn up on your own, you may get a game if another 'single' also turns up. Some clubs have a rule that the tournament director (commonly the owner) will play if necessary and then everybody is guaranteed a game.

Other clubs insist that you come with a partner and if you turn up alone you must be prepared to be disappointed. In any case, it is advisable to ring up in advance so that the director knows the position. If another single does turn up, you will be offered a partner – and please try to look happy about it, irrespective of the capabilities of the person concerned. Nothing is guaranteed to give a worse impression than a single who arrives, is given a partner and, at the end of the evening, complains that the partner was not good enough. If there are several singles, directors will always try to match them by strength, but there can never be any sort of guarantee and, if two partners are of widely differing ability, the stronger is bound to be disappointed. However, on this occasion, you need not worry as you will have a partner – me.

Now how is the evening organized? There are two possible arrangements and the choice will almost invariably depend on how many people turn up. If there is a small number of tables, the Howell movement will be used. For a larger number, the Mitchell is preferred. The dividing line varies between clubs and the type of event but, in principle, four tables or less guarantees a Howell movement; eight tables or more guarantees a Mitchell; with five, six or seven, it could be either. We shall discuss both in detail.

Mitchell movement

Let us, first of all, assume we have gone to a big club and there are several tables; the Mitchell movement will be used. Each table is assigned a number (and, if there are two or more sections, each will be given a colour). Suppose, to keep it simple, that there is only one section and we sit down, East–West, at Table 3. Pairs sitting North–South take the table number as their pair number and East–West will add a certain number (usually the number of tables in play) to that table number to work out theirs. Let us assume that thirty-two people have turned up so that we have eight complete tables and are asked to add eight to our table number. We shall therefore be Pair 11.

An evening consists of a number of boards, ranging from 24–27.

With eight tables, it will be convenient to play 24 boards in eight rounds, three per round. Each round will be against new opponents. On the first round, each table is handed three boards and we shall be asked to deal, play and record. So we deal the cards in the normal manner and the dealer is named on the board, as we learnt earlier. The arrangement of the tables and boards would typically be as follows (with North at the top of the page):

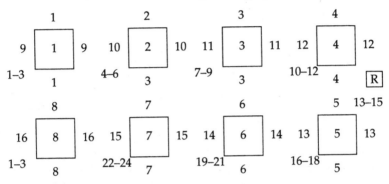

In the middle of each table, I have shown the table number (1–8) and, as you see, the tables are numbered clockwise round the room. You will always be told if they are numbered differently – it will always be some sort of 'circle' so that moving pairs go 'round' the room. As above, the North–South pairs have a number equal to the table number and East–West have eight more. The arrangement of the boards varies according to whether there is an odd or even number of tables. The 'odd' case is more convenient. Let us, for argument's sake, assume that nine complete tables had turned up. There would then have been 27 boards and Table 1 would have started with boards 1–3, Table 2 with 4–6 etc. up to Table 9 with boards 25–27. With an even number, as in our case, there will be problems in the movement if it is arranged in this way. In practice, an extra table is set up (which will not actually be used for playing but is considered a 'relay' table 'R'). The boards are handed out as shown above with Tables 1 and 8 sharing boards throughout the evening; i.e. they will share boards 1–3 on the first round, 4–6 on the second, and so on. Boards 13–15 will be placed on the relay table and will not be played on the first round.

The basic rate of play is based on eight boards per hour so that we shall be expected to complete a board in about 7½ minutes, a two-board round in about fifteen minutes, a three-board round in about twenty-two minutes, etc. As there is a certain amount of paperwork to be done, the first round usually takes a little longer and the director will allow for this.

With each board there are four cardboard 'curtain' cards and a sheet of paper known as a 'travelling score-slip' or, more concisely, 'traveller'. The blank curtain cards look like this:

North Board No.	East Board No.	South Board No.	West Board No.
♠ _____ ♡ _____ ◇ _____ ♣ _____	♠ _____ ♡ _____ ◇ _____ ♣ _____	♠ _____ ♡ _____ ◇ _____ ♣ _____	♠ _____ ♡ _____ ◇ _____ ♣ _____

The blank traveller looks either like this:

Section					Board No.			
N–S pair number	E–W pair number	Contract	Declarer	Result	+ Score –		Match-points	
							N–S	E–W
1								
2								
3								
4								
5								
6								
7								
8								
9								
10								
11								
12								
13								
14								
15								

or like this:

Section					Board No.			
N–S pair number	E–W pair number	Contract	Declarer	Result	+ Score –		Match-points	
							N–S	E–W

The choice varies from club to club and also between tournaments, much depending on whether a computer is being used to calculate results and how it is programmed. The difference is that, while on the first sheet, the North–South pair numbers are tabulated, on the second, both columns are blank. In the first case, which we shall assume here, our result is entered on the line of the North–South pair number – here 3 in the first round. In the second case, the result is entered on the first available line so that, in our case, the entry on the top line would be 3 and 11.

We now deal board 7 and play it. Suppose that, for argument's sake, it is the last hand we looked at in the defence section:

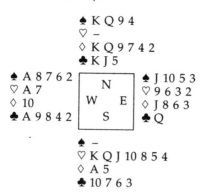

♠ K Q 9 4
♡ –
◊ K Q 9 7 4 2
♣ K J 5

♠ A 8 7 6 2
♡ A 7
◊ 10
♣ A 9 8 4 2

♠ J 10 5 3
♡ 9 6 3 2
◊ J 8 6 3
♣ Q

♠ –
♡ K Q J 10 8 5 4
◊ A 5
♣ 10 7 6 3

For a good start, let us defend it correctly against 3♡ and defeat it by one trick. At the end of play, each player takes his appropriate curtain card, numbers it with '7' (the board number) and fills in his hand. This is to ensure that, when the board arrives at the next table, the players can check their cards against the curtain card and mistakes can be rectified (typically if one hand has twelve cards and another fourteen) before play starts. It is the duty of the player sitting North to enter the score on the traveller and for his opponents to agree it. Therefore, at the end of play on this board, the curtain cards will be numbered and filled in (clearly and legibly) like this:

North Board No. 7	East Board No. 7	South Board No. 7	West Board No. 7
♠ KQ94	♠ J1053	♠ –	♠ A8762
♡ –	♡ 9632	♡ KQJ10854	♡ A7
◊ KQ9742	◊ J863	◊ A5	◊ 10
♣ KJ5	♣ Q	♣ 10763	♣ A9842

and our score will be filled in on the traveller thus:

Section					Board No. 7			
N–S pair number	E–W pair number	Contract	Declarer	Result	+ Score –		Match-points	
							N–S	E–W
1								
2								
3	11	3H	S	-1		100		
4								
5								
6								
7								
8								
9								
10								

The score is always written from the *North–South* point of view.
Here North–South scored -100 and the score is shown accordingly.
Had we misdefended and allowed the contract to be made, the
sheet would have looked like this:

Section					Board No. 7			
N–S pair number	E–W pair number	Contract	Declarer	Result	+ Score –		Match-points	
							N–S	E–W
1								
2								
3	11	3H	S	=	140			
4								
5								
6								
7								
8								
9								
10								

We play three boards against the first pair, complete the curtain
cards and enter the results on the respective travellers. Make sure

that both sides agree that the score entered is correct. Once a round comes to an end, the traveller entry must not be altered. If you subsequently discover that a mistake has been made, both tournament director and the opponents must be called (at a convenient moment – typically between rounds or the end of the evening) and all parties must agree on the alteration. To alter a traveller without such permission is considered cheating and a recent offender was suspended from competitive bridge for several months.

At the end of the round, the director will call a move, typically thus: 'East–West move to the next higher numbered table; stationary pairs move the boards down to the next lower numbered table'.

Now let us understand the consequence of the move in close detail. The East–West move simply means adding one for most pairs. However, the pair on the highest numbered table (here Pair 16 at Table 8) will move to Table 1. The boards will normally subtract one except that, with an even number of tables, the relay table counts and the North–South pair on Table 5 will pass their boards to the relay table (and those boards will be 'rested' for a round) while the North–South pair on Table 4 will take their boards from the relay table (and, in fact, they will have to be dealt, played and recorded for the first time). Boards 1–3, shared between Tables 1 and 8 on the first round, will go to Table 7. So the room will now look like this:

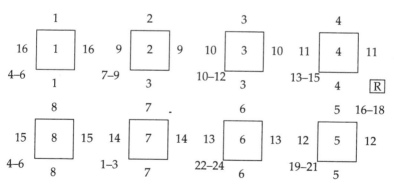

There will be eight such rounds during the evening so that, by the end, everybody will have played all the boards, albeit in different orders. For that reason, it is imperative to keep as quiet as possible so that vital information about a board is not overheard by neighbouring tables who may still have to play it. Post-mortems should be kept to an absolute minimum and be conducted in low whispers.

Behaviour in clubs varies a great deal. At the one extreme, there are those who regard the club as little more than a social venue (with the bridge very much 'by the way') and talk throughout the evening at the top of their voices, ensuring, almost as a matter of duty, that the entire club is updated with the latest gossip. They discuss hands at similar volume and have to be continually quietened by the director. At the other extreme, there are those who sit in total silence apart from bids, calling for a card from dummy (you must never touch dummy's cards in duplicate – always tell partner which card to play) and conventional explanations.

At the beginning of each round after the first, you are in a position to check that cards have been replaced properly in their respective pockets by first counting them and then comparing them with the curtain card. Call the director immediately if there is any irregularity. If you can attract his attention silently by raising your hand, well and good; if not, you may call 'Director!' and that is the only occasion when you are allowed to raise your voice in a bridge club. Never do so otherwise – to partner, opponents and, least of all, to the director, who has a difficult enough job as it is. One well-known player did so recently when accusing an opponent of unethical play and was rightly suspended for several months, even though – it has to be admitted – his complaint was not without justification. As a matter of common courtesy and to ensure that no information passes to a competitor, all complaints and queries must be made in a whisper.

Before moving for the last round, the director is likely to call an 'arrow switch'. (Some clubs arrow switch the last two rounds and others only arrow switch the first round). What this means is that the moving pairs will play the North–South rather than East–West cards, the board being rotated through ninety degrees. In that case, the result is entered on the line of the moving pair.

In our case, on the last round, we shall be at Table 2, playing boards 1–3. Seven results will already have been entered and we shall put our result on line 11. The sheet might look like this:

Section					Board No. 1			
N–S pair number	E–W pair number	Contract	Declarer	Result	+ Score –		Match-points	
							N–S	E–W
1	9	4H	S	=	420			
2								
3	13	5H	S	=	450			
4	15	4H	S	+2	480			
5	10	6Hx	S	-1		100		
6	12	6H	S	-1		50		
7	14	4H	S	=1	450			
8	16	4H	S	+1	450			
9								
10								
11	2	4H	S	+2	480			
12								
13								
14								
15								

Before arrow switches were introduced, the eight North–South pairs and eight East–West pairs were effectively being compared over a different set of cards and there were always two winners. Nowadays, with one or two exceptions, it is desirable to have one winner and an arrow switch of a small proportion (one or two rounds) is a way of mixing or 'scrambling' the Mitchell movement so that everybody can, at least on a proportion of hands, compete against everybody else. Now there is only one winner.

At the end of the evening, all the travellers are handed to the director and he calculates the score, usually on a computer. We must now learn match-point scoring in detail, as it is markedly different from rubber bridge. The basic rule is that a 'top' score on a board is calculated by $(n - 1) \times 2$ where n is the number of tables (or, more accurately, the number of times a board is played – if time does not permit the movement to be completed or, if there is an odd number of pairs and half the pairs have to sit out for one round). In our case, the top score is $(8 - 1) \times 2 = 14$. On a given board, each pair is awarded:

2 points for every pair they outperform;

1 point for every pair with whom they perform equally well.

So let us illustrate it by match-pointing that board 1 above on the above basis.

Pair 1:   Scored +420, beating N–S pairs 5 and 6 (i.e two others) to score 4 match points

Pair 2:   Scored -480, beating no other E–W pairs but equalling pair 15 (one other) to score 1 match-point.

Pair 3:   Scored +450, beating N–S pairs 1, 5 and 6 and equalling pairs 7 and 8. Therefore they score $(3 \times 2 + 2 \times 1) = 8$ match-points. Notice there is no difference between the score for $4\heartsuit + 1$ and that for $5\heartsuit$ bid and made exactly.

Pair 4:   Scored +480 beating N–S pairs 1, 3, 5, 6, 7 and 8 and equalling 11 to score $(6 \times 2 + 1 \times 1) = 13$ match-points.

Pair 5:   Scored -100, the poorest N–S score; they score no match-points – a 'bottom'.

Pair 6:   Scored -50, beating pair 5 to score 2 match-points.

Pair 7:   Scored +450 and, similar to pair 3, score 8 match-points.

Pair 8:   Scored +450 for 8 match-points as pairs 3 and 7.

Pair 9:   Scored -420, beating E–W pairs 2, 13, 14, 15, 16 to score 10 match-points.

Pair 10: Scored +100, beating all seven other E–W pairs to score a 'top' of 14 match-points.

Pair 11: We scored +480 (playing North–South on this board) to score 13 match-points in the same way as pair 4.

Pair 12: Scored +50 beating all other E–W pairs except pair 10 to score $6 \times 2 = 12$ match-points.

Pair 13: Scored -450, beating pairs 2 and 15 and equalling pairs 14 and 16 to score $(2 \times 2 + 2 \times 1) = 6$ match-points.

Pair 14: Scored -450 for 6 match-points in the same way as 13.

Pair 15: Scored -480 for 1 match-point in the same way as pair 2.

Pair 16: Scored -450 for 6 match-points in the same way as pairs 13 and 14.

Thus we can fill in the match-point awards for the board like this:

Section					Board No. 1			
N–S pair number	E–W pair number	Contract	Declarer	Result	+ Score –		Match-points	
							N–S	E–W
1	9	4H	S	=	420		4	
2								1
3	13	5H	S	=	450		8	
4	15	4H	S	+2	480		13	
5	10	6Hx	S	-1		100	0	
6	12	6H	S	-1		50	2	
7	14	4H	S	=1	450		8	
8	16	4H	S	+1	450		8	
9								10
10								14
11	2	4H	S	+2	480		13	
12								12
13								6
14								6
15								1
16								6
17								

The above calculations were a very long-winded way of working it all out and it can be done much more quickly. You might have noticed that, at any given table, 14 available match-points were shared:

Pair 1	scored	4	Pair 9	scored	10	
Pair 11		13	Pair 2		1	(arrow switched)
Pair 3		8	Pair 13		6	
Pair 4		13	Pair 15		1	
Pair 5		0	Pair 10		14	
Pair 6		2	Pair 12		12	
Pair 7		8	Pair 14		6	
Pair 8		8	Pair 16		6	
Total		56			56	

The totals of 56, i.e. n x (n -1) on both sides give a check on the accuracy. Therefore all the director has to do is to work out the scores for the North–South pairs in each case and deduct the answer from a top (here 14) to give the East–West score. These

Board No.	1	2	3	4	5	6	7	8	9	10	11	12
Pair Names No.												
1 P. England 4 Miss F. Scotland												
2 Mrs. L. Wales 1 G. Ireland												
3 Mrs. K. France 8 J. R. Italy												
4 A. Germany 13 S. Poland												
5 R. D. Portugal 0 Miss C. Malta												
6 H. Austria 2 Mrs. Y. Hungary												
7 Mrs. O. Rumania 8 Mrs. S. Bulgaria												
8 T. Switzerland 8 U. Sweden												
9 V. B. Finland 10 M. Denmark												
10 E. Spain 14 F. W. Andorra												
11 A. Reader 13 D. Roth												
12 P. L. Turkey 12 B. B. Greece												
13 Miss N. Holland 6 Miss H. Belgium												
14 Q. Luxembourg 6 Z. Albania												
15 A. Norway 1 I. Iceland												
16 S. Russia 6 J. Cyprus												
Column Total 112												

match-points are then entered on a main results sheet (see below). The director will have already entered the competitors' names from the wallet slips.

13	14	15	16	17	18	19	20	21	22	23	24	Boards	Total	%	Pos.

When he has all the travellers in, the director will be able to calculate the match-points on each one and fill in the results sheet. We shall do this in a moment as a practice exercise but, first of all, we are going to take a close look at our other two boards in the last set to illustrate the main differences between rubber bridge and match-pointed pairs. Remember that we are playing the North–South cards on this round. On Board 2, North–South are vulnerable, and suppose the traveller looks like this (of course we do not look at it until play at our table has been completed). Our result on line 11 has still to be entered.

Section					Board No. 2			
N–S pair number	E–W pair number	Contract	Declarer	Result	+ Score	–	Match-points N–S	E–W
1	9	1NT	E	=		90		
2								
3	13	2C	W	+1		110		
4	15	3C	W	-1	50			
5	10	3H	S	-1		100		
6	12	3Hx	S	-1		200		
7	14	4Cx	W	-2	300			
8	16	1NT	E	+1		120		
9								
10								
11								
12								
13								
14								
15								
16								
17								

As you can see, this was obviously a competitive part-score hand with our opponents having a club fit against our heart fit. The first noticeable feature is that, on two occasions, part-score contracts have been doubled, potentially into game, relatively rare in rubber bridge as the potential loss usually far outweighs the likely gain.

In match-points, it is a different story and we are going to do a few exercises to illustrate this point.

First, with the sheet as above, I should like you work out the match-points, assuming that our result against pair 2 was:

(a) 2H = (b) 2H + 1 (c) 3H – 1 (d) 3Hx – 1 (with you, South, as declarer)

(e) 2C = (f) 3C = (g) 3C – 1 (h) 3Cx – 1 (with us as defenders)

Each example should take you scarcely more than a minute, so that the whole test should be completed in well under ten minutes. Start your stop-watch.

We are going to work our way through the answers and it will be fascinating to learn that, in certain situations, little things mean a lot while, in others, a great deal means nothing.

(a)–(b)

Section					Board No. 2			
N–S pair number	E–W pair number	Contract	Declarer	Result	+ Score –		Match-points N–S	E–W
1	9	1NT	E	=		90	8	
2								2
3	13	2C	W	+1		110	4	
4	15	3C	W	-1	50		10	
5	10	3H	S	-1		100	6	
6	12	3Hx	S	-1		200	0	
7	14	4Cx	W	-2	300		14	
8	16	1NT	E	+1		120	2	
9								6
10								8
11	2	2H	S	=	110		12	
12								14
13								10
14								0
15								4
16								12
17								

A close inspection reveals two very important aspects of pairs' scoring – the possible importance of overtricks and doubles. First consider Pair 9. They played in 1NT, just making, to score 6 match-points, just below average. Had they made an overtrick, they would have beaten Pairs 13 and 10 and levelled with 16 to score 11 match-points, a huge difference. Similarly, looking at it from the other point of view, of Pair 8, they conceded 1NT with an overtrick to score only 2 match-points; had they held it to seven tricks, they would have beaten Pairs 5 and 3 and levelled with 1 to score 7 match-points, again a huge difference.

The two doubled contracts, defeated, brought in tops for the defending Pairs, 7 and 12, and it is particularly important to note Pair 12's score of 200. Had they failed to double, it would only have been 100, scoring only 9 match-points. When we tabulated our scores (including the part-score bonus of 50), we finished with a table in which scores for contracts of 2♡ (110) up to 4◊ (130) were greater than 100 but less than 200, and it is worth noting that game contracts which are made but not bid (e.g. 1NT + 2, 150; 2♠ + 2, 170; 3◊ + 2, 150) all fall into that range. Therefore, if you are playing against vulnerable opponents, it is very often worthwhile doubling them in competitive situations to try and score 200 rather than 100, even if it means accepting the risk of a certain bottom if their contract is made.

(b) however, shows the other side of the coin. Had we made 2♡ with an overtrick, apart from writing 140 instead of 110 on the above sheet, the match-pointing would have been identical. Once we were allowed to play 2♡, uncontested, we were already on a very good board, irrespective of result. Our opponents should have competed with 3♣.

So how does one know when overtricks (and undertricks) are important and when not? The truth of it is that, most of the time, we don't. However, when we have finished this exercise, we shall lay down some guidelines.

(c)–(d)

N–S pair number	E–W pair number	Contract	Declarer	Result	+ Score –		Match-points N–S	E–W
						Board No. 2		
1	9	1NT	E	=		90	10	
2								7
3	13	2C	W	+1		110	4	
4	15	3C	W	-1	50		12	
5	10	3H	S	-1		100	7	
6	12	3Hx	S	-1		200	0	
7	14	4Cx	W	-2	300		14	
8	16	1NT	E	+1		120	2	
9								4
10								7
11	2	3H	S	-1		100	7	
12								14
13								10
14								0
15								2
16								12
17								

Despite failing to make our contract, we have still scored an average because opponents have missed out by failing to double. That would have earned them 13, leaving us with 1 – a shared bottom.

(e)

Section					Board No. 2			
N–S pair number	E–W pair number	Contract	Declarer	Result	+ Score –		Match-points	
							N–S	E–W
1	9	1NT	E	=		90	9	
2								5
3	13	2C	W	+1		110	4	
4	15	3C	W	-1	50		12	
5	10	3H	S	-1		100	6	
6	12	3Hx	S	-1		200	0	
7	14	4Cx	W	-2	300		14	
8	16	1NT	E	+1		120	2	
9								5
10								8
11	2	2C	E	=		90	9	
12								14
13								10
14								0
15								2
16								12
17								

Conceding 2♣ for -90 would still have earned us above average.
Tight defence was important here; had we conceded an overtrick
for 2♣ + 1, 110 or 3♣ = also 110 (no difference), the sheet would
have looked like this:

(f)

Section					Board No. 2			
N–S pair number	E–W pair number	Contract	Declarer	Result	+ Score –		Match-points	
							N–S	E–W
1	9	1NT	E	=		90	10	
2								9
3	13	2C	W	+1		110	5	
4	15	3C	W	-1	50		12	
5	10	3H	S	-1		100	8	
6	12	3Hx	S	-1		200	0	
7	14	4Cx	W	-2	300		14	
8	16	1NT	E	+1		120	2	
9								4
10								6
11	2	3C	E	=		110	5	
12								14
13								9
14								0
15								2
16								12
17								

We have now scored well below average – a big difference.

(g)–(h)

Section					Board No. 2			
N–S pair number	E–W pair number	Contract	Declarer	Result	+ Score –		Match-points	
							N–S	E–W
1	9	1NT	E	=		90	8	
2								3
3	13	2C	W	+1		110	4	
4	15	3C	W	-1	50		11	
5	10	3H	S	-1		100	6	
6	12	3Hx	S	-1		200	0	
7	14	4Cx	W	-2	300		14	
8	16	1NT	E	+1		120	2	
9								6
10								8
11	2	3C	E	-1	50		11	
12								14
13								10
14								0
15								3
16								12
17								

Now we have a very good board but we notice that, had we doubled 3♣, we would only have earned one extra match-point by virtue of having beaten rather than levelled pair 4.

A look through these results seems very confusing to the duplicate beginner. Sometimes the overtricks or extra undertricks are crucial, sometimes worthless, and the position will become even more incredible when we move to Board 3. This time, East–West are vulnerable and we, as North–South, are not. On this occasion, there is a straightforward slam on for our opponents and, again with our result still to be entered, the sheet to date looks like this:

Section					+ Score –		Match-points		Board No. 3
N–S pair number	E–W pair number	Contract	Declarer	Result			N–S	E–W	
1	9	6S	E	=		1430			
2									
3	13	6S	E	=		1430			
4	15	6S	E	=		1430			
5	10	6S	E	=		1430			
6	12	6S	E	=		1430			
7	14	6S	E	=		1430			
8	16	6S	E	=		1430			
9									
10									
11									
12									
13									
14									
15									
16									
17									

Now, if the same happens at our table the board will be 'flat' and everybody will score an average of 7 points out of 14. But suppose we enter the bidding, find a diamond fit and decide to sacrifice in 7◊. Opponents will, of course, double and all now hangs on the result. If we go six off, we concede 1400 but look at the sheet!

Section					Board No. 3			
N–S pair number	E–W pair number	Contract	Declarer	Result	+ Score –		Match-points	
							N–S	E–W
1	9	6S	E	=		1430	6	
2								
3	13	6S	E	=		1430	6	
4	15	6S	E	=		1430	6	
5	10	6S	E	=		1430	6	
6	12	6S	E	=		1430	6	
7	14	6S	E	=		1430	6	
8	16	6S	E	=		1430	6	
9								8
10								8
11	2	7Dx	S	-6		1400	14	
12								8
13								8
14								8
15								8
16								8
17								

Incredible – we have lost 1400 points on the board but get an outright top!

But now let us point out something interesting. Had we only gone five off (conceding 1100) that would have saved 300 points but the match-point score would have been unaffected. The same applies if we had only gone four off (conceding 800), three off (conceding 500), two off (conceding 300), one off (conceding 100) or even made the contract to score + 1630! To the normal rubber bridge player, this seems beyond the bounds of sanity. We are in a grand slam, doubled and vulnerable and it makes not the slightest difference whether we make it or go six off! For a rubber bridge player, the difference in absolute bridge points is 1400 + 1630 = 3030. Playing at high stakes, that is the difference between begging on the Embankment and dining at the Palace.

In this hand, the trick that makes all the difference is the one between going six and seven off. Had we gone seven off, the sheet would have looked like this:

Section						Board No. 3		
N–S pair number	E–W pair number	Contract	Declarer	Result	+ Score –		Match-points	
							N–S	E–W
1	9	6S	E	=		1430	8	
2								14
3	13	6S	E	=		1430	8	
4	15	6S	E	=		1430	8	
5	10	6S	E	=		1430	8	
6	12	6S	E	=		1430	8	
7	14	6S	E	=		1430	8	
8	16	6S	E	=		1430	8	
9								6
10								6
11	2	7Dx	S	-7		1700	0	
12								6
13								6
14								6
15								6
16								6
17								

That one trick makes the difference between top and bottom and notice that the above match-point score remains unaltered if we go eight or more off – we still get zero – no more, no less. In other words, there is no difference between seven off (-1700) and thirteen off (-3500). Therefore it becomes even stranger that, on Board 2, we were making a tremendous fuss about 30 points – the difference between 1NT = and 1NT + 1 which, to the rubber bridge player, is scarcely worth talking about.

These two boards are very extreme cases, but they illustrate what a different game match-pointed pairs is. The first duty, therefore, must be to summarize the main differences and then consider how that is going to affect our tactics in bidding, play and defence.

However, let us first complete the main results sheet and look at the figures. We shall assume we made 2♣ on Board 2 and escaped for six off on Board 3.

Board No.	1	2	3	4	5	6	7	8	9	10	11	12
Pair Names No.												
1 P. England Miss F. Scotland	4	8	6	5	14	12	2	5	11	7	3	3
2 Mrs. L. Wales G. Ireland	1	2	0	5	10	10	2	11	2	7	3	3
3 Mrs. K. France J. R. Italy	8	4	6	4	4	9	5	5	6	0	11	8
4 A. Germany S. Poland	13	10	6	5	2	5	5	9	12	14	11	11
5 R. D. Portugal Miss C. Malta	0	6	6	5	2	0	2	11	14	2	3	11
6 H. Austria Mrs. Y. Hungary	2	0	6	13	10	5	14	5	8	12	8	3
7 Mrs. O. Rumania Mrs. S. Bulgaria	8	14	6	13	2	5	9	14	11	10	14	14
8 T. Switzerland U. Sweden	8	2	6	0	6	14	9	0	2	4	3	3
9 V. B. Finland M. Denmark	10	6	8	9	12	14	12	3	12	2	6	11
10 E. Spain F. W. Andorra	14	8	8	9	4	4	0	9	6	14	3	6
11 A. Reader D. Roth	13	12	14	1	4	9	9	9	8	4	0	0
12 P. L. Turkey B. B. Greece	12	14	8	10	10	5	5	0	3	0	3	3
13 Miss N. Holland Miss H. Belgium	6	10	8	1	12	9	9	5	2	10	11	11
14 Q. Luxembourg Z. Albania	6	0	8	9	12	9	5	14	12	7	11	11
15 A. Norway I. Iceland	1	4	8	14	8	0	12	9	3	12	11	3
16 S. Russia J. Cyprus	6	12	8	9	0	2	12	3	0	7	11	11
Column Total	112											

13	14	15	16	17	18	19	20	21	22	23	24	Boards	Total	%	Pos
14	14	3	5	3	2	3	2	14	13	12	0	24	165	49.11	9
2	0	10	5	12	11	0	12	10	12	13	12	24	155	46.13	13
7	8	10	11	12	11	10	8	2	6	13	10	24	178	52.98	5
7	8	3	0	3	7	3	2	2	1	2	2	24	143	42.56	16
12	2	0	5	8	14	6	6	7	12	8	2	24	144	42.86	15
2	4	3	9	11	14	10	2	2	6	10	8	24	167	49.30	8
10	2	10	11	12	4	4	2	2	12	6	6	24	201	59.82	1
12	8	3	14	3	7	14	12	7	8	12	12	24	169	50.30	7
7	6	4	3	2	10	11	12	12	6	2	2	24	182	54.17	4
4	12	11	14	11	7	0	2	7	1	2	14	24	170	50.60	6
7	6	4	0	11	7	11	12	0	2	6	12	24	161	47.92	11
2	6	11	9	11	12	8	8	7	2	1	2	24	152	45.24	14
0	0	11	9	6	0	14	2	4	8	4	6	24	158	47.02	12
2	12	14	9	2	3	4	12	12	8	1	4	24	187	55.65	3
12	14	4	5	3	0	4	6	12	2	8	8	24	163	48.51	10
12	10	11	3	2	3	10	12	12	13	12	12	24	193	57.44	2
													2688	799.61	

The director will normally announce the full list at the end of the evening and, on this occasion, we see that the leading positions were:

1	Mrs. O. Rumania & Mrs. S. Bulgaria	(Pair 7)	59.82%
2	S. Russia & J. Cyprus	(Pair 16)	57.44%
3	Q. Luxembourg & S. Albania	(Pair 14)	55.65%

We finished eleventh with 47.92%, a little below average – not too shameful for a first effort.

Let us take a closer look at those results and summarize what we can learn about pairs' scoring:

1 Most important of all: each board, irrespective of vulnerability, contract, whether doubled or not, (or the hand being passed out for that matter) is of equal importance. Therefore we must pay just as much attention to defending a modest undoubled part-score as to a redoubled vulnerable grand slam. On each board, 112 match-points are available to be shared among the 16 pairs, each table contesting 14. Therefore, in the above table, every vertical column must total 112 and the grand total must come to $112 \times 24 = 2688$.

2 It is usual for the result of each pair to be expressed as a percentage. Were a pair to score a 'top' (here 14) on every board, their total would be $24 \times 14 = 336$, and that would be a maximum 100%. The percentage is therefore calculated by dividing the total match-points of each pair by 3.36. A further check on accuracy is evident in that the total percentage must equal $16 \times 50 = 800$. Ours is slightly out because it is usual to round to two decimal places. Of course, with each pair playing the same number of boards, we could calculate a result by merely looking at the total match-points. However, had an odd number of pairs turned up, there would have been a 'ghost' pair and one table where moving pairs would have had to sit out for one round. They would therefore have played three boards fewer than the stationary pairs and one cannot obviously compare scores fairly over differing number of boards. The percentage is the recognized standard.

3 In practice, scores tend to vary, according to the size and quality

of the field, between about 35% to 65% In small fields of low standard, however, a much wider spread is possible but so too is a closer contest. I have seen pairs win an evening with 54% and others being disappointed with 65%!

4 You will have noticed that our results, on the boards we looked at in detail, had a considerable effect on those of other pairs. For that reason, even if a pair will not necessarily win an event, it can, right up to the last board, have considerable say in who does. It is accordingly written into the laws that pairs who are clearly not in contention for a prize are nevertheless expected to continue to play as well as they can so as not to spoil the event for others. Sadly, there are many who find it amusing to go in for eccentric bidding and other wild practices once it is clear that they are out of the running. This is clearly in breach of the proprieties of the game and, although it has to be admitted that this is very difficult to enforce in practice, you will very quickly earn yourself a bad name (very difficult to rectify) if you 'mess around', not caring about the result.

5 You will also have noticed that the luck element has by no means disappeared. Notably, if you pick up poor cards all evening, you will be almost completely in the hands of your opponents and if they bid their cards correctly, the chances are that you will be on a poor board, even with adequate defence. In practice, no pair wins a contest unless a fair amount is thrown at them. To give yourself a chance, you must avoid throwing unnecessary points away – even then, there is no guarantee.

6 The major difference between pairs and rubber bridge is that the question is *whether* you outperform another pair rather than by *how much*.

7 At pairs, it generally pays to be more competitive than at rubber bridge. If you get doubled for an enormous penalty, that is just one bad board and it will not ruin the whole evening. You have to consider not so much how *badly* you will be penalized but how *often*. Therefore you need not be quite so strict about requirements for overcalls and competing. It has been said that the successful pairs' players tend to be playing, rather than defending, most of the hands. There is an element of truth in

this, but allow me a couple of stories from my own experience, playing in good-standard fields on both occasions.

The first time I ever won at duplicate (as a very incapable teenager) I played with someone I had never seen before (even weaker than myself) and of the twenty-six hands played during the evening, one was passed out, I played two, he played one and we defended twenty-two. Recently, I was honoured to partner a gentleman (who had better remain nameless) who is generally accepted as one of the world's two or three best declarers, being particularly well-known in the pairs' game. The evening consisted of twenty-four boards of which I played two, he played four and we defended eighteen, winning the event comfortably. During the evening, he made three bids which – to put it kindly – might be described as 'debatable'. Had he bid those three hands in a more orthodox manner, there would have been a number of changes and I still would have played two hands (with one swap) he also would have played two, leaving twenty defended to win with an even higher percentage than our actual 65+.

8   It was demonstrated earlier that overtricks can be very important and, even though, on the odd occasion, they may mean nothing, it pays to fight for every trick. For that reason, passive defence tends to pay in the long run. Avoid taking desperate measures to defeat a contract if it means risking giving away an overtrick. It is also often justified to risk a contract (even a game or slam) for an overtrick rather than settle for a safety play. However, if the contract is doubled, we see the other side of the coin. If you double a contract and it is made, you will, at best, get a very bad board – almost invariably a bottom. For that reason, overtricks, in terms of match-points, will be of little importance. Once you double, you must defeat the contract at all costs.

9   Sacrifice positions are very important. According to vulnerability, you can afford to go off: one at unfavourable; two at equal; three at favourable, to prevent game.

In the small slam zone, the calculations are slightly more complicated:

At unfavourable, three in all situations;
At Love All, four in all situations;
At Game All, four against a minor-suit slam (worth 1370);
five against a major-suit or no-trump slam (worth over 1400);
At favourable, five against a minor-suit slam; six against a
major-suit or no-trump slam.

In the grand slam zone:

At unfavourable, five in all situations;
At Love All, six in all situations;
At Game All, seven in all situations;
At favourable, eight in all situations.

It is advisable to have these figures at your fingertips, but remember that, before sacrificing, you must be confident that the
opponents' contract is going to be made.

10 For game, you should be confident of odds of at least 50% –
remember that, in rubber bridge, the rewards are so high that
poorer odds are acceptable. However, at the other end of the
scale, it is not unreasonable to bid a grand slam on a finesse
(whereas it is at rubber bridge). However, this statement only
holds if you are confident that the rest of the room will be in at
least the small slam. This may hold in very strong fields but, in
practice, most of the time you will get a well-above-average
board if you bid and make a small slam. Greed rarely pays in
this area.

11 There is a tendency of many pairs to play major-suit fits in no-
trumps for the sake of the extra ten points if a similar number of
tricks are made. There is some sense in this but, in my experience, the practice loses at least as much as it gains, particularly
when you bear in mind that, if you have arrived at the correct
level, you should be expecting at least an above-average board.

12 With the same mentality, many pairs tend to forego looking for
minor-suit slams for fear of having to play in five of their minor
when ten or more tricks are cold in no-trumps. This is more
sensible and many pairs compromise by insisting that 4NT and
5NT are natural rather than Blackwood in this type of situation
so that they are not caught out. Again, this is sensible logic.

I could go on with this type of discussion for hours, but that will be enough for the time being. There are many good books written on match-point technique and they are well worth reading if only to learn how the mind of the match-point expert works.

However, there must be one word of caution. Match-point play revolves around trying to estimate what is happening at other tables and how to outperform those in the same seat there. In theory, some of the arguments are brilliant but, in practice, they are sadly off the mark. In my long experience as a director, it has not been uncommon for me to open a traveller and find that the board has been played at n tables in n different contracts! Trying to predict what ought to be happening at other tables is not that difficult. Trying to predict what is actually happening is like trying to forecast next week's football results. Although the experts do not like to admit it, this applies irrespective of the strength of the field. In a weak field, many pairs will be scarcely better than beginners and have little idea of what they doing. As soon as you approach the top – particularly nowadays when the vogue is very much for disruptive rather than disciplined and constructive bidding – the variety hardly shrinks. You only have to read magazine tournament reports for countless examples.

We conclude this chapter with two other methods of organizing tournaments.

Howell movement

The imaginary evening we have just discussed was run on a Mitchell movement, where you only play half the other pairs. Where there are very few tables, or in important competitions where the organizers think it is proper for pairs to play on an all-play-all basis, a Howell movement is used. The tournament director will place Howell movements card on each table which will look something like the ones below.

TABLE 1			
Rd	NS	EW	Boards
1	8	1	1–4
2	8	2	5–8
3	8	3	9-12
4	8	4	13-16
5	8	5	17-20
6	8	6	21-24
7	8	7	25-28

NS remain
EW to 3NS

TABLE 2			
Rd	NS	EW	Boards
1	5	4	5-8
2	6	5	9-12
3	7	6	13-16
4	1	7	17-20
5	2	1	21-24
6	3	2	25-28
7	4	3	1-4

NS to 2EW
EW to 4EW

TABLE 3			
Rd	NS	EW	Boards
1	7	2	9-12
2	1	3	13-16
3	2	4	17-20
4	3	5	21-24
5	4	6	25-28
6	5	7	1-4
7	6	1	5-8

NS to 4NS
EW to 1EW

TABLE 4			
Rd	NS	EW	Boards
1	6	3	17-20
2	7	4	21-24
3	1	5	25-28
4	2	6	1-4
5	3	7	5-8
6	4	8	9-12
7	5	9	13-16

NS to 2NS
EW to 3EW

Here we take our pair number from the top line of the card on the table. So again, if we sit East–West at Table 3, our pair number will be 2. There is one stationary pair, No. 8, sitting North–South at Table 1 and the others move, 2 following 1, 3 following 2 etc, with 1 following 7. Here boards have been divided into sets of four for twenty-eight to be played in the evening but, for a shorter evening, they can be divided into sets of three for twenty-one boards to be played.

Thus the card shows the table number (usually shown as a big numeral) with four columns, showing the round (Rd) number (here 1-7), the North–South pair number, the East–West pair number and the numbers of the set of boards. Boards 13–16 will be placed on a relay table between Tables 3 and 4 and Boards 21–24 and 25–28 between Tables 4 and 1. Boards will then move round the room decreasing the table number by one each round.

The important rule in a Howell movement is to double-check, each round, that you are at the right table, sitting in the right direction, with the right opponents and are playing the right set of boards. The move directions are at the bottom of the card and we shall move from 3EW to 1EW (playing against the stationary pair) to 3NS to 4NS to 2NS to 2EW (i.e changing direction at table 2) to 4EW.

When you play in a large Howell movement, there will be several stationary pairs. One will sit North–South throughout but others will switch to East–West once or twice during the evening. In those cases, the move on another table might simply say 'Go to Table 8' and you will be told which way to sit when you arrive there.

In big tournaments, most pairs' contests are played by scrambled Mitchell or a Howell where there are knock-out stages and an all-play-all final with a small number of pairs – typically twenty to thirty. The alternative arrangement is Swiss pairs.

Swiss pairs

The Swiss principle (often used in chess and other games as well) involves a random draw for the first round. After that, pairs are matched up according to how well they are doing, bearing in mind that two specific pairs can only meet each other once. This has a number of advantages, one of which is that those who perform poorly early on still have a chance to catch up against weaker opposition in the later rounds, while the more successful pairs are taking points off each other. The tournament is divided into several rounds and, in addition to the main prizes, there are usually ascenders' prizes, awarded to pairs who move up the greatest number of places in the second half of the competition. In fact, for administrative reasons, the first two rounds in Swiss pairs are randomly drawn and subsequent rounds are paired according to how well you were doing two rounds previously.

In all pairs' tournaments, you will be expected to 'make up' two boards at the beginning which you will not play and will be passed on to the next table. The director will hand you two sets of curtain cards and you will have two packs of cards already on the table. To save time, it is wise to order those packs into suits so that duplication is done quickly. You will make up the boards according to the curtain cards and then double-check that each hand has thirteen cards, that they are correct and that the curtain cards and playing cards go into the correct numbered board – the commonest mistake is to put the cards of Board 1 into Board 2 and vice versa. You will then pass those boards to the next table and receive some new ones already made up from another table. Again count your cards before looking at them and double-check that your own cards match up exactly to those on the curtain card.

The usual arrangement in Swiss pairs is that, for a given round, there will be ten boards in circulation, of which you will make up two and play the other eight. On the table you will find a blank result card which you will fill in and hand to the director at the end of the eight-board match. It will look something like this:

Round North–South pair No. East–West pair No.						
Board No.				Contract	By	+ North–South –
1	11	21	31			
2	12	22	32			
3	13	23	33			
4	14	24	34			
5	15	25	35			
6	16	26	36			
7	17	27	37			
8	18	28	38			
9	19	29	39			
10	20	30	40			
North–South initial East–West initial						

Now suppose this is the third round and we make up Boards 23 and 24 and play 21, 22 and 25–30. We cross out the board numbers not played, fill in the results and, when both sides have agreed the scores, initial the card. It is then handed to the director, looking something like this:

Round 3 North–South pair No. 126 East–West pair No. 78					
Board No.				Contract	By	+ North–South –	

Board No.				Contract	By	+ North–South –	
1	11	21	31	3NT + 1	S	630	
2	12	22	32	2H – 2	W	200	
3	13	23	33	–			
4	14	24	34	–			
5	15	25	35	6Dx =	E		1540
6	16	26	36	1NTxx + 1	N	1160	
7	17	27	37	Passed out			
8	18	28	38	3S + 1	W		170
9	19	29	39	4Dx – 2	N		500
10	20	30	40	7NT =	W		1520

North–South initial	JK
East–West initial	AR

Each board is match-pointed over the whole field (which could be a hundred tables) and the result is calculated according to how the match-points are shared between the two pairs at each table. So, for example, if the eight boards above were played at twenty-five other tables the top would be 50 and we would be playing the match for a total of 400 match-points. The results are fed into a computer. Suppose it calculates the results (relevant to our match) as follows:

Board No.	Match-points	
	N–S	E–W
21	30	20
22	48	2
25	1	49
26	50	0
27	17	33
28	12	38
29	2	48
30	10	40
Total	170	230

These totals are expressed as a percentage of the maximum 400. So this match would be 170/400 = 42.5% to 230/400 = 57.5% in favour of East–West. In practice, this is expressed in terms of victory points according to the following scale:

Percentage	Victory points	Percentage	Victory points
under 33.75	0	49.50–50.50	10
33.75–36.49	1	50.51–51.25	11
36.50–38.99	2	51.26–52.25	12
39.00–41.24	3	52.26–53.50	13
41.25–43.24	4	53.51–55.00	14
43.25–44.99	5	55.01–56.75	15
45.00–46.49	6	56.76–58.75	16
46.50–47.74	7	58.76–61.00	17
47.75–48.74	8	61.01–63.50	18
48.75–49.49	9	63.51–66.25	19
		over 66.25	20

Therefore about two thirds of the match-points will be enough to win all the victory points. Consequently, had we been sitting East–West in the above match, we would have won 16–4. Each round after the first two, we will be matched against another pair with a similar victory-point score. During round 4, we will receive a com-puter slip looking something like this (assuming that we had lost our first match 8–12 and won our second 19–1):

D. Roth, A. Reader Pair No. 178										
Scores in matches										Total
1	2	3	4	5	6	7	8	9	10	
8	19	16								43

Boards	21	22	23	24	25	26	27	28	29	30	
M.P.	20	2	–	–	49	0	33	38	48	40	230

In round 5, you will sit E–W at table 16 against Pair no. 43
Miss P. Gorgeous and Miss J. Delightful

In practice, one needs to win a little over 80% of the victory points to win a Swiss pairs' competition, which is normally played over three or four sessions with about ten to thirteen rounds.

Occasionally, though rarely nowadays, a club or tournament will stage an individual event. This is scored on a match-pointed pairs basis and you continually change partners, playing a very small number of boards (usually one or two). The movement will be clearly explained at the time by the director and there should be no special problem. The important points here are to keep the bidding simple and to consider it a 'fun' rather than serious event.

Team Events

Whereas, in pairs' scoring, a given pair is awarded credit according to the number of pairs (sitting in the same direction) they beat or level, in teams, we consider two tables only and the size of the score is taken into account. This is best illustrated by an example. Suppose a team of four ladies, Team A, consisting of Anne, Angela, Anthea and Arabella, challenge a team of four gentlemen, Team B, consisting of Bernard, Brian, Barry and Benjamin. The players might sit like this:

Each team sits North–South in one room and East–West in the other. Let us assume four hands are played. Each pair keeps a record, scoring plus or minus *from its own point of view*.

In Room 1 , the following happens:
Board 1: N–S bid 3NT and make it exactly:
   the ladies record +400
   the gentlemen record -400
Board 2: N–S bid 3NT and make it with an overtrick:
   the ladies record +630
   the gentlemen record -630

Board 3: E–W bid 6♠ and make it exactly:
                the ladies record   -1430
                the gentlemen record   +1430
Board 4 N–S bid 2♡ and make it with an overtrick:
                the ladies record   +140
                the gentlemen record   -140

In Room 2 , the following happens:
Board 1: N–S bid 3NT and make it exactly:
                the ladies record   -400
                the gentlemen record   +400
Board 2: N–S bid 3NT and go one off:
                the ladies record   +100
                the gentlemen record   -100
Board 3: E–W bid 4♠ and make it with two overtricks:
                the ladies record   +680
                the gentlemen record   -680
Board 4: E–W bid 3♣ and make it with an overtrick:
                the ladies record   +130
                the gentlemen record   -130

At the end of the match, the pairs return to their team-mates and score up. The ladies will compare as follows and calculate a net total:

Board No.	Room 1		Room 2		Net Total	
	+	−	+	−	+	−
1	400			400	0	0
2	630		100		730	
3		1430	680			750
4	140		130		270	
			Grand total		1000	750
			Margin		250	

Similarly, the gentlemen will calculate as follows:

Board No.	Room 1		Room 2		Net Total	
	+	**–**	**+**	**–**	**+**	**–**
1		400	400		0	0
2		630		100		730
3	1430			680	750	
4		140		130		270
			Grand total		750	1000
			Margin			250

On Board 1, the scores were identical and there was no *swing*.

On Board 2, there was a swing of 730 to the ladies.
On Board 3, there was a swing of 750 to the gentlemen.
On Board 4, there was a swing of 270 to the ladies.

The total swing turned out to be 250 to the ladies, and they win the match by that margin. The above method is known as *aggregate scoring* and is used in a small number of competitions. It is very close to rubber bridge scoring, except that honours do not normally count and part-scores are not carried over. The disadvantage of this type of scoring is that one sensational board (for example a grand slam, made in one room and defeated in the other) could cause a swing of such magnitude that the match is virtually decided on that board alone. This is obviously undesirable and, in nearly all teams' matches, a scale of International Match Points (always referred to as 'imps') is used. Let us tabulate it and we shall see that it has the effect of *dampening down* large swings:

Swing	IMP	Swing	IMP	Swing	IMP
0–10	0	370–420	9	1500–1740	17
20–40	1	430–490	10	1750–1990	18
50–80	2	500–590	11	2000–2240	19
90–120	3	600–640	12	2250–2490	20
130–160	4	750–890	13	2500–2990	21
170–210	5	900–1090	14	3000–3490	22
220–260	6	1100–1290	15	3500–3990	23
270–310	7	1300–1490	16	4000 and over	24
320–360	8				

At the lower end of the scale, the differences between imps are of the order of 30 or 40 while at the other end, in the third column, they are 250 and then 500. Therefore imp scoring is a compromise between rubber bridge (where points are everything) and match-pointed pairs, where every board is of equal importance, irrespective of the number of points at stake. However, it is much nearer to the rubber bridge extreme and it is important to go for game, to ensure making your contract rather than risk it in search of overtricks. Defenders should attempt to defeat a contract even if it means risking giving away overtricks.

So can you rescore the above four-board match using imps? The ladies' card would look like this:

Board No.	Room 1		Room 2		Net Total		IMP	
	+	−	+	−	+	−	+	−
1	400			400	0	0	0	
2	630		100		730		12	
3		1430	680			750		13
4	140		130		270		7	
					Grand total		19	13
					Margin		6	

The men's card would look like this:

Board No.	Room 1		Room 2		Net Total		IMP	
	+	−	+	−	+	−	+	−
1		400	400		0	0	0	
2		630		100		730		12
3	1430			680	750		13	
4		140	130			270		7
					Grand total		13	19
					Margin			6

The ladies win by 6 imps.

In practice, the net totals are never written out; they are just shown here for clarity.

There are various ways of organizing teams' contests depending on numbers entering and whether play takes place on one evening or over a weekend congress. We shall look at the three most important.

The knock-out match

This is a straightforward 'head-to-head' match of the type described above. The length of the match can vary according to time available – 24, 32, 48 or 64 boards being typical. Teams can be of four, five or six players and boards are typically played in sets of 6, 8, 12 or 16. In each set, the two tables take half the boards each and exchange boards on completion. At the end of each set, teams have the right to change their line-up as they wish, relevant rules varying according to the competition.

In a typical league match, 24 boards will be divided into two sets of 12. For the first 12 boards, the two teams would sit as diagrammed earlier. Customarily, refreshments are taken at half-time and, for the second half, the team playing at home changes seats, the visitors remaining stationary. So, if the gentlemen were entertaining the ladies, the line-up for the second half might look like this:

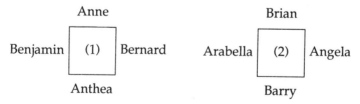

A 32-board match is played in sets of 8. A coin is tossed at the beginning and the winning captain can choose to 'seat' in first and third sessions (or allow his opponents to do so), allowing the losing captain to choose opponents in those sessions, while he chooses opponents in the second and fourth. So, in the above match, suppose the ladies had won the toss and chosen to 'seat' first, they would take their seats:

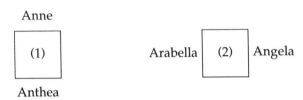

and now the men would have the choice of where to sit for the first session. For the second session, the men would be obliged to 'seat':

and now the ladies would have the choice of opponents. The room in which a team sits N–S is considered its 'home table'. In this match, Room 1 would be the ladies' home table and, at the end of a session, they reconvene to score up in that room. Scores are agreed with opponents before the next session commences.

The multiple teams event

In tournaments where large numbers of teams participate, there are two approaches in addition to the knock-out. In multiple teams, the entry is divided up into sections, usually denoted by a colour and consisting of about thirteen teams. The idea is that each team plays two boards against every other team and the winners are the team with the highest net imp score, although there is a possible modification which we shall look at in a moment.

At the start, each team sits at one table and takes its number from the table number. North–South pairs remain stationary while East–West move. At the beginning, the director will instruct the moving pairs where to go for the first couple of boards. Typically, he might say: 'East–West add 5 or subtract 8; deal, play and record.' What that means is that you add 5 or subtract 8 from your table number, bearing in mind that the answer must lie between 1–13 inclusive. Therefore, in practice, the East–West pairs of teams numbered 1–8 will add 5 and go to 6–13 and those numbered 9–13 will subtract 8 and will go to 1–5.

In the second and subsequent rounds, the move is always the same – what is known as an *American whist movement*. East–West pairs move down two tables, i.e. from 13 to 11, 12 to 10, etc… 2 to 13, 1 to 12, dropping the boards they have just played on the table they skip. Scoring is done at the about the halfway stage. There will then be another director's instruction (typically 'East–West add 6 or subtract 7') and the American whist movement continues thereafter. There will be one 'double' move so that team-mates do not play against each other – here the director will instruct East–West pairs to go down four tables, dropping the boards off at their team-mates' table.

At the end of play, a traveller will be assigned to each team and you will be expected to provide two legibly completed cards (one from the North–South pair and the other from East–West) and a summary of your results on that traveller. So let us try doing that as a stop-watch exercise. I am going to show you two cards as they would be completed by the North–South and East–West pairs and show you how to complete the details of one 'two-board' match. I should like you to score the remaining boards to find the swing and express it in imps. You should then total the net imps against each team and enter it on the traveller, giving your total net imp, indicating the sign (+ or –) at the bottom.

A typical personal scorecard, filled in by North–South, might look like this (assuming that the team number is 11):

Board		Opponents' Pair No.	Final Contract	By	Lead	Tricks (result)	Score		Match -points	
No.	Vul.						+	−	+	−
1	–	12	4S	S	HK	+1	450			
2	NS		5Dx	W	CQ	−3	500			
3	EW	1	Passed	out			–		3	
4	ALL		2S	E	HQ	+2		170		1
5	NS	3	3H	S	C4	+2	200			
6	EW		2D	N	C2	−2		100		
7	ALL	5	7C	W	C3	=		2140		
8	–		6Hxx	S	C6	+1	1620			
9	EW	7	3NT	W	S7	=		600		
10	ALL		1NTx	N	S8	−2		500		
11	–	9	2NT	S	SJ	+1	150			
12	NS		6H	E	DA	−1	50			
13	ALL									
14	–									
15	NS	13	3NT	E	DK	+3		490		
16	EW		4H	N	DK	=	420			
17	–	2	1NTxx	S	DQ	−2		600		
18	NS		4Hx	E	DJ	−3	500			
19	EW	4	2C	S	D10	+1	110			
20	ALL		2S	S	C10	−1		100		
21	NS	6	6NT	N	C6	=	1440			
22	EW		1D	E	C4	+2		110		
23	ALL	8	5C	S	C2	−3		300		
24	–		3D	W	H5	+1		130		
25	EW	10	3S	W	H2	+1		170		
26	ALL		3NTx	W	SA	−4	1100			

The vulnerability is given to help check the score. The opening lead column is there purely for personal convenience to help with discussions and it is not necessary to fill it in. Notice that we do not play boards 13 and 14 (which would hypothetically have been against our team-mates). Now let us look at the card filled in by East–West for the same boards:

Board		Opponents' Pair No.	Final Contract	By	Lead	Tricks (result)	Score		Match -points	
No.	Vul.						+	−	+	−
1	−	12	4S	S	HK	+1		450		
2	NS		5Dx	W	CQ	-2		300		
3	EW	1	1NT	W	C5	+1	120		3	
4	ALL		2S	E	HQ	+1	140			1
5	NS	3	4H	S	D6	=		620		
6	EW		3D	N	C10	-3	150			
7	ALL	5	7C	W	SJ	=	2140			
8	−		4H	S	CJ	+3		510		
9	EW	7	3NT	W	H5	-1		100		
10	ALL		1NTx	N	S8	-3	800			
11	−	9	3NT	S	SJ	=		400		
12	NS		6H	E	SQ	=	980			
13	ALL									
14	−									
15	NS	13	3NT	E	DK	+2	460			
16	EW		4H	N	D5	+1		450		
17	−	2	1NTx	S	DQ	-2	300			
18	NS		4H	E	CA	-2		100		
19	EW	4	2C	S	D8	=		90		
20	ALL		2S	S	C10	=		110		
21	NS	6	6NT	N	H8	-2	200			
22	EW		3NT	E	CJ	-1		100		
23	ALL	8	5Cx	S	HK	-3	800			
24	−		3D	W	HQ	+1	130			
25	EW	10	3S	W	CK	=	170			
26	ALL		3NTx	W	SA	-3		800		

I have filled in the results against Team No. 1 and you see that we gained 3 imps on board 3 and lost 1 imp on board 4, leaving a net gain of 2 imps for the two-board match. The traveller looks like this (overleaf):

Team No. 11 Opponents' number	Net swing (imps) +	-	Victory points
1	2		
2			
3			
4			
5			
6			
7			
8			
9			
10			
11			
12			
13			

We shall discuss victory points in a moment but, for the time being, I should like you to fill in the imp swings on the above cards and the net swings on the traveller in under two minutes. Start your stop-watch.

Now check your answers against the following:

Board No.	Vul.	Opponents' Pair No.	Final Contract	By	Lead	Tricks (result)	Score +	Score -	Match-points +	Match-points -
1	–	12	4S	S	HK	+1	450		0	0
2	NS		5Dx	W	CQ	–3	500		5	
3	EW	1	Passed out		–				3	
4	ALL		2S	E	HQ	+2		170		1
5	NS	3	3H	S	C4	+2	200			9
6	EW		2D	N	C2	–2		100	2	
7	ALL	5	7C	W	C3	=		2140	0	0
8	–		6Hxx	S	C6	+1	1620		15	
9	EW	7	3NT	W	S7	=		600		12
10	ALL		1NTx	N	S8	–2		500	7	
11	–	9	2NT	S	SJ	+1	150			6
12	NS		6H	E	DA	–1	50		14	
13	ALL									
14	–									
15	NS	13	3NT	E	DK	+3		490		1
16	EW		4H	N	DK	=	420		1	
17	–	2	1NTxx	S	DQ	–2		600		7
18	NS		4Hx	E	DJ	–3	500		9	
19	EW	4	2C	S	D10	+1	110		1	
20	ALL		2S	S	C10	–1		100		5
21	NS	6	6NT	N	C6	=	1440		17	
22	EW		1D	E	C4	+2		110		5
23	ALL	8	5C	S	C2	–3		300	11	
24	–		3D	W	H5	+1		130	0	0
25	EW	10	3S	W	H2	+1		170	0	0
26	ALL		3NTx	W	SA	–4	1100		7	
						Total	92	46		
						Net	+46			

Board		Opponents' Pair No.	Final Contract	By	Lead	Tricks (result)	Score		Match -points	
No.	Vul.						+	−	+	−
1	–	12	4S	S	HK	+1		450	0	0
2	NS		5Dx	W	CQ	-2		300	5	
3	EW	1	1NT	W	C5	+1	120		3	
4	ALL		2S	E	HQ	+1	140			1
5	NS	3	4H	S	D6	=		620		9
6	EW		3D	N	C10	-3	150		2	
7	ALL	5	7C	W	SJ	=	2140		0	0
8	–		4H	S	CJ	+3		510	15	
9	EW	7	3NT	W	H5	-1		100		12
10	ALL		1NTx	N	S8	-3	800		7	
11	–	9	3NT	S	SJ	=		400		6
12	NS		6H	E	SQ	=	980		14	
13	ALL									
14	–									
15	NS	13	3NT	E	DK	+2	460			1
16	EW		4H	N	D5	+1		450	1	
17	–	2	1NTx	S	DQ	-2	300			7
18	NS		4H	E	CA	-2		100	9	
19	EW	4	2C	S	D8	=		90	1	
20	ALL		2S	S	C10	=		110		5
21	NS	6	6NT	N	H8	-2	200		17	
22	EW		3NT	E	CJ	-1		100		5
23	ALL	8	5Cx	S	HK	-3	800		11	
24	–		3D	W	HQ	+1	130		0	0
25	EW	10	3S	W	CK	=	170		0	0
26	ALL		3NTx	W	SA	-3		800	7	
							Total	92	46	
							Net	+46		

Team No. 11 Opponents' number	Net swing (imps) +	Net swing (imps) -	Victory points
1	2		
2	2		
3		7	
4		4	
5	15		
6	12		
7		5	
8	11		
9	8		
10	7		
11			
12	5		
13	0	0	
Total	62	16	
Net	+46		

At the end of play, the results will be summarized on a main results' sheet. Teams' results are more difficult to predict than pairs' as much depends on the nature of the boards. If there are a large number of 'flat' boards (e.g. 3NT easy to bid and make) there may be few swings and a team could win an event with as little as +30 imps. With very distributional hands there are likely to be lots of doubles and sacrifices, and one could well be disappointed with scores over +70 imps. Our result above is quite respectable and, on average, the team would finish second or third in this typical summary:

Opponents' Number	1	2	3	4	5	6	7	8	9	10	11	12	13	Total +	Total −	Psn.
Team Number																
1	X	+3	+6	−8	−13	0	−5	−1	0	+9	−2	−4	−1		16	10
2	−3	X	+6	+9	+9	−1	+18	+7	−6	−7	−2	+12	+14	56		1
3	−6	−6	X	0	0	+1	+6	−4	−2	−1	+7	−1	0		6	6
4	+8	−9	0	X	−5	+5	−3	+8	+6	+2	+4	−17	−1	2		5
5	+13	−9	0	+5	X	−9	−8	−3	−2	0	−15	+5	+1		22	11
6	0	+1	−1	−5	+9	X	−14	−13	−10	0	−12	+2	+2		41	13
7	+5	−18	−6	+3	+8	+14	X	+5	−6	−1	+5	−3	−3	3		4
8	+1	−7	+4	−8	+3	+13	−5	X	+7	−1	−11	−1	−2		7	7 =
9	0	+6	+2	−6	+2	+10	+6	−7	X	+9	−8	+20	+1	35		3
10	−9	+7	+1	−2	0	0	+1	+1	−9	X	−7	−8	−6		31	12
11	+2	+2	−7	−4	+15	+12	−5	+11	+8	+7	X	+5	0	46		2
12	+4	−12	+1	+17	−5	−2	+3	+1	−20	+8	−5	X	+3		7	7 =
13	+1	−14	0	+1	−1	−2	+3	+2	−1	+6	0	−3	X		8	9

Therefore the leading positions would be displayed as:

1 Team 2 +56
2 Team 11 +46
3 Team 9 +35

We are now going to introduce victory points. This is effectively a further dampening in that every two-board match is considered of equal importance, so that one disastrous or sensational result does not have too big an effect on the final placings. The victory point scale varies with the number of boards played in a match. In each match, 20 victory points or 'VPs' are at stake. Here we have two boards per match and the scale, relevant to two or three boards, reads as follows:

IMP difference	VP	IMP difference	VP
0	10–10	11–12	16–4
1–2	11–9	13–14	17–3
3–4	12–8	15–16	18–2
5–6	13–7	17–18	19–1
7–8	14–6	19 or more	20–0
9–10	15–5		

Therefore, if we win a match by 6 imps, we score 13 victory points, but if we lose it by 14 imps, we only score 3 victory points. Our next exercise is to rescore the above teams' session in victory points and it will be interesting to see if it makes any difference. I should like you fill in the traveller for Team 11 including the victory points and then rescore the above table, putting in the victory points instead of the imps with the plus or minus sign. You should check the accuracy of your result by remembering that, while with imps the net total should be zero (the above positive and negative columns both totalled 140), with victory points the average is 10 per match and your grand total should be 13 x 12 x 10 = 1560. Aim for under ten minutes. Start your stop-watch.

Now compare your answers with those below.

Team No. 11 Opponents' number	Net swing (imps) +	-	Victory points
1	2		11
2	2		11
3		7	6
4		4	8
5	15		18
6	12		16
7		5	7
8	11		16
9	8		14
10	7		14
11			
12	5		13
13	0	0	10
Total	62	16	144
Net	+46		

Opponents' Number	1	2	3	4	5	6	7	8	9	10	11	12	13		Total		Psn.
Team Number															+	−	
1	X	11	13	6	3	10	7	9	10	15	9	8	9		110		10
2	9	X	13	15	15	9	19	14	7	6	9	16	17		149		1
3	7	7	X	10	10	11	13	8	9	9	14	9	10		117		6 =
4	14	5	10	X	7	13	8	14	13	11	12	1	9		117		6 =
5	17	5	10	13	X	5	6	8	9	10	2	13	11		109		11
6	10	11	9	7	15	X	3	3	5	10	4	11	11		99		13
7	13	1	7	12	14	17	X	13	7	9	13	8	8		122		4
8	11	6	12	6	12	17	7	X	14	9	4	9	9		116		8 =
9	10	13	11	7	11	15	13	6	X	15	6	20	11		138		3
10	5	14	11	9	10	10	11	11	5	X	6	6	7		105		12
11	11	11	6	8	18	16	7	16	14	14	X	13	10		144		2
12	12	4	11	19	7	9	12	11	0	14	7	X	12		118		5
13	11	3	10	11	9	9	12	11	9	13	10	8	X		116		8 =

There are a few changes in position, notably in the middle of the table. The difference here is small, but can be considerable when there a lot of big swings around.

Victory points are always used in our third type of organization.

Swiss teams

These are very popular tournaments and have large entries. This time, you play a series of matches (typically six for a one-day event or a dozen or more over a weekend), usually over 7, 8 or 9 boards. After agreeing the imp difference, the teams share twenty VPs on the following scale:

IMP difference	VP	IMP difference	VP
0	10–10	14–16	16–4
1–2	11–9	17–19	17–3
3–4	12–8	20–23	18–2
5–7	13–7	24–27	19–1
8–10	14–6	28 or more	20–0
11–13	15–5		

There is no need to memorize these scales: they will always be on display. At the beginning, you will be expected to fill in an assignment card, which will give your team number, and looks something like this:

Team No. 11		Names	A. Reader			D.Roth								
			T. Mate			Mrs. T. Mate								
Round No.	1	2	3	4	5	6	7	8	9	10	11	12	13	14	15
Opponents	12														
N–S	R6														
E–W	B6														
IMP															
VP															
Running Total															

The draw will be random in the first round – in fact, Teams 1 and 2 will play on Table 1; Teams 3 and 4 on Table 2, etc., bearing in mind that each 'table' comprises two tables in different section colours, usually placed a few tables apart so that there is no chance of overhearing. Here, we have been drawn as Pair 11 and our North–South pair will sit at red 6 while our East–West pair will sit at blue 6; our opponents of Team 12 occupying the other seats. Thus red 6 will be our 'home' table, while blue 6 will be theirs. After the first round, teams are matched up against those doing equally well and, by the end, our card might look something like this (for a weekend tournament of fourteen rounds).

| Team No. 11 | | Names | A. Reader | | D.Roth | | | | | | | | | |
| | | | T. Mate | | Mrs. T. Mate | | | | | | | | | |

Round No.	1	2	3	4	5	6	7	8	9	10	11	12	13	14	15
Opponents	12	24	87	43	2	61	47	116	128	13	75	72	5	99	
N–S	R6	R24	B36	B26	B33	R28	B24	R18	B25	R27	R28	R24	R29	R24	
E–W	B6	B24	R36	R26	R33	B28	R24	B18	R25	B27	B28	B24	B29	B24	
IMP	+9	-2	+45	-18	+18	+12	+31	-38	0	+1	+14	-25	+27	-4	
VP	14	9	20	3	17	15	20	0	10	11	16	1	19	8	
Running Total	14	23	43	46	63	78	98	98	108	119	135	136	155	163	

There was overkill of 17 imps in match 3 and of ten in match 8. Remember again that you cannot be drawn against the same team more than once and you should notify the director immediately if you are.

To win such an event, you will normally need to average about 14-15 VPs per match, but the above score would certainly win a prize in a big field. In practice, the field is divided up into three or four sections – random for the first round but according to score thereafter. Before the start of each session, a notice displaying the playing area applicable to your score range will be clearly displayed and you collect your assignment card from one end of that room. After each match, the winning captain returns both assignment cards to the control table and waits until captains are called to collect their assignment cards for the next round.

Having discussed pairs' and teams' scoring, we conclude this chapter with two 'compromises'.

The pairs' event with teams' scoring: The Butler method

It is often difficult to get four people together to form a team and yet many like to play with IMP in preference to match-point scoring. The Butler method gives a pair a chance to practice for important team events without their team-mates being present. The principle is to compare the score of each individual pair with an average or *datum* score on the board and express any difference in imps. Let us illustrate with an example. Suppose there are thirteen tables. On Board 1, there is an easy 3NT available to North–South at Love All, but some pairs have tried for a dubious slam in clubs. The traveller might look like this:

Section								Board No. 1	
N–S pair number	E–W pair number	Contract	Declarer	Result	+	N–S – Score		Match-points N–S	E–W
1	14	3NT	S	+1	430				
2									
3	18	3NT	S	+2	460				
4	20	3NT	S	+2	460				
5	22	3NT	S	+2	460				
6	24	6C	N	-1		50			
7	26	6Cx	N	-1		100			
8	15	6C	N	=	920				
9	17	5C	N	+1	420				
10	19	5C	N	=	400				
11	21	6Cx	N	=	1090				
12	23	3NT	S	+1	430				
13	25	6C	S	-1		50			
14									
15									
16	2	3NT	S	+2	460				
17									
18									
19									
20									
21									
22									
23									
24									
25									
26									

There is no firm rule, but the datum score is typically calculated by ignoring the two most eccentric scores and taking an average of the remainder. On the above traveller, the highest North–South score was +1090 and the lowest was -100 so those two are ignored and the datum is calculated as: $1/11(430 + 460 + 460 + 460 - 50 + 920 + 420 + 400 + 430 - 50 + 460) = 394.55$ taken as 390 when rounded to the nearest multiple of 10. Now all North–South scores are compared against +390 and all East–West scores are compared against -390. So Pair 1 will score 430–390 = +40 for a 1 imp gain and Pair 2 (who played this board as East–West on the arrow switch) will score $-460 - (-390) = -70$, for a 2 imps loss. You should now calculate the scores for the other pairs and confirm that the final table for this board will look like this:

Section						Board No. 1			
N–S pair number	E–W pair number	Contract	Declarer	Result	+	N–S – Score	Match-points N–S	E–W
1	14	3NT	S	+1	430		+1	
2								-2
3	18	3NT	S	+2	460		+2	
4	20	3NT	S	+2	460		+2	
5	22	3NT	S	+2	460		+2	
6	24	6C	N	-1		50	-11	
7	26	6Cx	N	-1		100	-11	
8	15	6C	N	=	920		+10	
9	17	5C	N	+1	420		-1	
10	19	5C	N	=	400		-2	
11	21	6Cx	N	=	1090		+12	
12	23	3NT	S	+1	430		-1	
13	25	6C	S	-1		50	-11	
14								-1
15								-10
16	2	3NT	S	+2	460		+2	
17								+1
18								-2
19								+2
20								-2
21								-12
22								-2
23								+1
24								+11
25								+11
26								+11

As in a pairs' contest, the scores for all boards are tabulated on a master sheet and a net plus or minus score calculated for each pair, the pair with the highest positive total net score winning the tournament.

The teams' event with pairs' scoring: 'point-a-board' or 'board-a-match'

This method goes to the other extreme, effectively playing match-pointed pairs on two tables. As before, every board is of equal importance and you either win it, tie it or lose it, irrespective of the difference in points. However, there is one change in that a difference of exactly 10 points (e.g. 3NT + 1 (non-vulnerable), scoring 430 against 4S =, scoring 420) which would be a victory for the no-trump players at pairs, is now considered a tie in the UK (in America, it is still a win for the no-trump players). You score two points for every board you win and one for every tie. The winning team is obviously the one with the higher number of points accumulated over the whole match.

SECTION 3

Bidding Systems

The System Card

We now come to the considerable task of sorting out a bidding system and preparing ourselves to face the almost endless variety of systems used by opponents in the heat of the battle.

The laws of duplicate insist that both members of a partnership produce identically filled-in bidding system cards. The entire section on bidding that follows will be devoted to filling in that card, studying the types of system that you are likely to meet in clubs and tournaments, and recommended defences against them.

If you are going to have any long-term success in the world of duplicate bridge, you will have to build up one or more regular partnerships and a considerable amount of effort will be needed in deciding which conventions you intend to play. In this respect, partnerships have to strike a balance between, on the one hand, being content with relatively few 'gadgets' and relying on their judgment and, on the other, learning a large a number of conventional bids, allowing them to deal with a widening range of hands while accepting an increasing strain on the memory. To begin with, it is probably wise to be content with relatively few. As the partnership blossoms and you increase your practice, you can add to your armoury.

A bridge partnership is one of the more testing relationships in life, particularly over the long term and, although there are many who stick together over decades, it is perhaps advisable to change the air from time to time, if only to avoid an unpleasant strain.

The principle problem with long-term bridge partnerships is the attitude towards mistakes. Many players consider that having to admit responsibility for a bad result is a serious stain on the ego, particularly as it occurs in the presence of opponents and sometimes – even worse – spectators (or as they are known in bridge jargon, *kibitzers*). They therefore either try to justify their actions or, worse still, put the blame on to their partners and how sad it is that long-established married couples are very often the worst offenders in this respect!

As in all other branches in life, one learns by mistakes and they should therefore be treated as treasures to be remembered rather than disasters to be forgotten or blamed elsewhere as soon as possible. A mistake remembered is one which will not be repeated and a player improves his game not so much by learning to play spectacular endplays, deceptions and squeezes, but far more by eliminating the shower of stupidities reliably on view at any club or tournament. You only had to watch a number of series on television to see players, reputedly the world's best, throwing points away like droplets in a waterfall with mistakes which ought to put a beginner to shame.

In fact, the most reliable way to assess a player is to watch his attitude towards mistakes. In my experience, the better the player, the quicker he is to point out *his own* mistakes. Mistakes, of course, invite criticism, which is often made in a less than polite manner, and this is the cause of many unnecessary, and often unpleasant, partnership dissolutions.

Mistakes should be discussed in detail for ease of memory but it is best done away from the table and in a constructive manner, with a view to 'knowing what to do next time'. I stressed in many of my previous books that the chances of a particular hand turning up twice are negligible, but situations *requiring similar handling* recur regularly and the best players are those who can recognize them, remember their mistakes from last time and produce the correct solution at the second and subsequent attempts.

This constructive approach is the key to establishing a successful long-term partnership and once you have chosen one or more people whom you wish to partner on a regular basis, you must sit down and sort out your bidding and defensive signalling systems. I have no intention of advising you on which system to play. I shall, however, show you how to complete a system card on the basis of what we have learnt so far and detail the various approaches currently in use. I shall then recommended possible defensive counters which you will need to know, irrespective of the system you choose yourself.

System cards – which must cover defensive signalling methods in addition to bidding – vary in design and comprehensiveness, but a typical example will be printed on both sides and look something like this:

BASIC SYSTEM			Name Partner	
OPENING BIDS	POINT RANGE	MIN. LENGTH	CONVENTIONAL MEANING	SPECIAL RESPONSES
1♣				
1◇				
1♡				
1♠				
1NT				
2♣				
2◇				
2♡				
2♠				
2NT				
3 bids				
4 bids				

DEFENSIVE BIDS			
OVER-CALLS	MEANING	OPPONENTS OPEN	DEFENSIVE METHODS
SIMPLE		STRONG 1♣	
JUMP		WEAK 1NT	
CUE-BID		STRONG 1NT	
1NT	Direct Protective	WEAK 2 BIDS	
	Responses	WEAK 3 BIDS	
2NT	Direct Protective	4 BIDS	
		MULTI	

ACTION AFTER OPPONENTS INTERVENE WITH				
SIMPLE OVERCALL		DOUBLE		BIDS
JUMP OVERCALL		DOUBLE		BIDS
DOUBLE	REDOUBLE	NEW SUIT	JUMP IN NEW SUIT	2NT
OTHER DOUBLES				

SLAM CONVENTIONS	MEANING OF RESPONSES	ACTION OVER INTERFERENCE
NAME		

OTHER CONVENTIONS:

OPENING LEADS	v suit contracts		4th; 3rd and 5th		
Attach red spot or hatch over if using non-standard leads Other leads	A <u>K</u> K <u>10</u> 9 <u>10</u> 9 x H x x <u>x</u> x	<u>A</u> K x Q J 10 9 8 7 x H x x <u>x</u>	<u>K</u> Q 10 Q J x 10 x x <u>x</u> <u>x</u> x	<u>K</u> Q x J 10 x H x x x x x <u>x</u> x	K J 10 10 x <u>x</u> H x x <u>x</u> x x x <u>x</u> x x
	v NT contracts		4th; 3rd and 5th		
	<u>A</u> K x (x) K <u>10</u> 9 10 x x <u>x</u> H x x <u>x</u> x	A J 10 x Q J 10 <u>10</u> 9 x H x x <u>x</u>	<u>K</u> Q 10 Q J x 9 8 7 x <u>x</u> x	<u>K</u> Q x J 10 x H x <u>x</u> x <u>x</u> x	K J 10 10 x <u>x</u> H x x x x x x <u>x</u> x x

(In all card combinations shown, circle the card normally led if different from standard, i.e underlined card.)

CARDING METHODS Describe primary method. State alternative in brackets	
ON PARTNER'S LEAD	
ON DECLARER'S LEAD	
WHEN DISCARDING	
EXCEPTIONS TO ABOVE	

Both members of the partnership must have identically completed convention cards. Cards must be exchanged with opponents for each round.

We shall now go through the card in detail, first entering our own choices, based on what we have learnt in the *Expert* series, and then considering the various styles we are likely to meet and how to counter them. As indicated above, both players must have identical cards and, each time we meet new opponents, the two pairs exchange these cards, briefly summarizing their main bidding methods but mentioning anything unusual.

Playing a straightforward Acol-style, the top part of our card will look like this:

BASIC SYSTEM			Name: A. Reader Partner: D. Roth	
OPENING BIDS	POINT RANGE	MIN. LENGTH	CONVENTIONAL MEANING	SPECIAL RESPONSES
1♣	11–19	4		
1◊	11–19	4		
1♡	11–19	4		
1♠	11–19	4		
1NT	12–14			Stayman
2♣	23+	0	Game-forcing	2◊ negative
2◊}	eight	5	forcing	2♡ negative
2♡}	playing	5	one	2♠ negative
2♠}	tricks	5	round	3♣ negative
2NT	20–22			Stayman
3 bids	weak	7		
4 bids	preempt	7		

As we go through the details, you will see that we have merely written down the general partnership agreements. The 2♣ opener, as we know, is not categorically forcing to game; we can stop in 2NT after 2♣ 2◊ 2NT but it is unnecessary to go into such detail. Similarly one-level openings may be made occasionally on 10 points or 20 – one does not have to stick absolutely rigidly to what is written on the card; all that needs to be shown is the approximate partnership agreement. Specific point-ranges are important for no-trump openings but irrelevant for preempts and, unless a partnership *specifically agrees* not to preempt above or below a certain point-count, there is no need to fill in that part of the card in detail. It is sufficient to indicate to opponents whether a pre-emptive bid is weak, intermediate or strong if such an agreement is made.

Similarly, the 'MIN LENGTH' column refers to the minimum length of the suit bid – again one does not have to be rigid. Sometimes a preemptive bid could be made on a good six-card suit, particularly in third position at favourable vulnerability. Pairs who do so might write down 6 in that column to cover that position but, as long as the partner understands that a seven-card suit is promised in principle (as will be the case nine times out of ten) and replies on that assumption, it is reasonable to write down 7 – the common partnership *understanding* is what matters.

Let us now work our way through defensive bidding. The first important distinction arises where we draw the line between simple and jump overcalls, i.e. if an opponent opens 1♢, how strong we have to be to bid 1♡ and how much stronger to bid 2♡. In the earlier books, we drew the line at about 14 points, bearing in mind that suit quality and length is relevant. Our entry would therefore look something like:

DEFENSIVE BIDS			
OVER CALLS	MEANING	OPPONENTS OPEN	DEFENSIVE METHODS
SIMPLE	9-13, 5+ suit	STRONG 1♣	
JUMP	14-17, 5+ suit	WEAK 1NT	

our intention being to double and bid again afterwards (or cue-bid) with stronger hands.

We make a cue-bid on strong hands where a take-out double is inappropriate and our entry there will look something like:

CUE-BID	Strong–forcing to suit agreement	STRONG 1NT

We now define our 1NT overcall. 'Direct' means that the opponent on your right opens, say with 1♠, and you immediately overcall 1NT. We defined that as 15–17. 'Protective' means that your left-hand opponent opened, again say with 1♠, and the next two hands passed. Now we defined 1NT as 12–14 points. We can still play Stayman after either of these bids and so we can include that under 'Responses'. Our entry will then look like this:

| 1NT | Direct Protective 15-17 12-14 Responses Stayman | WEAK 2 BIDS |
| | | WEAK 3 BIDS |

Now for the 2NT overcall: we agreed that it would show at least 5–5 in the two lowest outstanding suits – the 'unusual' no-trump – in both direct and protective positions. Our entry will look like this:

| 2NT | Direct Protective Unusual – two lowest out- standing suits | 4 BIDS |
| | | MULTI |

Regarding action after opponents intervene, we agreed that a double would be for penalties and bids would be forcing. Therefore, if we sit North–South, the sequence:

W	N	E	S
			1♠
2♡	Dble		

would be for penalties (as partner has already bid), and

W	N	E	S
			1♣
2♣	2♢		

would be forcing, as South has previously passed. The same applies over jump overcalls so our entry would look like this:

ACTION AFTER OPPONENTS INTERVENE WITH		
SIMPLE OVERCALL	DOUBLE Penalty	BIDS Forcing
JUMP OVERCALL	DOUBLE Penalty	BIDS Forcing

When opponents double, we redouble with about 10 points and a misfit. Bids are now non-forcing and jump bids are preemptive. The 2NT bid shows a good raise to three of partner's bid suit. Our entry would look like this:

DOUBLE	REDOUBLE 10+ with misfit	NEW SUIT Non-forcing	JUMP IN NEW SUIT Preemptive	2NT Good raise to three

We have not agreed on any other doubles so we shall leave that entry blank for the moment.

The strong club we have not yet met and, although it is played by a minority of players, you are likely to have to play against it once or twice in a session, particularly in the stronger clubs and tournaments. We shall discuss it in more detail later but, for the moment, it will be sufficient to say that, while we play 2♣ as our strong forcing bid, strong club players play 1♣ as forcing (but for one round only), promising 16 or 17 points minimum, according to style. Our 2♣ bid makes no promise about clubs and the same applies to the strong 1♣. There is, therefore, little point in playing the take-out double. A simple defence would be to play that a double promises at least 5–4 in the majors; 1NT promises at least 5–4 in the minors; and any suit bid is natural. Strength is of little importance as we are primarily trying to cause disruption to opponents, who have probably got the balance of the points. The important factors are vulnerability and the necessity to have honours in the implied suits, i.e. hold a playing or *offensive* hand rather than a defensive hand. Our entry would now look like this:

SIMPLE	9-13, 5+ suit	STRONG 1♣	Double for majors 1NT for minors

Against an opening bid of 1NT, we are bidding natural suits:

| JUMP | 14-17, 5+ suit | WEAK 1NT | Natural |
| CUE-BID | Strong – forcing to suit agreement | STRONG 1 NT | Natural |

Against weak two bids, normally in the majors (but occasionally in diamonds), there are a number of defences, but it is simple to treat them as preempts and use the double for take-out.

1NT	Direct Protective 15-17 12-14 Responses Stayman	WEAK 2 BIDS	Take-out Dble
		WEAK 3 BIDS	Take-out Dble
2NT	Direct Protective Unusual – two lowest out- standing suits	4 BIDS	Take-out Dble
		MULTI	Dixon

The defence to the 'multi' (named after its inventor, the English international Chris Dixon) will be explained later.

For slam bidding, we learnt Blackwood, although we shall use it with the maximum of discretion, i.e. as little as possible! We must also learn what to do if opponents interfere between the 4NT enquiry bid and the ace- showing reply. The usual procedures are DOPI and ROPI. Suppose one of us bids 4NT and the next hand, planning a sacrifice, bids 5◊. The procedure is follows:

Double: No aces i.e. 0 (or 4) aces – hence the 'DO' of 'DOPI'
Pass: One ace, i.e. 1 ace – hence the 'PI' of 'DOPI'
Next bid up (here 5♡): 2 aces, etc.

ROPI applies if 4NT is doubled (some pairs use that double to show a minor two-suiter or the two lowest outstanding suits if we have obviously agreed a minor). Now:

Redouble: No (or 4) aces – 'RO' of 'ROPI'
Pass: One ace – 'PI' of 'ROPI'
5♣:   Two aces
5◊:   Three aces

Our entry will therefore read:

SLAM CONVENTIONS	MEANING OF RESPONSES	ACTION OVER INTERFERENCE
NAME Blackwood	5♣: 0 or 4 5♢: 1 5♡: 2 5♠: 3	DOPI, ROPI

We have not agreed any 'OTHER CONVENTIONS' to date, so that can be left blank for the moment.

Regarding defensive methods, we are expected to mark our card clearly with a red or other distinguishing mark if we play anything unusual. We are going to play normally, so we simply delete what does not apply. The only additions I would recommend at the moment is the lead of the queen from A K Q. Also I prefer the 9 from 9 8 7 x against no-trumps and my chosen lead from 10 x x and other small-card holdings will vary according to the message I wish to send:

OPENING LEADS	v suit contracts		4th; 3rd and 5th		
Attach red spot or hatch over if using non-standard leads	A K̲ K 1̲0̲ 9 1̲0̲ 9 x H x x x x	A̲ K x Q J 10 9 8̲ 7 x H x x x̲	K̲ Q 10 Q J x 10 x x x̲ x x	K̲ Q x J̲ 10 x H x x x̲ x x x̲ x	K J̲ 10 10 x x̲ H x x x x x x x̲ x x
Other leads Q from A K Q	v NT contracts		4th; 3rd and 5th		
	A̲ K x (x) K 1̲0̲ 9 10 x x x H x x x̲ x	A J̲ 10 x Q J 10 1̲0̲ 9 x H x x x̲	K̲ Q 10 Q J x̲ ⑨8̲ 7 x x x	K̲ Q x J̲ 10 x H x x̲ x x̲ x	K J̲ 10 10 x x̲ (vary) H x x x x̲ x x
(In all card combinations shown, circle the card normally led if different from standard, i.e underlined card.)					

For the 'CARDING METHODS' section, we use discretion on partner's lead in the following order of priority. Encouragement/

discouragement of the suit led, count, McKenney suit preference and other information. When following to declarer's lead, count and suit preference will usually be relevant in that order and we play natural discards (high to encourage; low to discourage).

CARDING METHODS Describe primary method. State alternative in brackets	
ON PARTNER'S LEAD	Encourage/discourage, (count, McKenney, other) in that order of priority
ON DECLARER'S LEAD	Count, (McKenney, other) in that order of priority
WHEN DISCARDING	Natural
EXCEPTIONS TO ABOVE	

That would complete an acceptable card. We must now work through it again and discuss the large number of alternatives commonly played.

First, we shall consider the most common variations on the Acol-style and that primarily means the incorporation of weak two-bids in the major suits. Straightforward Acol players do not include them but suitable hands occur far more frequently than those appropriate to a strong Acol two-bid and it is therefore very useful, from both the constructive and disruptive points of view, to be able to cater for both varieties. There are three ways of proceeding:

1 Benjaminized Acol – usually referred to as 'Benji';
2 Reversed Benjaminized Acol – usually referred to as 'Reversed Benji';
3 Acol with a Multi.

Exact point ranges and suit requirements vary but a weak two in a major would normally promise exactly six cards in the suit, usually headed by at least one of the top three honours and about 6–10 points. However, some pairs vary their practice and degree of strictness on the above requirements according to seat and vulnerability. Many allow much weaker hands, particularly in third seat at favourable vulnerability, and most insist that, especially in first or second seat, a weak two denies four cards in the other major (to reduce the chances of missing game in that suit).

Benji and reversed Benji

In Benji, the two-bids are as follows:

2♣: A strong Acol two in a suit *as yet unspecified*, forcing for one round; some pairs also use it for balanced hands of 19–20 points and they will specify a closer range for their 2NT opening, 21-22 points.

2♢: Game-forcing, as 2♣ is in straightforward Acol.

2♡ and 2♠:Weak as defined above.

In reversed Benji, the 2♣ and 2♢ bids exchange duties. When replying, the following normally applies:

Benjaminized

2♣: Has 2♢ as its negative, but some pairs use it as relay, irrespective of strength. After that, the opener will specify his strong suit (or bid 2NT with 19–20 points, balanced), and bidding will proceed naturally (or with the use of conventions over a normal 2NT opening) thereafter.

2♢: Has 2♡ as its negative.

2♡ and 2♠ are, of course, non-forcing but, if the partner wishes to bid, then:

  (i) A raise in the bid major is purely preemptive and should be passed.

 (ii) A change of suit is natural and forcing and, particularly if the response is in a minor, 3NT will be the likely goal as opposed to four of the major; responder is likely to be singleton or void in the opener's major. Opener is now expected to support the responder's suit or show a feature in an unbid suit with a view to 3NT.

(iii) 2NT is a forcing relay, asking for specification regarding point-range, suit quality or possibly side-suit features with a view to a more accurate valuation of the hand.

Reversed Benjaminized

2♣:   Treated as the normal Acol game-forcing bid.
2◊:   Has 2♡ as negative but some pairs use it as relay, irrespective of strength.
2♡ and 2♠:Treated as with Benji.

The best way to illustrate it all is to work through some examples – we shall simply listen to opponents' bidding (suppose they are sitting North–South with South as dealer) Let us start with the pair playing Benji:

(1) S   N
     2♣   2◊
     2♡

Here South has shown an Acol two in hearts. The bidding now depends on the meaning of North's 2◊ bid. If it is a negative, there is no need to repeat it and therefore any bid is natural. Some pairs, however, who insist that a strong Acol two is categorically forcing, will allow a second negative (here 2♠ or 2NT according to agreement). Where the 2◊ was merely an unspecified relay, most pairs will now specify 2♠ or 2NT as the first negative at this point, treating it as though the opener had opened an Acol strong two in hearts.

(2) S   N
     2♣   2◊
     2NT

Here South has effectively 'opened' a 19–20 point 2NT and, irrespective of the meaning of the 2◊ response, bidding proceeds normally thereafter.

(3) S   N
     2♣   2◊
     3♣

Here South has shown an eight playing-trick hand in clubs. If the partnership specifies a second negative, that will probably be 3◊. Natural bidding follows.

(4) S   N
     2♣   2♠
     3◊

Here North has made a positive response and therefore has forced to game. South specifies his suit (or no-trumps if applicable) and natural bidding follows. North is likely to have a five-card spade suit and South an eight playing-trick hand in diamonds.

(5) S   N
    2♣   2NT
    3♠

Another positive response played by a pair who treat 2◊ as negative. North will have a balanced hand of about 8 points minimum (or an ace and a king) and South an eight playing-trick hand in spades. As North has implied a minimum of a doubleton spade, the partnership is likely to agree that any bid on the four-level by North will be a cue-bid, with a view to a spade slam, rather than a suit, which would probably be of four cards only.

(6) S   N
    2◊   2♡
    2NT

This is equivalent to   S   N
                      2♣   2◊
                      2NT

in straightforward Acol, except that the 2◊ bid may not be negative. Effectively, therefore, bidding will proceed as though South had 'opened' 2NT, showing 23–24 points.

(7) S   N
    2◊   2♡
    3♣

Here South has a game-forcing hand with a long club suit. If 2♡ was an agreed negative, there may a second negative available (3◊) otherwise natural bidding follows. If 2♡ is merely a relay, then the pair are likely to play 3◊ as negative. Natural bidding follows thereafter, as with   S   N   in straightforward Acol.
                           2♣   2◊
                           3♣

(8) S   N
     2◊   2♠
     2NT

Here North has replied positively and South shows a balanced hand. This is the same as   S   N

                                       2♣   2♠
                                       2NT

in straightforward Acol.

(9) S   N
     2♡   3♡
     Pass

South has shown a weak two and North, probably short on defensive power, has raised the preempt. South should not bid again, irrespective of his hand within the weak two range. Had North wanted a more accurate description, he could have asked for it with 2NT.

(10) S   N
     2♠   2NT

This is an enquiry and forcing for one round. There are a number of approaches and opponents must tell you which they are adopting. They are as follows:

   (a) American:
      (i) If minimum in the point range, repeat major suit.
     (ii) If maximum in the point range with a solid suit, e.g.

          ♠ A K Q x x x
          ♡ x x
          ◊ x x x
          ♣ x x   bid 3NT.

    (iii) If maximum in the point-range without a solid suit, show a side-suit feature. Therefore, with

          ♠ K Q x x x x
          ♡ x x x
          ◊ K x
          ♣ J x

        bid the feature, here 3◊. (If you have two side-suit features, bid the lower-ranking first).

(b) Shortages:
    (i) With no solid suit and no singleton or void outside, repeat major suit.
    (ii) With a solid suit and no singleton or void outside, bid 3NT.
    (iii) With a singleton or void outside the suit, bid it at the three-level. Therefore, with

       ♠ K Q x x x x
       ♡ J x x
       ◇ x x x
       ♣ x   bid 3♣.

(c) Blue club responses – show point-range and suit quality in steps. There are several possibilities but the following would be typical:

    (i) Minimum points, less than 5 points in the suit:
       ♠ K x x x x x
       ♡ Q x
       ◇ J x x
       ♣ J x   bid 3♣.

    (ii) Minimum points, 5 or more points in the suit:
       ♠ A Q x x x x
       ♡ J x x
       ◇ x x
       ♣ x x   bid 3◇.

    (iii) Maximum points, less than 5 points in the suit:
       ♠ K x x x x x
       ♡ A x x
       ◇ Q x
       ♣ x x   bid 3♡.

    (iv) Maximum points, 5 or more points in the suit:
       ♠ A K x x x x
       ♡ Q x x
       ◇ x x
       ♣ x x   bid 3♠.

    (v) Maximum points, solid suit
       ♠ A K Q x x x
       ♡ J x
       ◇ x x x
       ♣ x x   bid 3NT.

After that, responder will either start cue-bidding or choose the final contract, usually three or four of the major or 3NT. There are countless variations on the above but you can see the idea and you will always be told what is going on.

Against the pair playing reversed Benji, the 2♣ opener is the same as in straightforward Acol, so there is nothing further to discuss. The weak twos are the same as in Benji so the same applies.

(11) S   N
    2◇   2♡
    3♡

Here South has shown an eight playing-trick hand in hearts and now much will depend on whether the 2♡ bid was merely a relay or a negative. In the former case, 3♠ may be played as a negative, otherwise natural bidding follows.

(12) S   N
    2◇   2♡
    2NT

Here South has shown 19–20 points, balanced, and irrespective of the meaning of the 2♡ response, bidding proceeds as though South had opened a 19–20 point 2NT.

How do we defend against all these conventions? With the strong twos, we shall rarely want to compete, but there are opportunities for lead-directing and suggestion of a sacrifice. A basic simple guide is: if a bid is conventional, a double indicates a strong holding in the suit actually named while, if a bid is natural, as with the weak two, a double is for take-out. (You can agree to play it for penalties but, until you learn to play more complicated take-out conventions against preemptive bids, I recommend that you stick to take-out doubles throughout for the time being.)

Therefore a double of 2♣ or 2◇ (against Benji or reversed Benji), which do not necessarily mean the respective minor suit will be for penalties, usually showing a strong holding in that suit (say K Q 10 x as a minimum). Similarly, where 2◇ or 2♡ are explained as minimum hands and/or relays, a double would show the respective red suit. Similarly, after a weak two, a double of a bid showing a feature or a point/suit range rather than a suit will also be for penalties.

The bid of 2NT should be 'unusual' (at least 5–5 in the minors) against a Benji or reversed Benji strong bid (i.e. 2♣ or 2♢), but natural, showing about 17–20 points, against a weak two in a major.

The bid of a suit against 2♣ or 2♢ (Benji or reversed) is natural and non-forcing. In the unlikely event of your having a strong hand against a strong two opener in either version, I recommend passing and bidding after you have found out what the big hand has. Remember that, with a strong hand, you are unlikely to be unduly worried about defending so there is no desperate rush to enter the bidding. Both the other hands are likely to be near Yarboroughs and it will be unlikely that your opponents can make very much.

Let us conclude this section with a stop-watch test. For each sequence, I should like you to write down what you understand by opponents' bidding and what, if anything, you propose to bid against it, stating the likely aftermath and final contract(s) anticipated. Each example should take about fifteen seconds so you should complete the test in about fifteen minutes. South will always be the dealer and you should assume the score is Love All but state whether any changes to the vulnerability would affect your answers. Start your stop-watch.

(1) You are West. South, playing Benji, opens 2♣. What do you bid on:

(a) ♠ A K x	(b) ♠ A K x x	(c) ♠ J x x	(d) ♠ x x
♡ A Q x x	♡ x	♡ x x	♡ x x x
♢ x x x	♢ A K x x	♢ K x	♢ x x x
♣ x x x	♣ Q J x x	♣ A K Q x x x	♣ A K J 10 x

(e) ♠ –	(f) ♠ A K Q J x	(g) ♠ x	(h) ♠ A x
♡ A K Q x x x x	♡ x	♡ x	♡ A
♢ x x x	♢ x x	♢ K Q x x x	♢ x x x x x
♣ x x x	♣ Q J x x x	♣ K Q x x x x	♣ J 10 x x x

(2) You are East. South, playing Benji, opens 2♣, partner passes and North replies with 2◊, an unlimited relay. What do you bid on:

(a) ♠ A x x   (b) ♠ x x   (c) ♠ J x x   (d) ♠ x x x
    ♡ A Q x x   ♡ x x x   ♡ x x   ♡ x x x
    ◊ K x x   ◊ A K Q x x   ◊ K Q J 10 x x x   ◊ x x x
    ♣ J x x   ♣ Q J x   ♣ Q   ♣ A K Q J

(e) ♠ K Q J 10 x x x (f) ♠ A Q J x   (g) ♠ –   (h) ♠ A Q 10 x x
    ♡ x   ♡ x   ♡ J x   ♡ A Q 10 x
    ◊ x   ◊ A x x x   ◊ A K Q J x   ◊ x
    ♣ Q x x x   ♣ A Q J x   ♣ A Q x x x x   ♣ 10 x x

Would it make a difference to any of your answers if the 2◊ bid were categorically a negative?

(3) You are East. South, playing reversed Benji, opens 2◊, partner passes and North bids 2♠, a positive response promising a five-card suit. What do you bid on:

(a) ♠ A K J x x (b) ♠ x   (c) ♠ –   (d) ♠ x
    ♡ x x   ♡ A J x x   ♡ A K x x x   ♡ x x
    ◊ x x x   ◊ A J x x   ◊ x x   ◊ x x
    ♣ x x x   ♣ A J x x   ♣ A Q x x x x   ♣ A K Q J 10 x x x

(4) You are East. South, playing reversed Benji, opens 2◊, partner doubles and North bids 2♡, an unlimited relay (according to your opponents' methods, a pass from him would have indicated a diamond suit and willingness to play 2◊ doubled). What do you bid on:

(a) ♠ K Q J x   (b) ♠ A K x x x   (c) ♠ J x   (d) ♠ x x
    ♡ Q J x x   ♡ x   ♡ A Q 10 x x   ♡ A K J 10 x
    ◊ x   ◊ Q J 10 x x x   ◊ x   ◊ Q x x
    ♣ A x x x   ♣ x   ♣ x x x x x   ♣ 10 x

(5) You are East. South, playing Benji, opens 2♣ and the bidding goes:

S	W	N	E
2♣	Pass	2◊	Pass
2♠	Dble	Pass	?

North's 2◊ is an unlimited relay. What do you bid now on:

(a) ♠ x x x x   (b) ♠ A Q 10 x   (c) ♠ Q J 10 x   (d) ♠ x x
    ♡ A Q J x x   ♡ x   ♡ x x x   ♡ x
    ◊ –   ◊ x x x   ◊ x x x   ◊ J x x x x
    ♣ K x x x   ♣ J x x x x   ♣ x x x   ♣ J 10 x x x

Would any of your answers be altered if North, instead of passing at his second turn (i) redoubles (ii) bids 3♠ (iii) bids 4♠?

(6) You are West. South deals and opens 2♡ (weak). What do you bid on:

(a) ♠ A Q x   (b) ♠ x x   (c) ♠ A J x x   (d) ♠ K x x
    ♡ A Q x x   ♡ K J 10 x x   ♡ x   ♡ K Q x x
    ◊ J x x   ◊ K x x   ◊ A K x x   ◊ K Q x x
    ♣ J x x   ♣ J x x   ♣ Q x x x   ♣ A 10

(e) ♠ A K Q x x   (f) ♠ A Q J x   (g) ♠ A K x x   (h) ♠ Q x
    ♡ x x   ♡ x   ♡ x x   ♡ A
    ◊ A x x   ◊ x x   ◊ K Q x x x   ◊ A K Q x x x x
    ♣ x x x   ♣ K Q J x x x   ♣ K Q   ♣ Q x x

(7) You are East. South deals and opens 2♠, West passes and North makes an enquiry with 2NT, expecting blue-club responses. What do you bid on:

(a) ♠ A K J x   (b) ♠ x   (c) ♠ x   (d) ♠ x x
    ♡ A x x   ♡ x   ♡ A K x x   ♡ x
    ◊ A x x   ◊ A x x x   ◊ A K x x   ◊ K Q J 10 x
    ♣ x x x   ♣ K Q J 10 x x x   ♣ Q x x x   ♣ A K J 10 x

(8) You are West. South opens 2♡, you pass and North makes an enquiry with 2NT, expecting American-style responses. Partner passes and South bids 3◊. What do you bid now on:

(a) ♠ K x	(b) ♠ K x x	(c) ♠ x x x
♡ Q J x x	♡ x x x	♡ x x
◊ K J x	◊ K Q J 10 x	◊ A K x
♣ x x x x	♣ x x	♣ K Q 10 x x

(9) You are East. South opens 2♠, partner passes and North bids 3♣. What do you bid on:

(a) ♠ A Q J x	(b) ♠ x x x	(c) ♠ x x	(d) ♠ x
♡ x	♡ A	♡ A K Q x x	♡ A Q 10 x
◊ x x x x	◊ A Q 10 x x x	◊ K Q J 10 x	◊ K J 9 x
♣ K Q J x	♣ J x x	♣ x	♣ A Q 10 x

(10) You are East. South opens 2♠, partner doubles and North passes. What do you bid on:

(a) ♠ A K J x	(b) ♠ K Q x	(c) ♠ Q J x x	(d) ♠ x x
♡ Q x x	♡ x x	♡ x x	♡ K J x x
◊ x x x	◊ x x	◊ x x x	◊ x x x
♣ x x x	♣ A K J x x x	♣ Q x x x	♣ A 10 x x

(e) ♠ K x	(f) ♠ x x x x	(g) ♠ J x	(h) ♠ x x
♡ A Q x x x	♡ K J 10 x x	♡ x x x	♡ A K x
◊ x x x	◊ K Q x	◊ K Q J x x x x	◊ x x x
♣ x x x	♣ x	♣ Q	♣ A K J 10 x

Let us work through the answers:

(1)(a) Here we have 13 points and would certainly have opened but there are a lot of losers in the minor suits and we have no good suit of our own. In any event, we shall have another chance to bid but the chances are that we would be better off defending. I recommend a pass.

(b) This time, South is likely (but no promises) to have an eight-playing-trick hand in hearts. In that case, this hand is probably worth a take-out double but remember partner is likely to have little or nothing and there will only be a success if he has a very long suit. We pass for the time being and await confirmation of South's hand. Should he turn up with a hand other than an Acol-two in hearts, we shall continue to pass, electing to defend.

(c) This time, we have a very good suit of our own and, if those clubs do not stand up, our defensive prospects may be minimal. There are two options: double showing clubs, or 3♣, attempting to cut down opposing bidding space. I recommend 3♣, non-vulnerable; double, vulnerable. Some would even risk 4♣ at favourable vulnerability.

(d) Here we have an ideal hand to double to show clubs. At favourable vulnerability, there might be a case for a preemptive 3♣, but there are a lot of losers and the bid might suggest a sacrifice at the five-level or higher, which may be too expensive.

(e) South is likely to have a strong two in spades and here we should preempt as far as possible – we have a good suit and may have little or no defence if South is short of hearts. I recommend 4♡, except at unfavourable vulnerability when 3♡ is probably enough.

(f) Here the position is less clear. We have a lot of playing strength but could play in one of two suits. Also if partner is very short of spades, we could have adequate defence against a red-suit game or slam. I recommend starting with 2♠, to ensure the correct lead in the event of North becoming declarer. (For example, were we to pass, North might relay with 2◇, finding his partner with an Acol two in diamonds.) There might be an opportunity to show the clubs later. North might bid 3◇ over 2♠ and then, if South turns up with an Acol two in hearts, we can double for take-out.

(g) This hand has a lot of playing strength and possibly little or no defence and therefore we want to declare. There are two possible approaches. An immediate 2NT would show both minors. The alternative is to double 2♣ now, intending to bid no-trumps (unusual) next time round. The immediate 2NT has the advantage of reducing opponents' bidding space, while the latter approach clarifies that the clubs are longer and that could be important if partner has two clubs and three diamonds. In that case, clubs should be preferred as a forcing game could result in loss of trump control and a heavy penalty if diamonds are trumps.

It is a close decision and a good case can be made on both sides. I would suggest double first at favourable vulnerability when the sacrifice is most likely. At any other vulnerability, I would recommend an immediate 2NT.

(h) This hand has the correct shape for an unusual no-trump but the points are in the short suits and there is plenty of defence. This is therefore no time to suggest a sacrifice and I recommend a pass.

(2)(a) Here we have a good defensive hand with little playing strength and therefore no wish to compete. I recommend a pass.

(b) Here we have strong diamonds and can indicate a lead with a double in a similar situation to (1d). South is likely to be declarer in a major-suit game.

(c) Here we want to preempt. I recommend 4◊ non-vulnerable; 3◊ vulnerable.

(d) We would like to indicate a club lead this time but it is difficult to do so. 3♣ on a four-card suit is too dangerous and might propel partner into a sacrifice which is phantom or too expensive. I recommend a pass.

(e) Here again, we want to preempt with a one-suited hand with few losers outside. I recommend 4♠, non-vulnerable; 3♠ vulnerable.

(f) This hand is at the other extreme. 4441 hands do not play well at the best of times, least of all when our points are badly placed under the strong hand. I recommend a pass now but, if South bids 2♡ and this is passed round to us, or North gives a raise to 3♡, we can take the view that partner is likely to have length in at least one of the non-heart suits and compete with a take-out double.

(g) This is a very powerful hand and there are three approaches. Unfortunately, to double now for the correct lead against a major-suit game, intending to bid clubs afterwards, would show longer diamonds than clubs, and this is dangerous. An immediate 2NT would show equal length in principle, causing trouble if partner has three diamonds and two clubs, or two diamonds and one club. I would take the view that we are likely to be playing this hand rather than defending and risk 3♣ now, intending to bid no-trumps next time round. An eventual club lead against a major-suit game will not be fatal as we have the ace.

(h) Here we have plenty of defence against the majors and opponents will have to play at the five-level or (more likely) 3NT for game. Our honours are likely to be badly placed and we have no reason to bid. I recommend a pass.

There is little reason to alter any of these answers if the 2◊ bid is categorically a negative.

(3)(a) Here a double would be for take-out and the last thing we would want to do is warn opponents of a bad split when they are committed to game at least. I recommend a pass.

(b) This hand, shapewise, is more suited to a take-out double but I should advise against it. We have 15 points and it is obvious that, with a strong hand over us (making all three jacks virtually worthless) and a positive response on our right, partner will turn up with nothing. We are therefore better suited to defence and I recommend a pass, hoping opponents get too high. 3NT is their most likely contract but they may find it difficult to stop there and be in trouble when suits are breaking badly.

(c) With a great deal of playing strength, this is a different story. A take-out double would be dangerous if partner is long in diamonds, so I would recommend bidding 3♣ now and hearts later. If opponents bid diamonds before the bid comes back to us, a take-out double would show this hand. How far we will compete depends on vulnerability but, once we have shown our two suits, it is for *partner* to decide.

(d) Again, we have massive playing strength and possibly no defence if there is a void of clubs against us. Preemptive bidding is therefore in order and I would recommend 5♣ except at unfavourable vulnerability, when 4♣ is probably enough although, even now, there is a good case for 5♣.

(4)(a) This is a misfit and therefore we want to defend. The opponents are in a forcing situation and will surely run into trouble. I recommend a pass.

(b) This hand is at the other extreme – a super fit with a good side-suit. It is important to bid spades to ensure a spade lead against a club or heart contract, and I recommend 4♠ now, intending to remove to 5◊ if doubled. After that, it will again be partner's decision whether to defend or sacrifice and his length in spades will probably be a critical factor.

(c) It may be tempting to double 2♡ for a heart lead but I would advise against it, primarily because the hearts are broken. A double, which takes no bidding space away, will help opponents to value their heart honours accurately. With partner having implied diamonds, there is plenty of defence and I recommend a pass.

(d) Here a double is more important. We can compete in diamonds later and partner will be better placed to decide whether to defend or sacrifice against a black-suit game or slam.

(5) The first point here is that partner should have a very good hand to compete against an Acol two bid, with a singleton or void spade a virtual must.

(a) Here we have a tremendous hand and should bid 4♡, intending to compete further if necessary. This could well be a hand where, if partner is strong in clubs and weak in diamonds, a slam could be on for both sides. It is usually best to compete vigorously in these situations, preferring the little mistake (both sides going one off in their contract – unnecessary loss of 200) to the serious mistake (both sides making their contract with that loss up to 2000). For that reason, it is probably worth going to the grand slam level but, as partner may be weak in clubs and strong in diamonds, there is no need to rush at this stage.

(b) This hand is poor from the playing point of view but it would be a mistake to leave the double or bid 2NT to advertize the fact. I recommend simply answering the double with 3♣ and awaiting further developments.

(c) This is a nightmare, but again we must simply answer the double with 3♣ and hope for the best.

(d) There is a case for making 2NT 'unusual' in this position as it is hard to imagine a hand where one wants to play 2NT against an Acol two bid. Otherwise, it is debatable whether this hand is worth two bids, vulnerability being important. At favourable, a sacrifice at the five-level will probably be worthwhile and I would recommend 3◊ now and clubs later. Otherwise a simple 3♣ is probably best.

  (i) If North redoubles, then he is announcing strength to his partner – and a possible intention to defend – and has promised another bid. Now there is no rush and in:

    (a) A simple 3♡ will do. We shall compete further later, if necessary.

    (b) No change – we simply bid our long suit, 3♣.

    (c) Now we do not need to choose and can pass, leaving it to partner.

    (d) This time, 2NT is categorically unusual – we would never bid it seriously in this situation.

  (ii) This time, North has confirmed a fit:

    (a) We compete with 4♡, as explained earlier.

    (b) There is now no need to bid on a hand with which we are likely to want to defend.

    (c) We pass gratefully.

    (d) This is less clear and vulnerability is important. Non-vulnerable, I should recommend a sacrifice and make the position clear to partner now with an unusual 3NT. Partner can then elect to defend 4♠ if his hearts are very strong, or compete if he prefers. At Game All, it is more debatable, but I should be inclined to do the same. At unfavourable vulnerability, even though partner should be that much stronger, I would prefer a pass but be prepared to be wrong.

  (iii) Now in (a), (b) and (c), a void of spades with partner is a virtual certainty.

    (a) I should recommend putting pressure on opponents with an immediate 6♡ at any vulnerability. It may well not be clear to a distributional South who is supposed to be sacrificing against whom – let him guess at a high level where a mistake will be expensive.

(b) Here we are happy to defend and I recommend a pass.

(c) same applies as in (b).

(d) This is less clear but I would go for the sacrifice with an unusual 4NT. This is unlikely to cost much and could well gain a lot in pushing opponents up to 5♠, which may go down if partner has very strong hearts.

(6)(a) This is a flat hand with little playing strength, particularly as our long suit has been bid by opponents. I recommend a pass, hoping to defend.

 (b) Here there is even less reason to bid. We pass and hope partner reopens with a take-out double, which we will be delighted to convert to a heavy penalty.

 (c) This an ideal take-out double and we hope for game in a non-heart suit or (less likely) 3NT if partner has a double-stop in hearts.

 (d) Here we have 17 points with the hearts well stopped in a balanced hand. 2NT is ideal, hoping to finish in 3NT.

 (e) This time, a straightforward overcall of 2♠ will invite 4♠ or 3NT. Note that overcalls should, generally speaking, be a little stronger at the two-level, and even more so at the three-level, than one would expect at the one-level.

 (f) This is an awkward hand. It would be a pity not to make a take-out double with a view to finding a 4–4 spade fit for 4♠, probably the most likely game. Against that, the double risks partner going too high in diamonds, with an embarrassing penalty likely if North bounces in hearts. It is probably safer to bid 3♣, hoping to bid spades later if we get another chance. The position will then be much clearer to partner, who can choose between 4♣ and 5♣ if he has sufficient strength.

 (g) This time, with a stronger hand and at least good tolerance for clubs, a take-out double is more appropriate. A club response can be corrected to diamonds *at the same level* and the risk of a disaster is much reduced. We are primarily hoping for 4♠ or 5◊, but 3NT may be there if partner has the hearts well stopped.

(h) Except in the unlikely event of a bad diamond split, we have eight tricks in our own hand and every prospect of making 3NT if partner has anything at all. We therefore bid it direct.

(7)(a) Here we shall be delighted to defend against the expected spade contract and pass, awaiting further developments.

(b) This time, we shudder at the thought of defending as opponents are likely to be heading for at least game, if not slam. If partner has any support for either minor, we could make a lot of tricks and I recommend an immediate 5♣ non-vulnerable, 4♣ vulnerable, although there is a case for 5♣ at Game All.

(c) Here we have a strong hand, good enough for a take-out double, hoping to play in a non-spade suit at a level appropriate to partner's strength.

(d) Here we are prepared to play in four of a minor (or more if partner is strong) and say so with an 'unusual' 3NT.

(8)(a) It will be our lead against a heart contract and doubling on this relatively poor and broken diamond holding is more likely to help opponents than partner. I recommend a pass.

(b) Here, with a solid holding, a double is unlikely to cost and could be important if opponents decide to play in 3NT. There could also be a worthwhile sacrifice in 5◊ at favourable vulnerability if partner is very short of hearts.

(c) This time, we shall want a club, rather than a diamond, lead against 3NT; indeed, a diamond could help set up South's ◊ Q J 10. We therefore pass.

(9)(a) Here, with all our points in opponents' suits, we are keen to defend and, particularly with opponents in a forcing situation, we pass and await further developments.

(b) Here it may be tempting to come in but the 3♣ bid (in preference to the enquiring 2NT) suggests a search for 3NT and therefore a misfit. With three cards (the worst possible holdings) in both opponents' suits, it is wiser to pass and hope to defend. North's attempt to find game, despite a likely misfit, suggests a strong hand and we are unlikely to able to make very much, even with the diamond honours well placed.

(c) This time, we have plenty of playing strength outside opponents' suits and can compete with a take-out double, hoping to play in a part-score or game in a red-suit.

(d) This is less clear. Again, we could have a red-suit contract on but the shorter broken suits are less suitable. This hand has excellent defensive prospects, particularly as partner is likely to be long in spades. We pass, hoping to defend.

(10) (a) It may be tempting to stand the double, but risky to do so. If partner is void of spades, we might only make two trump tricks and the loss could be considerable. It is safer to bid 2NT with a view to a possible no-trump game.

(b) Here it is likely that the club suit will come in for six tricks and now 3NT is very likely to be made. We bid it direct.

(c) This is a very poor hand and we can do no more than answer the double with 3♣, hoping to play there. 2NT would show a stronger hand – about 8 points with a potential double stop as a minimum.

(d) This is a close decision. 3♡ would promise no points at all but the upper limit is less clear. There are a lot of losers in this hand and I suggest that 3♡ is enough, although there is a case for 4♡.

(e) Here we have one more heart and one more point than before but the ♠K is unlikely to be of much value. The minor-suit holdings could hardly be worse and again, I recommend that 3♡ is enough.

(f) This hand has far more playing strength and now I recommend 4♡.

(g) Here we need eleven tricks for game and this hand is very short of top cards. I recommend inviting with 4◊. 3NT could be on if partner has a spade stop and the ◊A but there is no practical way to find out.

(h) Here we shall certainly be insisting on game and a slam is not out of the question. It is best to start with an unassuming cue-bid of 3♠ to allow partner to describe his hand further. We shall raise 3NT to 4NT (quantitative). Otherwise, we shall bid 5♣ over a red suit bid to show this type of hand.

Multi-coloured two diamonds

We now turn to the 'multi', the generally accepted shortening for the convention, initiated by Terence Reese and Jeremy Flint, as the *multi-coloured two diamonds*. This was the pioneer in the world of two-way or multi-purpose bids which have become very popular nowadays. There are a number of ways of playing it and the opening bid of 2◊ is forcing and can show any of:

1 A weak-two in either major;
2 An eight playing-trick hand in either minor;
3 A balanced hand of 19–20 points.
4 Some pairs, (notably those playing a strong 1♣ opening) also use it for a strong 4441 shape, singleton yet unspecified) but this is rare and can be ignored for the time being.

Therefore pairs announcing 'Acol with a multi' will use 2♣ for the normal Acol game-force and two of a major for the usual eight playing-trick hand in the bid suit. 2NT will normally promise 21–22 points.

In practice, the multi (except in fourth position where a strong hand is most likely and, with neither yourself nor your partner able to open, you are unlikely to want to enter the bidding anyway) will show a weak two in a major about eight times out of ten and it is reasonable to plan your defensive bidding on that assumption. It is first necessary to understand how the opponents will probe for their best contract.

On hearing a multi, the partner must first decide his likely final contract on the assumption that there is a weak two in a major opposite. His procedure (assuming no interference for the moment) is as follows:

1 If he is happy to play in 2♡ opposite a weak two in hearts, he

bids 2♡. The multi hand is then is expected to pass if he indeed has a weak two in hearts but correct to 2♠, 2NT or 3 of a minor if he has the appropriate hand. Where 2NT is bid, the bidding continues (with Stayman if appropriate) exactly as if the multi hand had opened with a 19-20 point 2NT.

2 If he is happy to play in 2♠ opposite a weak two in spades but has sufficient heart support (three to an honour would be a typical minimum) to be able to play in 3♡ (or more) opposite a weak two in hearts, he bids 2♠. The multi hand is now expected to pass with a weak two in spades, correct to 3♡ with a weak two in hearts, or correct to 2NT, 3♣ or 3♢ with the appropriate strong hands. Again, where 2NT is bid, the bidding continues (with Stayman if appropriate) exactly as if the multi hand had opened with a 19–20 point 2NT.

3 If he is happy to play in three of either major and/or has game ambitions, he 'relays' with 2NT, an enquiry for more detailed information, which is forcing for one round. The multi hand is now expected to specify his type. There are a number of approaches of which these two are the most common:

(i) 3♣ shows an eight playing-trick hand in clubs,

3♢ shows an eight playing-trick hand in diamonds,

3♡ shows a weak two in hearts,

3♠ shows a weak two in spades,

3NT shows 19–20 points, balanced.

However, one can be more accurate within the weak two range by using a further two-way bid and second relay:

(ii) 3♣ shows *either*:

a weak two in hearts (but the strong end of the weak-two range)

or an eight playing-trick hand in clubs).

3♢ shows *either*:

a weak two in spades (but the strong end of the weak-two range)

or an eight playing-trick hand in diamonds.

3♡ shows a weak two in hearts (weak end of the range)

3♠ shows a weak two in spades (weak end of the range).

Here, in the cases where 3♣ or 3♢ are bid, the responder relays again with the next suit up and now the sequence:

2◊   2NT

3♣   3◊

3♡   confirms the weak two in hearts (strong end),

while

2◊   2NT

3♣   3◊

3♠   confirms the eight playing-trick hand in clubs.

Similarly, the sequence:

2◊   2NT

3◊   3♡

3♠   confirms the weak two in spades strong end),

while

2◊   2NT

3◊   3♡

3NT confirms the eight playing-trick hand in diamonds.

Before considering how to defend against this swarm of double Dutch, it will be advisable to simply listen to our opponents' bidding for a few hands and write down exactly what they mean. Then, at least, we can get used to the general idea. Let us assume that we are East–West. South deals and North–South announce that their range for the weak two is 5–9 points, (minimum 5–7, maximum 8–9) and that they are using method (ii) above.

(1) S   N

     2◊   2♡

     Pass

Here South has confirmed a weak two in hearts (exact strength within the 5–9 range unspecified) and North is happy to play there. The implication is that either North is weak (in which case it could be costly not to compete) or that he is strong with an intense dislike of hearts (in which case it could be very expensive to do so) – an unpleasant decision!

(2) S   N

     2◊   2♠

     Pass

Here South has confirmed a weak two in spades (again the exact strength within the 5–9 range is unspecified) while North has indicated a willingness to play 3♡ (had the multi been a weak two in hearts). Again, he could be weak, or strong with a spade misfit, and the same dilemma exists for opponents.

(3) S   N
    2◊   2♡
    2♠   Pass

South has confirmed a weak two in spades (exact strength unspecified) and North is happy to play there.

(4) S   N
    2◊   2♡
    2NT   Pass

Here South has confirmed 19–20 points, balanced and North must be very weak.

(5) N   S
    2◊   2♠
    2NT   Pass

Here again, South has confirmed 19–20 points, balanced, and again North will be weak but is likely to have a reasonable heart holding.

(6) S   N
    2◊   2♡
    3♣   Pass

Here South has confirmed an eight playing-trick hand in clubs and North is obviously desperately weak.

(7) S   N
    2◊   2♠
    3◊   Pass

Here South has confirmed an eight playing-trick hand in diamonds and again North is obviously desperately weak but will have a heart holding.

Some pairs play these last two sequences as forcing and, in that case, they will probably use the next suit up as a negative, i.e. 3◊ over 3♣ or 3♡ over 3◊.

(8)   S   N
      2♢   2♠
      2NT   3♣
      3♡   3♠
      3NT   Pass

South has shown a 19–20 point balanced hand and has been asked about majors via Stayman. He has shown four hearts and North has shown a four-card spade suit in case South started with four cards in *both* majors. Clearly South does not have four spades. Note that, through his bid of 2♠ over the multi but his failure to support the heart bid, North is almost certainly marked with exactly three hearts.

(9)   S   N
      2♢   2NT
      3♣   3♢
      3♡   Pass

South has confirmed a weak two in hearts, 8–9 points. That appears to be insufficient for North to proceed to game.

(10) S   N
      2♢   2NT
      3♣   3♢
      3♠   3NT
      Pass

South has confirmed an eight playing-trick hand in clubs and the partnership is now in a game-forcing situation as North has promised some strength with his 2NT bid. Note that North is now in charge of the auction as he knows South's hand while South knows little or nothing about North's.

(11) S   N
      2♢   2NT
      3♣   3♢
      3♠   4♣
      4♡   4♠
      6♣   Pass

South has again confirmed the eight playing-trick hand in clubs and North's 4♣ bid initiates cue-bidding. South showed the ♡A while denying the ◇A and North showed the ♠A. South, clearly rich in trumps and controls, bids the slam.

(12) S   N
    2◇   2NT
    3♣   3◇
    3♠   5♣
    Pass

South again confirmed the eight playing-trick club hand, but North, by going straight to game, when 4♣ would have been forcing, has denied all interest in a slam, which South should normally respect.

(13) S   N
    2◇   2NT
    3◇   3♡
    3♠   4♣
    4♠   Pass

South has confirmed a weak two in spades but is at the strong end of the range (8–9 points). 4♣ is a cue-bid, agreeing spades. South, having nothing to cue-bid, can do no more than bid 4♠ and North does not wish to proceed further.

(14) S   N
    2◇   2NT
    3◇   3♡
    3NT   Pass

South has shown an eight playing-trick hand in diamonds and North is content to play 3NT.

(15) S   N
    2◇   2NT
    3♡   Pass

South has confirmed a weak two in hearts and is at the weak end of the range (5–7 points).

(16) S   N
    2◇   2NT
    3♠   4♠

South has confirmed a similar hand, in spades this time, but North feels strong enough to go to game.

(17) S   N
   2◇   2NT
   3NT 4♣
   4♡   4♠
   4NT Pass

South confirmed 19–20 points, balanced, and now 4♣ is the Stayman bid. South has four hearts but North tries 4♠, in case South started with both majors; then 6♠ may be on. As it is, South does not have a four-card spade suit and note that 4NT is natural and passable in this sequence.

We could go on for hours but this should be enough to give you the general idea. We now have to consider our counter-measures. The most common is the Dixon defence. First, let us consider the defender sitting immediately over the multi hand. We work on the assumption that the opener has a weak-two in a major.

Double shows 13–16 points and a balanced hand.

2♡   means that we are working on the assumption that opener has a weak two in spades and we are making a 'take-out double' against that hand. Ideally, we have opening or greater strength up to about 20 points and a 1444 shape. The bid is non-forcing.

2♠   means that we are working on the assumption that opener has a weak two in hearts and we are making a 'take-out double' against that hand. Ideally, we have opening or greater strength and a 4144 shape – again non-forcing.

2NT shows 17–20 points, balanced. Bidding proceeds as though we had opened 2NT on that range and Stayman applies as usual.

3♣   is a natural, non-forcing overcall but remember that we are on the three-level so a good suit is crucial and at least opening strength in points is required. Vulnerability is obviously relevant.

3◇   natural overcall in the same way as 3♣.

3♡   and 3♠ are natural and preemptive. Some pairs play them as strong jump overcalls; others vary it with vulnerability.

3NT is natural.
Higher bids are natural and preemptive in all suits.

Now, as the multi is forcing, we have the option to pass and bid on the next round. Therefore after

	(i)	2◇	Pass	2♡	Pass
		Pass	?		
or	(ii)	2◇	Pass	2♠	Pass
		Pass	?		
or	(iii)	2◇	Pass	2♡	Pass
		2♠	?		

Double is for penalties, although some pairs agree to play it as weak take-out double (on hands where it would be dangerous to come in first time with the partner of the multi as yet unlimited).

2♠ in case (i) is natural and non-forcing.
2NT shows a minor two-suiter (at least nine cards in the two suits, but preferably ten or more).
3♣ or 3◇ shows nine or more cards in the bid minor and the other major.
3♡ over 2♠ is natural and strong but non-forcing.
A cue-bid (i.e. 3♡ over 2♡ or 3♠ over 2♠) is strong and forcing at least to suit agreement – at this level, that inevitably means game. In the first place, it is an invitation to 3NT if partner can stop the major suit announced by the multi.

For the player sitting to the right of the multi, the options are limited in that he may not have a second chance to speak. Therefore the 'pass and bid later' tactic is ruled out. He will therefore have to be more daring on occasions but, unlike his partner, he has the immediate cue-bid available:

After   2◇   Pass   2♡   ?

Double 13–16 points, balanced as before.
2♠ is the take-out double against an assumed weak two in hearts as before.
2NT shows 17–20 points, balanced as before.
3♣ or 3◇ are natural overcalls as before.

3♡ is a cue-bid, forcing, invitational to 3NT but may be a strong two- suiter.
3♠ is a strong jump overcall, non-forcing.
3NT is natural.

After   2◇   Pass   2♠   ?

Double 13–16 points, balanced as before.
2NT shows 17–20 points, balanced as before.
3♣ or 3◇ are natural overcalls as before.
3♡ is a natural overcall, non-forcing.
3♠ is a cue-bid forcing to game, in the first place, inviting 3NT.
3NT is natural.

Therefore, with the intermediate two-suiters, he may have to bid one immediately, hoping to bid the other later but, if he has hearts and another suit and it is likely that after 2◇ Pass 2♡ Pass, the multi hand will correct to 2♠, then:

Double is for take-out (unless agreed otherwise – penalty is unlikely as we are sitting under the long suit.
2NT is the minor two-suiter as before.
3♣ shows clubs and hearts as before.
3◇ shows diamonds and hearts as before.

We now turn to situations where the partner of the multi bids 2NT as a strong relay. Now it is far less likely that we shall want to enter the bidding. But, for the rare occasions where it may be appropriate, the basic rules are that:

A no-trump bid or a double of a no-trump bid is unusual – for the minors.
A double of a suit which means or may mean what it says, is for take-out.
A double of a suit which is merely used for relay is for penalties, with a view to lead-direction and/or sacrifice.

To give some examples:
(1) 2◇   Pass   2NT   Dble   is for minors.
(2) 2◇   Pass   2NT   Pass
      3♣   Dble   is for take-out.

(3) 2◊   Pass   2NT   Pass
    3♣   Pass   3◊   Dble   is for penalties.

Let us now try a test on what we have just learnt. In each case, state
what information the opponents have exchanged so far, what you
intend to bid, how you expect the auction to proceed and what
final contract(s) you envisage. Again, you should be aiming to get
under fifteen seconds per example, to complete the test in about
fifteen minutes. Assume South deals at Love All but state what
difference to your answers, if any, a change in vulnerability would
make. Start your stop-watch.

(1) You are West. South opens 2◊. What do you bid on:

(a) ♠ A K x x	(b) ♠ x	(c) ♠ A K x	(d)♠ K x
♡ x x	♡ K Q J x	♡ K x x x	♡ x x x
◊ K Q x x	◊ K Q J x	◊ K x x x	◊ x x
♣ J x x	♣ J x x x	♣ Q x	♣ A K J 10 x x

(e) ♠ A K x x	(f) ♠ x	(g)♠ J x	(h)♠ K Q J x x
♡ K Q x	♡ J x	♡ K Q x x x	♡ x x
◊ K Q x	◊ A K Q J x	◊ x	◊ x x
♣ J x x	♣ A J x x x	♣ A Q J x x	♣ A K x x

(i) ♠ A K Q J x	(j) ♠ K x	(k)♠ K Q	(l) ♠ x x
♡ x	♡ K x	♡ K Q	♡ A K Q x x x
◊ A K Q x x x	◊ x x	◊ Q x x x x	◊ A K x
♣ x	♣ A K Q J x x x	♣ Q x x x	♣ x x

(2)You are East. South opens 2◊, partner passes and North bids
  2♡. What do you bid on:

(a) ♠ K Q x x	(b) ♠ x	(c) ♠ A Q x	(d)♠ K x
♡ x x	♡ A Q J x	♡ Q J x x	♡ x x x
◊ Q x x	◊ A Q x x	◊ Q J x	◊ K x
♣ A J x x	♣ Q x x x	♣ K x x	♣ A Q 10 x x x

(e) ♠ A K x x	(f) ♠ x x	(g)♠ A K Q J x	(h)♠ K x
♡ A K x	♡ x	♡ x	♡ A K Q x x x
◊ K x x	◊ K Q J x x	◊ A K Q x	◊ x x
♣ Q x x	♣ A J x x x	♣ Q x x	♣ 10 x x

(3) You are West. South opens 2♢ and you double. North bids 2♡ and partner doubles – this is for penalties as you have approximately described your hand. South corrects to 2♠. What do you bid now on:

(a) ♠ K x
   ♡ Q x x
   ♢ K Q x x
   ♣ A J x x

(b) ♠ A x
   ♡ K Q J x
   ♢ K x x x
   ♣ x x x

(c) ♠ A K J x
   ♡ J x x
   ♢ K x x x
   ♣ Q x

(d) ♠ J x x x
   ♡ K Q x x
   ♢ A K x
   ♣ K x

(4) You are East. South opens 2♢, partner bids 2♡ and North passes. What do you bid on:

(a) ♠ A K J x
   ♡ x x
   ♢ x x x x
   ♣ J x x

(b) ♠ 10 x x
   ♡ x x x
   ♢ J x x
   ♣ J x x x

(c) ♠ A K x
   ♡ x x
   ♢ x x
   ♣ K Q J x x x

(d) ♠ x x x x
   ♡ A K x x
   ♢ Q x x
   ♣ Q J

(e) ♠ x x
   ♡ x x
   ♢ Q x x x x
   ♣ J x x x

(f) ♠ K Q J x x x
   ♡ x
   ♢ x x x
   ♣ x x x

(g) ♠ x
   ♡ x x
   ♢ K Q x x x x x
   ♣ Q x x

(h) ♠ K x
   ♡ A x x x
   ♢ x x x
   ♣ A x x x

Would any of your answers be altered if North doubles 2♡? This would mean that he intends to play in 2♡ doubled if his partner has a weak two in hearts or the 19–20 no-trump hand. Otherwise opener should correct to another suit.

(5) You are West. The bidding goes:

S	W	N	E
2♢	Pass	2NT	Pass
3♣	?		

What do you bid now on:

(a) ♠ A K x x
   ♡ A K x x
   ♢ K x x x
   ♣ x

(b) ♠ A K J x x
   ♡ J
   ♢ K Q J x x
   ♣ x x

(c) ♠ x x
   ♡ K
   ♢ A K x x x
   ♣ A Q x x x

(d) ♠ A K x x x
   ♡ x
   ♢ x x
   ♣ A K 10 x x

(6) You are East. The bidding goes:

S	W	N	E
2♢	Pass	2NT	Pass
3♣	Pass	3♢	?

What do you bid now on:

(a)♠ A K x x   (b) ♠ A x   (c) ♠ A x x
   ♡ x x   ♡ J x   ♡ K x x
   ◊ Q J x x   ◊ K Q J x   ◊ K J x x
   ♣ x x x   ♣ J x x x x   ♣ x x x

(7) You are East. The bidding goes:

S	W	N	E
2◊	Pass	2♡	Pass
Pass	Dble	Pass	?

The double is agreed as penalties. What do you bid now on:

(a)♠ K x x x   (b) ♠ x x x x x x (c) ♠ K Q J 10 x x x   (d) ♠ x x x
   ♡ x x   ♡ –   ♡ –   ♡ x x x
   ◊ K x x x   ◊ Q J x x x   ◊ x x x   ◊ x x x
   ♣ Q x x   ♣ J x x   ♣ x x x   ♣ x x x x

(8) You are East. The bidding goes:

S	W	N	E
2◊	Pass	2♡	Pass
Pass	2NT	Pass	?

(a)♠ K J x   (b) ♠ K Q x x x   (c) ♠ A J x x x
   ♡ K J x   ♡ K Q x x   ♡ x
   ◊ x x x   ◊ x x   ◊ x x
   ♣ J x x x   ♣ x x   ♣ Q J x x x

Would any of your answers be altered if North doubles 2NT for penalties?

(9) You are East. The bidding goes:

S	W	N	E
2◊	Pass	2♡	Pass
Pass	3◊	Pass	?

What do you bid now on:

(a)♠ A K x x x (b) ♠ K x x x x   (c)♠ x x x   (d) ♠ x x
   ♡ x   ♡ A   ♡ x x   ♡ K Q x x x
   ◊ x   ◊ K x x x   ◊ x x   ◊ x x x
   ♣ J x x x x x   ♣ J x x   ♣ K Q J x x x   ♣ K J x

Let us work through the answers:

(1) (a) Here we are just about good enough for a take-out double against a weak two in hearts and we show this hand with a non-forcing 2♠, hoping for 4♠ or (less likely) 5◊. 3NT may

be possible if partner is strong with the hearts well stopped.

(b) This is ideal for a take-out double against a weak two in spades and we bid 2♡, hoping for game in a non-spade suit, 4♡ being favourite.

(c) Here we are balanced in the 13–16 range and show it with a double. After that, let partner decide the final contract, 4♡ (assuming there is a weak two in spades against us) and 3NT being favourites.

(d) Here we have a good suit and it is safe to overcall with 3♣ non-vulnerable. When vulnerable, it is more debatable, but the quality of the suit makes it unlikely that we shall be doubled. The risk of missing a cold vulnerable game in no-trumps (certainly favourite) outweighs that of a heavy penalty and I would risk it at any vulnerability. The position would be more debatable, however, if partner had already passed.

(e) Here we are balanced in the 17–20 point range and ideal for a natural, non-forcing 2NT, hoping primarily for 3NT.

(f) This time, with a minor two-suiter, we pass first time round, intending to bid 2NT next round to show this type of hand. We hope for game in a minor or 3NT if partner can stop both majors.

(g) With a club and heart two-suiter, we work on the assumption that the multi is a weak two in spades. We pass now, intending to bid 3♣ next round to show the bid suit with the other major. We hope to finish in 4♡ or 5♣.

(h) Similarly, with a club and a spade two-suiter, we pass now, intending to bid 3♣ next time over a likely 2♡.

(i) This time, we have a spade and diamond two-suiter but to pass now, intending to bid 3♦ next time to show this type of hand against an assumed weak two in hearts, is not good enough because 3♦ is non-forcing. We must pass now and then cue-bid whatever the opponents bid (probably 2♡) to force to game. North will probably bid 2♡ and that will be passed round to us. On our 3♡ bid, partner will probably bid clubs, which we will correct to diamonds to show this type of hand.

(j) With seven solid club tricks and both major suits stopped, we have a likely 3NT contract and should bid it direct. There is always the option to remove to 4♣ (unlikely to go down too heavily) should South double, sitting there with an eight playing-trick hand in diamonds!

(k) Here we are in the 13–16 point range but most of the points are very badly placed in short suits and the playing strength of the hand is very poor. Particularly as both long suits are minors, I would deem it unlikely that game will be missed if partner cannot bid, and pass, particularly when vulnerable. One might risk a double, non-vulnerable, especially at pairs scoring, where we might want to compete for a minor-suit part-score. Even that is probably unwise.

(l) Here, if we have agreed that a direct 3♡ is preemptive, we must pass and bid the suit next time. Some pairs play an immediate 3♡ as strong and, in that case, this hand is ideal.

(2) (a) With 12 points, this is just about a take-out double against a weak two in hearts and we might risk 2♠ to show this hand, non-vulnerable. Vulnerable, opposite a partner who has, so far, proved unable to speak, it is more debatable and I would prefer a pass, particularly with those scattered honours.

(b) This is a much better take-out double against the spade suit. At the moment, we cannot bid but South is likely to correct 2♡ to 2♠ and we can reopen with a take-out double if and when this is passed round to us. We hope for game in a non-spade suit, 4♡ being favourite.

(c) Here we are high in the 13–16 point range with a balanced hand and show it with a double, hoping primarily for 3NT.

(d) Here we might consider coming in with an overcall of 3♣ but, particularly with a broken suit and our major-suit holdings likely to be poor, irrespective of which suit South has, I would advise against it, particularly when vulnerable, although it has the advantage of taking bidding space away from South, leaving North wondering which major his partner is holding. However, even if it escaped a heavy penalty, the bid might help opponents re- or devalue club honours and lengths/shortages if they have most of the points.

(e) Here we are in the 17–20 point range, balanced, and show the hand with a non-forcing 2NT, hoping for 3NT.

(f) This is awkward in that, while we could easily show this hand as West (passing and bidding an unusual no-trump afterwards), we cannot do so here. Nevertheless, with good playing strength, it would seem a pity not to come in. There are several approaches. One is to pass anyway, hoping (slightly against the odds on our hand) that South has spades after all. We will then be able to bid 2NT (unusual) to play in 3♣ or 3◊ according to partner's choice. The other advantage in passing is that partner has another chance and may have a spade – minor two-suiter. A second approach is to bid our better suit, 3◊ (less likely to be doubled than 3♣) and hope for the best – we are more likely to prefer a diamond to a club lead if hearts are trumps unless partner has a singleton club. A third approach is to bid 3♣, leaving room to run to 3◊ if doubled – that way, we get both suits in. My choice would be 3◊ (non-vulnerable), pass (vulnerable), but many would disagree.

(g) This is an ideal take-out double against the presumed heart suit but we cannot bid 2♠ here as it is non-forcing and we are near to game on our own. It is best to cue-bid 3♡, effectively game-forcing, with the intention of supporting diamonds or bidding 4♠ over 4♣. The alternative approach would be to bid 3♠ now if it were agreed as strong. However, we agreed to play it as preemptive and, even if it were strong, it would still be non-forcing and the risk of missing game, opposite the minimal values partner would need, is too high.

(h) Here South is likely to correct the 2♡ bid to 2♠. Therefore we pass now and, if 2♠ is passed round to us, we can reopen with 3♡ to show this hand.

(3) (a) Here we are near-maximum for our bid and should be taking some action (unless a pass in this position is agreed as forcing) but exactly what is more difficult. Partner does not need more than four good hearts for his double. We do not know whether he is able to double 2♠ or is merely

doubling with a view to competing in hearts. With most of the points in the long suits of the partnership, I would suggest opting to play, rather than try to defend at a low level, and offer a choice of games with 3♠. Partner can now choose 3NT if he has spades after all or game in a non-spade suit.

(b) This time, we certainly prefer to play and invite with 3♡, showing a minimum with good heart support.

(c) Here, with the heavy trump stack, we have no hesitation in doubling 2♠ for penalties.

(d) This is less clear. We have easily enough for 4♡ but could be in trouble if two or more of the outstanding spades are in partner's hand, leaving North with a singleton or void. Rather than take a categorical decision on 4♡ immediately, I would prefer 3♠, intending to stand 3NT, if partner has a spade value. Otherwise we can always play in 4♡.

(4) Here partner has made a take-out double against an assumed weak two in spades.

(a) The hand is something of a misfit but 2NT is reasonable, hoping for 3NT.

(b) We prefer clubs to hearts but there is little point in raising the level of bidding to show this as we are probably in trouble already. With North having passed, South may well have a strong hand and it is wise to pass 2♡, almost certainly assured of at least a 4–3 fit.

(c) Here we have a double spade stop and a club suit which is very likely to run. 3NT is favourite for final contract and we bid it direct.

(d) Partner has shown interest in the non-spade suits and all our points are working. We have little interest in any other contract than 4♡ so we bid it direct.

(e) This is a poor hand and we must simply answer the take-out double with our longest suit, 3◊, hoping to play there.

(f) This looks like a disastrous misfit and it is not at all clear what South's multi is based on. Despite partner's bidding, it is more likely to be a weak two in hearts than in his 'expected' spades. This kind of situation, where it is not clear which major is implied by the multi, crops up frequently and I have lost count of the number of times opponents have finished up in the 'wrong' major on a 3–2 'fit' or worse! This time, however, we are in trouble. If we bid 2♠ and find South with that suit, the penalty could be enormous. On the other hand, if we pass 2♡ and find South with that suit, we are likely to be allowed to play there undoubled and escape for a few fifties. Bidding 2NT or three of a minor is likely to invite trouble. My recommendation is to hope to find partner with 0544 and pass, aiming for the best of a bad job. We can always remove to 2♠ if South doubles; partner should respect this.

(g) Here we appear to have a diamond fit but, with a hand sadly lacking in tops, game is a long way off. Nevertheless, it would be timid not to at least invite it and I suggest a non-forcing 4♢. 3NT could be on if partner has the ♢A and stops in both majors but it is difficult to investigate it.

(h) This hand has a heart fit and is rich in tops. However, with a weak two sitting over us and our hand going down on dummy, the ♠K is of dubious value. I suggest inviting with a non-forcing 3♡.

If North doubles 2♡, we can pass on (d), awaiting further developments. We can always bid 4♡ later and do not mind defending with so many points. On (f), the position is more dangerous and it is probably wise to bid 2♠ immediately. If it is doubled, i.e. South has spades after all, we can either decide to stick it or rescue to 2NT, intending to redouble for SOS with a view to playing in three of a minor. On (h), we can pass, intending to bid 3♡ if necessary later. Most players would agree that an immediate 3♡ now would be preemptive rather than constructive.

(5)(a) Here, at the moment, South is showing an eight playing-trick hand in clubs or a 'strong-end' weak two in hearts. Our high point-count suggests the heart hand but our shape favours the clubs. Even if South has the strong club hand, it is worth competing with a take-out double as partner is almost certain to fit one of our suits. Even if he is very low on points (as is likely) game could be on in any non-club suit (four of a major being favourite) if he has a five-card or longer major suit.

(b) Here we were hoping for 2♡ from North to be passed round to us so that we could bid 3◊ to show the diamond-spade two-suiter. This option has now gone but, with South having shown clubs or hearts, we can still bid 3◊ and partner should realize why we did not come in the first time. Of course, if he is short in both majors, he could mistakenly take us for a diamond-heart two-suiter, but he is unlikely to go wrong. If opponents bid 3♡ and stop there, I should recommend competing further with 3♠. They are most unlikely to double either this contract or 4◊.

(c) Here we were hoping for an unusual no-trump and now it is wise to wait. If opponents stop in 3♡, we can then try an unusual 3NT.

(d) Again, we must wait, intending to bid 3♠ if opponents stop in 3♡.

At favourable vulnerability, in both these last two cases, we might decide to compete, even over 4♡.

(6)(a) With insufficient strength and distribution, we have no reason to compete and, as we prefer a spade lead to a diamond, we pass.

(b) This time, we shall want a diamond lead against a likely heart contract, so we make a lead-directing double.

(c) This is less clear but, with a broken holding, a double might be more helpful to the opposition than partner and I recommend a pass.

(7) Here South has confirmed a weak two in hearts and partner has doubled for penalties.

(a) We have no reason to argue and pass, expecting a large penalty.

(b) This is less clear but it is most likely that, if we run, it will be to a contract in which we have little chance and we could be doubled for an enormous penalty. I should recommend hoping that partner has a heavy trump stack and short diamonds so that we might contribute a trick and recommend a pass. If this turns out to be wrong, we have, at least, respected partner.

(c) Here the case for removing the double is much stronger. This hand is unlikely to have much defence and will be worth six tricks with spades as trumps even if partner is void. I recommend 2♠. Partner should realize that we have this type of hand.

(d) Here we have three trumps more than we might have had and no better contract to suggest. We pass and hope partner is enormous while North is void of hearts.

(8) This time, partner has shown a minor two-suiter.

(a) Here most of our points are in the wrong suits and we should quietly show our preference with 3♣. It is likely to be a mistake to leave or raise the no-trumps. Not only are we going to be on dummy but, even if we were not, there would be lots of losers in at least one major suit.

(b) This is a dreadful misfit and it is now a question of whether to quietly bid 3♣ and hope to get away with it or leave 2NT, which will probably be defeated but is most unlikely to be doubled by the very limited multi hand. I prefer the pass. It is not out of the question that partner has A x in spades, in which case we might come near to making 2NT.

(c) This time, we have a massive club fit and should invite game with 4♣, hoping partner is able to raise to game.

If North doubles 2NT for penalties, he is obviously intending to take similar action over a rescue to a minor. I recommend sticking to 3♣ on (a). A pass on (b) leaves partner to take the choice. On (c), 3♣ is probably enough as game at the five-level is now most unlikely. If we are really lucky 3♣ will be doubled and South will sit there wondering whether to stand it with his void – he should respect his partner.

(9) This time, partner has shown diamonds and the other major, here spades.

(a) We have a sensational fit and there should be good play for 4♠, so we bid it direct.

(b) Here we have a double fit. Again 4♠ should present no problem but there could be a slam on. It costs nothing to bid

3♡ first. Partner will, in the first place, take it as an invitation to bid 3NT but, whatever he bids, we will *then* bid 4♠ and he will realize that our 3♡ bid was an advanced cue-bid. 6♠ may now be reached.

(c) This is a poor hand but it is important not to advertize the fact. We have been asked for preference between diamonds and spades and should quietly give it with 3♠, hoping to play there.

(d) This is a nightmare and the first temptation to resist is 3NT. Yes, we have all the suits well stopped but, particularly with a six-card heart suit sitting over us, very few tricks. Especially if partner has bid on distribution rather than high-card strength, we could be on for a hiding and it is best to be grateful that there has been no double so far and pass quietly, thereby giving preference between diamonds and spades.

Cue-bidding

We are now going to turn to alternative uses of the cue-bid. In the earlier books, we defined our method as a very strong hand, unsuitable for take-out double by virtue of being one- or two-suited. The choice by partner of our other short suit(s) could make matters awkward, not to mention the chance of the double being left in on a hand better suited to declaring rather than defending.

The strong, highly distributional hands suitable for the cue-bid crop up very rarely and therefore the cue-bid, in the opinion of many, is grossly under-used. The Michaels cue-bid is a sound alternative. Suppose South deals and opens, West shows at least 5–5 in two suits as follows:

S	W	N	E	
1♣	2♣			shows both majors;

S	W	N	E	
1◇	2◇			also shows both majors;

S	W	N	E	
1♡	2♡			shows spades and a minor (as yet unspecified);

S	W	N	E	
1♠	2♠			shows hearts and a minor (as yet unspecified).

Strength varies considerably between partnerships. Some vary it with vulnerability, specifying: weak at favourable; intermediate (about opening bid strength) at equal; and strong at unfavourable. Others play it as either weak or strong (intending to bid twice in the latter case) and bidding the suits in natural order with intermediate hands. A third group plays it with unspecified strength, reasonable as the bid is forcing, but will tend to vary the minimum requirement with vulnerability.We shall not spend time going into the pros and cons of the three methods; our concern is how to play against them.

In cases where we have opened a major and have heard a cue-bid on our left, the partner of the cue-bidder will normally either bid the other major to play there or bid 2NT (forcing) to find out which minor his partner has. So let us listen to a few sample sequences by the opponents.

(1)	S	W	N	E
	1♣	2♣	Pass	2♡
	Pass	Pass		

West shows 5–5 in the majors and East chooses to play in 2♡.

(2)	S	W	N	E
	1◊	2◊	Pass	2♠
	Pass	Pass		

West again shows 5–5 in the majors and East chooses to play in 2♠.

(3)	S	W	N	E
	1♣	2♣	Pass	2♡
	Pass	3♡		

West shows a major two-suiter and is strong by the minimum standards for his first bid – he may also be more distributional than 5–5.

(4)	S	W	N	E
	1♣	2♣	Pass	2◊
	Pass	2♠	Pass	

West has another major two-suiter but East has equal length in the two majors and can throw the choice back to his partner. West has longer and/or stronger spades. Note that this option is not available if we open in diamonds for lack of bidding space. In that case, East must take a decision unless he is strong enough to venture to the three-level.

(5)
S	W	N	E
1♡	2♡	Pass	2♠
Pass	Pass		

West has shown 5–5 in spades and an unspecified minor. East decides to play in 2♠, irrespective of the minor. The implication is that he has a spade fit and/or a serious dislike of one of the minors and is terrified of going to the three-level, risking more serious trouble.

(6)
S	W	N	E
1♡	2♡	Pass	2NT
Pass	3♣	Pass	Pass

West has shown 5–5 in spades and clubs and East is happy to play in 3♣.

(7)
S	W	N	E
1♠	2♠	Pass	2NT
Pass	3♢	Pass	3♡
Pass	4♡		

West has shown 5–5 in the red suits and East was strong enough to go to the three-level. Perhaps he was intending to go to 4♡ direct had West shown clubs. As it was, East was content to stop in 3♡ but West is considerably stronger than his stated minimum and goes to game.

These should be enough to give the general idea of what opponents are doing. So far, we have kept North quiet but, in this type of situation where West has announced considerable playing strength and is likely to be relatively poor on defence, there is scope, not only for disruption of opponents' bidding space, but also for using the information given to increase the accuracy of our own bidding. My suggested defence is as follows:

1 A double shows a modest raise to the two-level – probably only three trumps.
2 A raise in partner's suit is purely preemptive and may be done on weaker hands than usual. With the cue-bidder unlimited, opponents may be cold for anything up to a grand slam and therefore I allow considerable license in this area. Obviously vulnerability and length of the trump suit are very important.

Such raises should be considered obstructive rather than constructive and opener should allow for this when considering whether to continue bidding.

3 In cases where we have opened with a minor and the cue-bid clarifies both suits, then the bid of the fourth suit is natural and non-forcing at any level. The implication is that partner has at least tolerance for our suit (say three cards or a doubleton honour as a minimum).

4 Still in cases where both suits are specified, i.e. the majors, the chances are that, if we are going anywhere at all, 3NT is our first consideration. A bid of one of them shows a stop in it and denies a stop in the other. A bid of no-trumps would obviously show stops in both. The minimum strength required must, of course, be enough to go to no-trumps at the two-level, i.e. about 11 points.

5 In cases where only one suit is specified, i.e. where we have opened a major and the cue-bid has promised the other major and an unspecified minor, then the bid of the major shows a stop as before, while a new suit is natural and non-forcing.

6 However, if we want to be more sophisticated – and I am all for it against these 'clever' cue-bids – we can use the cue-bids two-way with the same rationale as the fourth-suit-forcing advanced cue-bid that we learnt in an earlier book. In the first place, it should be understood as a stop for no-trumps. But then, if partner bids no-trumps and we return to opener's suit, the cue-bid merely showed a feature for a *trump* contract, i.e. a singleton. Where we jump immediately in one of the opponents' suits, we show a void. This can be extremely useful if the bidding soars to dizzy heights.

7 A pass followed by a double is for penalties.

8 A pass followed by support or a new suit shows the ability to defend and therefore probably poor trump support e.g. x x x x and honours in opponents' suit(s).

This has all been something of a mouthful so let us listen to some more example sequences, this time allowing partner to enter the fray.

(8) S   W   N   E
    1♣   2♣   Dble

West has shown the majors and North has modest trump support, probably three to an honour.

(9) S   W   N   E
    1♣   2♣   3♣

West again has the majors and North is trying to preempt. He should have four trumps as bad splits have been advertized but minimal strength is sufficient. ♣ A Q x x and little else is enough.

(10) S   W   N   E
    1♣   2♣   4♣

This time, North is extending the preempt even further – a five-card or longer trump support is likely.

(11) S   W   N   E
    1♣   2♣   2♦

North is now showing a diamond suit, non-forcing, and probably has tolerance for clubs.

(12) S   W   N   E
    1♣   2♣   3♦

North is now showing a longer diamond suit and his interest in clubs will probably be stronger than before as he must be prepared to play in 4♣ if we have long clubs and dislike diamonds intensely.

(13) S   W   N   E
    1♣   2♣   2♡

North has a heart stop but no spade stop and is willing to play 2NT or more if South can stop the spades. South can bid 2NT (or more) himself with a full stop (or 2♠ with a half-stop if bidding space allows). If South cannot stop spades, North is responsible if he has to return to 3♣, even on a four-card suit.

(14) S   W   N   E
    1♣   2♣   2♠

North has a spade stop but no heart stop and is willing to play 2NT (or more) if South can stop hearts. South can bid 2NT (or more) with a heart stop. Otherwise, he must return to 3♣. Only in the case where he is strong enough to play 3NT or 4♣ can he use 3♡ to show a half-stop.

(15) S   W   N   E
    1♣   2♣   2NT
This is natural, showing stops in both majors.

(16) S   W   N   E
    1♣   2♣   3♡
This shows a willingness to play at least 4♣ and a void of hearts.

(17) S   W   N   E
    1♣   2♣   4♣
This shows a willingness to play at least 5♣ and a void of spades.

These two sequences could well pave the way for anything up to a grand slam in clubs on minimal high-card values.

(18) S   W   N   E
    1♡   2♡   3♢
This is natural and non-forcing with a likely tolerance of hearts.

(19) S   W   N   E
    1♡   2♡   2♠
This is forcing, showing a spade stop, and is strong enough for at least 2NT. South is invited to show minor-suit features, for a possible 3NT, or return to hearts.

(20) S	W	N	E	(21) S	W	N	E
1♡	2♡	Pass	2♠	1♡	2♡	Pass	2NT
Pass	Pass	Dble		Pass	3♢	Dble	

These are both for penalties. Note the application of the rule of passing with a strong defensive hand when opponents are in a forcing situation. We learnt this when studying the handling of opponents' take-out doubles in the beginners' book and the same applies here.

(22) S   W   N   E
    1♠   2♠   Pass   3♡
    Pass   Pass   3♠
North has shown modest trump support but did not bid the first time because of his defensive values – points in short suits outside

spades. Bidding 3♠ first time would suggest a wish to sacrifice – the last thing North wants.

We could go on for hours with the number of sequences almost unlimited, but this should have given you the idea and enough information for a test. Again, you should be aiming for a maximum of fifteen seconds per example, to complete the test in about ten minutes. As before, assume that South is dealer at Love All but state any differences in your answers were the vulnerability to be changed. Start your stop-watch.

(1) You are North. South deals and opens 1◊; West cue-bids with 2◊ What do you bid on:

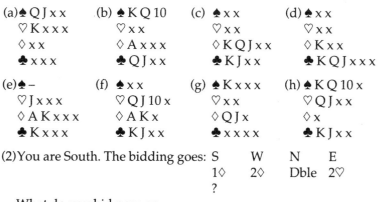

(a) ♠ Q J x x
   ♡ K x x x
   ◊ x x
   ♣ x x x

(b) ♠ K Q 10
   ♡ x x
   ◊ A x x x
   ♣ Q J x x

(c) ♠ x x
   ♡ x x
   ◊ K Q J x x
   ♣ K J x x

(d) ♠ x x
   ♡ x x
   ◊ K x x
   ♣ K Q J x x x

(e) ♠ –
   ♡ J x x x
   ◊ A K x x x
   ♣ K x x x

(f) ♠ x x
   ♡ Q J 10 x
   ◊ A K x
   ♣ K J x x

(g) ♠ K x x x
   ♡ x x
   ◊ Q J x
   ♣ x x x x

(h) ♠ K Q 10 x
   ♡ Q J x x
   ◊ x
   ♣ K J x x

(2) You are South. The bidding goes:

S	W	N	E
1◊	2◊	Dble	2♡
?			

What do you bid now on:

(a) ♠ K J x
   ♡ x
   ◊ A Q x x x
   ♣ K x x x

(b) ♠ K Q 10
   ♡ x x
   ◊ A K J x x
   ♣ A J x

(c) ♠ x x
   ♡ x x
   ◊ K Q J x x x
   ♣ A K x

(d) ♠ x x
   ♡ A K 10
   ◊ A Q x x x x
   ♣ A Q

(e) ♠ x
   ♡ J x x
   ◊ A K Q x x x
   ♣ K Q x

(f) ♠ x x x
   ♡ –
   ◊ A K J x x x
   ♣ A Q J x

(g) ♠ K J x
   ♡ K J x
   ◊ A K Q x x
   ♣ J x

(h) ♠ x
   ♡ K J x
   ◊ A x x x x
   ♣ K Q x x

(3) You are South. The bidding goes:

S	W	N	E
1♡	2♡	2♠	Pass
?			

What do you bid now on:

(a) ♠ x
  ♡ K Q x x x
  ◊ K Q x
  ♣ K J x x

(b) ♠ x x
  ♡ A K x x x
  ◊ x x
  ♣ A K x x

(c) ♠ x x
  ♡ A K J x x
  ◊ K Q x x
  ♣ x x

(d) ♠ K x
  ♡ A K J x x
  ◊ x x x x
  ♣ Q x

(4) You are South. The bidding goes:

S	W	N	E
1♣	2♣	2♡	Pass
?			

What do you bid now on:

(a) ♠ x x x
  ♡ K x
  ◊ K x
  ♣ A Q x x x x

(b) ♠ x
  ♡ A x x
  ◊ K x x
  ♣ A J x x x x

(c) ♠ x x
  ♡ A x
  ◊ K Q x x
  ♣ A Q x x x

(d) ♠ –
  ♡ K x x x
  ◊ K Q J x
  ♣ A J x x x

(5) You are North. The bidding goes:

S	W	N	E
1♣	2♣	2♡	Pass
2♠	Pass	?	

What do you bid now on:

(a) ♠ x x x
  ♡ K Q 10
  ◊ K x x
  ♣ K x x x

(b) ♠ Q x
  ♡ K Q x
  ◊ A Q x x
  ♣ x x x x

(c) ♠ J x x
  ♡ K J x
  ◊ A x x x
  ♣ Q J x

(d) ♠ x
  ♡ A K x
  ◊ K Q x x x
  ♣ J x x x

(6) You are South. The bidding goes:

S	W	N	E
1◊	2◊	4◊	4♠
?			

What do you bid now on:

(a) ♠ K J x
  ♡ K
  ◊ Q x x x x
  ♣ A x x x

(b) ♠ –
  ♡ K Q x x
  ◊ A K x x x x
  ♣ J x x

(c) ♠ A x x
  ♡ A x x
  ◊ K Q x x x x
  ♣ –

(d) ♠ –
  ♡ A K Q x
  ◊ A 10 x x x x
  ♣ K Q x

(7) You are South. The bidding goes:

S	W	N	E
1♠	2♠	4♡	5♡
?			

So partner has shown a void of hearts and East obviously has a considerable fit with his partner in that suit. What do bid now on:

(a) ♠ K Q J x x	(b) ♠ Q 10 9 x x	(c) ♠ A Q x x x	(d) ♠ A K x x x
♡ x x x	♡ K Q 10	♡ K x x	♡ K x x x
◊ K Q	◊ K J x	◊ Q x x	◊ x
♣ A Q x	♣ Q x	♣ Q x	♣ Q J x

(8) You are North. The bidding goes:

S	W	N	E
1♡	2♡	2♠	2NT
Pass	3◊	?	

What do you bid now on:

(a) ♠ K Q x x	(b) ♠ A Q x	(c) ♠ K Q J	(d) ♠ K J x
♡ x x x	♡ x x x	♡ Q x x	♡ K Q x
◊ K J	◊ Q J 10 x	◊ x x	◊ x x x
♣ Q x x x	♣ Q x x	♣ K x x x x	♣ A Q x x

Let us work through the answers:

(1)(a) Here we have a poor hand, length in West's implied majors and a misfit for diamonds. We are therefore keen to defend and have no reason to bid.

(b) With 12 points, we have enough to bid 2NT but are worried about the hearts. If partner cannot stop them, we are willing to play in 3◊ or more. We therefore bid 2♠, forcing for one round, to show this type of hand.

(c) With length in diamonds and no defence against either major suit, we shudder at the thought of defending and are advised to bounce the bidding. How far is more debatable as we have very poor holdings in the two majors, the doubletons suggesting several potential losers. Nonetheless, I would have no hesitation in bidding at least 4◊ (which opponents are most unlikely to double at any vulnerability) and I think there is a good case for 5◊ at favourable. Opponents do not know that our major-suit holdings are so bad and may well decide to compete in a major at the five-level for fear of conceding a game when they can make one themselves. That may be well one level too high for them.

(d) Again, we want to declare rather than defend but the position is less clear-cut as partner may only have four diamonds; if he has a singleton or void in clubs, we shall want to defend after all. We make this clear with 3♣, non-forcing, prepared to play there or in 3◊, according to partner's choice.

(e) This time, there could be anything up to a grand slam on in diamonds. At the same time, opponents could be making a lot of tricks in spades, notably if, as likely, one of them is void of diamonds. As we are prepared to play at least in game, our best bid is 4♠ to show the void. Partner can take matters from there, cue-bidding the ♣A, or rejecting with 5◊ if he has values in spades and heart losers.

(f) This time, we have enough for game and 3NT is uppermost in our mind. We start with 2♡, forcing for one round, to see if partner can stop the spades. If he cannot, we might have to try for 5◊ or possibly stay out of game, despite the apparently adequate point-count.

(g) Here, we can just about scrape up a raise to 2◊ and show it with a double. The ♠K in opponents' suit is hardly a working card but with the trump honours, it is probably worthwhile. Make it

♠ K x x x
♡ x x
◊ x x x
♣ Q J x x

and I should prefer a pass.

(h) We have a very unpleasant stack against West in both his suits and are looking forward to defending. We pass now, intending to double whatever contract opponents reach.

(2) East has merely given preference for his longer major (he had the option to pass with equal length) and it is not clear whether the opponents intend to go any higher.

(a) The cue-bid has devalued our spade holding and it is

unlikely that we can defeat 4♡. 5◊ could be a worthwhile sacrifice at favourable vulnerability but it is likely to cost at least 300. I suggest passing now, hoping they do not reach game. To compete in diamonds may well push them into it.

(b) Here we have a much stronger hand and although the spade honours are still badly placed, we may well be able to set 4♡. However, it is unlikely that we can make 3NT, even if partner has a heart stop, as we will not be able to run nine tricks once that stop has been knocked out. I suggest competing with 3◊ now, being prepared to go up to 4◊ in competition but willing to defend 4♡.

(c) This hand has poor defensive prospects and, although it is likely, there is no guarantee that West will be able to follow both clubs. Bouncing is in order and I should recommend 5◊ at favourable and 4◊ otherwise. In the latter case, we might buy it at the four-level, but have reserved the option to sacrifice at equal.

(d) Here we might make 5◊ unless the ♣K is with West, but there is no harm in looking for 3NT first. We cue-bid 3♡, in the first place asking partner if he has a spade stop. (He bids 3NT with a full stop but 3♠ with a half-stop.) If he hasn't, we shall try 5◊.

(e) 5◊ will now depend on partner's length in hearts. There are two possible approaches. One is to bounce to 4◊ or 5◊, according to vulnerability, on the argument that this hand has very poor defensive prospects, and this is a reasonable action. The other is to bid 2♠ now, initially showing a spade for no-trumps and asking for a heart stop from partner. When partner answers, we then repeat diamonds to indicate that we were cue-bidding the singleton. I prefer the first option, except at unfavourable vulnerability when there is little to be gained by bouncing.

(f) Although there could be up to four losers in 5◊, a slam could be on if partner has singleton spade and the ♣K is not in the West hand. I recommend the void-showing bid of 4♡, leaving partner to sign off in 5◊ or bid the slam with a spade control.

(g) Here we have both majors well stopped but could still have difficulty in making 3NT if partner has doubled on a weak hand. I suggest inviting with 2NT, allowing partner to pass, sign off in 3◊ or bid 3NT if he has a couple of useful club honours in addition to the ◊Q.

(h) This time, we would be willing to compete with 3◊ but have little interest in going higher.

(3) Here partner has, at the moment, made an unassuming cue-bid and is suggesting spade control for no-trumps. If we are also interested in no-trumps, we are expected to show minor-suit stops.

    (a) Here we have both minor suits stopped but we are aceless and one of our holdings (more likely to be diamonds) will be badly placed under the long suit. A case can be made for 3NT on our 14 points but, with bad splits advertized, I would favour 2NT.

    (b) Here we simply carry on describing our hand with 3♣.

    (c) Same applies – this time 3◊.

        Both (b) and (c) are forcing as partner has committed us at least to suit agreement.

    (d) Here we have neither minor stopped and can do little but bid 3♡.

(4) This time, West has specified the majors and partner has advertized a heart stop but no spade stop.

    (a) We are in a similar position and repeat our clubs with 3♣.

    (b) This hand is stronger by virtue of the singleton spade. We could still bid 3♣, which is forcing, but there is a better bid. We can try 2♠, which partner will understand as asking for a half-stop. If he then bids no-trumps, we return to clubs, clarifying that we had bid spades for another reason – to show the singleton (with a void, we bid an immediate 3♠). This may pave the way for game or even a slam in clubs.

    (c) Here 3NT is ruled out but 5♣ could still be on. With our extra strength and doubleton spade, there is no harm in reversing into 3◊. Partner should realize that we have this type of hand and choose 4♣ or 5♣.

    (d) As explained in (b), we can show a void with a direct 3♠. Anything up to a grand slam in clubs could be on.

(5) Here partner is asking for a half-stop in spades for no-trumps, although, as explained earlier, he might be intending to show a singleton with an advanced cue-bid.

   (a) Here we cannot oblige and must support the clubs with 3♣; this agrees the suit and is therefore non-forcing.

   (b) Here we have a half-stop in spades and an opening bid so we can bid 3NT, hoping to play there.

   (c) Another half-stop but, with only 12 points, 2NT is enough.

   (d) This time, five clubs or more could be on – for the moment, we can bid our diamond suit with 3◊ (forcing, as no suit has yet been agreed). We will support clubs later and probably finish in 5♣ or 6♣.

(6) Here partner has bounced the bidding, presumably desperately short of defence against one, if not both, majors.

   (a) With so many points badly placed in opponents' suits and very poor minors, this hand is a disaster and we have no reason to bid any more. I recommend a pass. A point of discipline here is that partner should almost certainly also pass. If he intended to bid 5◊, he should have done so first time round, giving East a very nasty problem. This is an extension of the basic principle that, once a player has made a preemptive bid, he should not bid again unless his partner forces him to do so.

   (b) Here our length and tops in diamonds opposite announced length with partner suggest that we have little defence against 4♠, apart from a probable heart trick. We therefore sacrifice in 5◊.

   (c) This is a dream of a hand and it is likely that partner has a singleton spade. There will therefore be no black-suit losers and partner is likely to have the ◊A. That leaves hearts where there may be two losers. There are a number of approaches. One is to cue-bid 5♣ but we see that partner is not going to be able to cue-bid anything and indeed, in the unlikely event of his having the ♣A, he will be positively discouraged into signing off in 5◊. Here, despite the void, the ♣A would be a useful card as we could discard one of our heart losers on it. Even the ♣ K Q could be crucial. On a spade lead, we could go to dummy, run a club honour, discarding a heart, later discarding our other heart on the other club honour. Even on a heart lead, we are still all right if East has the ♣A. My suggestion would be a direct 6◊. Partner may have a doubleton heart in a 1255 shape but even if he hasn't, it is probable, with a great deal of distribution around, that opponents will sacrifice in 6♠, costing little, rather than risk losing over 900 in 6◊. This particularly applies if we are vulnerable and they are not. Unfavourable vulnerability is the best position for this kind of 'punting'. Now, by refusing to sacrifice, opponents risk losing nearly 1400, while the sacrifice may only cost 300, if not less. In this situation, it is nearly always right to 'take out insurance' even at the risk of looking silly occasionally when it proves to be a phantom.

(d) Here we can virtually guarantee the small slam and it is a question of the grand. The easiest approach is a cue-bid of 5♡. This commits the partnership to at least 6◊ and partner should therefore realize that he is invited to cue-bid black-suit controls. If he can bid 6♣, we bid 7◊. If not, we settle for 6◊.

(7) Here partner has confirmed a void of hearts and East has tried to preempt us.

(a) This is a dream of a hand with every point working. We shall insist on at least 6♠ and it is a question of whether a grand slam is on. We cue-bid 6♣ and see if partner can cue-bid 6◊.

(b) This is at the other extreme; we are seriously short of top cards and are best advised to double 5♡ as there is no guarantee that we can make even 5♠. If partner overrules us, that is his responsibility.

(c) This is less clear and, as we have a minimum opening bid and little more to add, it is wise to pass and leave the decision to partner.

(d) Here West is likely to have a spade-diamond two-suiter and we have far fewer losers than (c). I suggest competing with 5♠, clarifying that we should prefer to declare than defend but are not too excited.

(8) East's 2NT was a request to his partner to specify his minor. Note that, as this was a free bid, East must have tolerance for *both* minors, unless he is intending to support spades later and merely wants more information about his partner's hand to help decide how high to go in spades.

(a) Here we have most of our points in opponents' suits and are better advised to defend. We are not strong enough to double and indeed, if East has long diamonds and a singleton spade, they could be close to game in diamonds.

(b) This time, we have a most unpleasant surprise for West in both his suits and, with an opening bid opposite, it looks tempting to double, despite the heart length. However, it is likely that East will be supporting spades after all and merely bid 2NT to establish his partner's shape and now it is less clear. Let us think further. If East intended to play in 3◊, partner has, at most, a singleton in the suit and is probably void and yet he made no attempt to compete with a distributional hand – stronger evidence that East intends to play in spades. I recommend a pass.

(c) Here it is more likely that East intends to play in diamonds but, with so many points in spades and a minimum point-count for the 2♠ bid, I again recommend a pass. Partner has another chance.

(d) With 15 points we must insist on game and the best way to tell partner is with 3♠. The message here will be that we prefer 3NT if he can stop the diamonds and has only four hearts. In the absence of a diamond stop, it will have to be 4♡.

Strong Club Systems

We now turn to defence against the strong 1♣ opening. In Acol, the big forcing bid is 2♣, which crops up very rarely and therefore tends to be under-used. Strong 1♣ systems try to draw the dividing line between 'stronger' and 'weaker' opening bids at a more realistic level so that there is greater use of the 'strong' bid and there is the considerable advantage of the weak bids being more strictly limited.

Strong club systems fall into two main categories:

1 Precision, pioneered by the Taiwanese shipping magnate C.C. Wei, where you need 16 or more high-card points to open 1♣.
2 Blue, popularized by the Italian world champions of the sixties era, where you need 17 high-card points (in an unbalanced hand) or 18 in a balanced hand, to open 1♣.

In both cases, 1♣ is forcing for one round but not necessarily to game. Whole books have been written on both systems and you are advised to read them if you really want to be fully familiar. Within each, there are countless variations and styles. For this book, however, it will be sufficient to go through the main points before recommending possible defences.

The first point is that, as 1♣ is forcing, you have the option of bidding immediately or passing, being guaranteed another chance. The accepted approach is to come in immediately on weak hands, in an attempt to disrupt some very accurate bidding sequences, (notably for the slam zone), which are part of these systems. With strong hands, where you do not mind defending and it is unlikely that the opponents have much on anyway, it is reasonable to pass and await further developments.

It will probably be easiest to work our way down the card to illustrate the differences between Acol and the strong club systems. A 'five-card' suit means, of course, five-card or longer unless otherwise stated.

	Precision	*Blue*
1♣	16+	17+ (unbalanced)
		18+ (balanced)
1◊	11–15	11–16

(May be a short suit – some allow down to a void; nevertheless I recommend treating it as a natural suit).

1♡ or 1♠	11–15 (five-card suit)	11–16 (four-card suit) There may be a longer suit outside – the *canapé* principle of bidding two suits.
1NT	13–15	16–17 or 13–15 with exact shape of 3334 or 3325.
2♣	11–15 five-card suit with exactly one four-card major or six-card suit with or without one four-card major.	11–16, six-card suit
2◊	Can be multi or 11–15 three-suited hand with short diamonds (e.g. 4414, 4315, 3415, 4405).	Can be multi, including 17+ points, 4441 shape (singleton unspecified).
2♡	Can be weak (as in Benji) or 11–15 with exactly four-card suit in bid major plus five-card club suit. Some play it as short diamond hand under 2◊ above.	Can be Flannery or reverse Flannery, specifying a 5–4 shape in the majors or weak (as in Benji).

2♠	As 2♡ but short-diamond hand ruled out.	Can be Flannery or reverse Flannery this time, referring to the black suits; or weak as in Benji.
2NT	22–23 balanced	21–22 balanced.

2NT (Some pairs in both styles play it as 5–5 in the minors; others play it as an unspecified single-suit preempt.)

3♣	Preemptive as usual	Preemptive or (more often) played as less than 17 points but with at least 7–8 playing tricks in clubs.
3◊ 3♡ 3♠	Preemptive as usual	Preemptive as usual.

The two systems also differ in the manner of replying to 1♣. Both play 1◊ as a negative (in a similar manner to 2♣ 2◊ in Acol) but with different definitions based on points; as in Acol, the bid has nothing to do with diamonds. But while Precision's positive responses are, in principle, natural, Blue Club is more concerned with showing controls (for slam purposes), preferring to discuss denomination later. Therefore:

1♣ 1◊	0–7 (some pairs allow an impossible negative, 8+ points with an exact 4441 shape, singleton as yet unspecified).	0–5
1♣ 1♡	8+, five-card suit, game-force.	6+, less than three controls, counting an ace as two controls, king as one control; forces at least to 2NT.
1♣ 1♠	8+, five-card suit, game-force.	Exactly three controls, game-force.
1♣ 1NT	8+ upper limit, if any, varies. Some play 8–10, others 8–13; game force, except that the partnership may stop in 2NT with precisely 16 opposite precisely 8.	Exactly five controls, game force.

| 1♣ 2♣ | 8+, five-card suit, game-force. | Exactly six controls, game-force. |
| 1♣ 2◊ | 8+, five-card suit, game-force. | Exactly seven controls, game force – slam almost certain. |

This is an enormous mouthful and it is best to summarize it briefly. Precision divides the positive/negative answer between 7 and 8 points. If the partnership has 16 + 8 = 24 points, minimum, between them, and at least one five-card suit, it is deemed to be in a game-forcing situation and, from then on, bidding can proceed *slowly* for maximum exchange of information with a view to a possible slam. The system uses the *principle of fast arrival* frequently and, if one partner jumps to game suddenly in a game-forcing situation, i.e. unnecessarily, he is stating that he wishes no further discussion on a possible slam.

Blue Club concentrates on controls. All first responses have nothing to do with the suits actually named and the strong hand is the first to name a suit on the second round of bidding.

Other notable features include the insistence of opening only five-card majors by the Precision players, and most of them insist that a reply of 1NT is unlimited and forcing. The opener, with a 5332 or 3532 shape, will very often have to bid a three-card minor at his second turn.

In both systems, a two-over-one bid after an opening of one of a non-club suit, shows 11+ and, in Blue Club, it forces the partnership to at least 2NT. This means that the opener can proceed slowly even with a strong hand in the 12–16 range, leaving more room for discussion.

Precision often includes trump-asking sequences; for example
1♣   1♡
2♡

agrees hearts as trumps and asks for length and suit quality in steps.

We could go on for hours but our prime concern is how to defend against all this. There are two basic defences to a strong 1♣. The simplest is to stipulate that a double shows majors (in principle at least nine cards and it is advisable to have points in the suits implied), while a bid of no-trumps shows at least nine cards in the minors, willing to play at the next level. All other bids are natural and merely obstructive, i.e. sign-offs.

However, a more accurate approach is the Truscott convention. After a strong 1♣:

Double shows clubs and hearts
1♦	diamonds and hearts
1♡	hearts and spades
1♠	spades and clubs
1NT	spades and diamonds
2♣	clubs and diamonds

In other words, each suit bid shows the suit and the next one up, the 'sandwich' combinations being shown by double and 1NT. Where the bidding goes: 1♣ Pass 1♦ ?, then the 1♦ bid for the red suits has been lost and 2♦ is used for the diamonds and hearts. Note that it is advisable to be slightly stronger to enter the bidding in this situation, for two reasons. First, you are now sitting under the strong hand; second, once there has been a negative response, it is much less likely that the opponents can make anything sensational and therefore there is less need to cause disruption. All higher bids in both cases are one-suited preempts in the suit named.

When does one come in against a strong 1♣? Philosophy varies. Some take the view that, as the opposition has been kind enough to tell you that they have the strength, it is unwise to come in unless you have one or two good suits with serious ambition to play the hand, successfully or as a cheap sacrifice. Competing on weaker hands is likely to give opponents useful information.

Others take the view, notably at favourable vulnerability, that, with the high accuracy of control-showing and trump-asking sequences, it pays to be disruptive at almost any price. They consequently come in on virtually anything. In the top-class game, it is this second philosophy that predominates and aggressive bidding is all the rage against most systems, with the prime objective of taking away as much bidding space as possible.

My own view, for what it is worth, is that, while one has to respect the fact that most people at the top are playing the aggressive style and they cannot all be wrong, in my own experience this approach loses at least as much as it gains and I, personally, have lost very little over the years by pursuing the more conservative attitude, preparing to accept missing out on the occasional spectacular gain. What few people realize is that successful disciplined bidding tends to go on unnoticed while bids on very poor hands which work well get no end of publicity.

Rather than have a stop-watch test, I am going to go through a few examples with you, listening to opponents' bidding and advising on where I would come in. As indicated before, the basic rule, apart from the strong 1♣ itself, is: a double of a bid which means the suit named is for take-out; a double of bid which does not necessarily refer to that suit is for penalties, in practice lead-directing or possibly suggesting a sacrifice should the vulnerability commend it.

In each case, I shall clearly state the meaning of opponents' bidding, as would be explained at the table in practice.

Let us start with some examples against the Precision version. Sitting over a 1♣ opener, I suggest competing on the following, playing Truscott, non-vulnerable (a stronger hand is expected when vulnerable):

♠ x x	♠ x x	♠ Q J x x x	♠ K Q x x	♠ K Q x x x
♡ K Q 10 x x	♡ K J x x x	♡ K J x x	♡ x x x	♡ Q
◇ x x	◇ Q x x x x	◇ Q x	◇ x	◇ J 10 x x x
♣ K J x x	♣ x	♣ x x	♣ A x x x x	♣ x x
(1) Double	(2) 1◇	(3) 1♡	(4) 1♠	(5) 1NT

♠ x	♠ x	♠ x	♠ K Q J 10 x x x
♡ x x x	♡ K Q 10 x x x	♡ x x x	♡ x
◇ A J x x	◇ x x x	◇ x x x	◇ Q J x x
♣ K J x x x	♣ J x x	♣ A Q J x x x	♣ x
(6) 2♣	(7) 2♡	(8) 3♣	(9) 4♠

The first six examples show the two-suiters and the other three, one-suiters. I should, however, prefer to pass on:

♠ K x	♠ A K Q	♠ A Q	♠ A Q J x	♠ Q J x x
♡ x x x x x	♡ K x x	♡ J x x x x	♡ x	♡ J 10 x x
◊ Q x x x	◊ Q 10 x x	◊ K J	◊ K Q x x	◊ x
♣ A x	♣ K x x	♣ x x x x	♣ K J x x	♣ K Q x x
(10)	(11)	(12)	(13)	(14)

In examples (10) and (12), the points are in the short suits and the hands are better suited to defence. (11) is balanced and again more suitable for defence. (13) is stronger and the best way to describe the hand is to wait for the opponents to bid hearts and then make a take-out double. If they fail to do so, it will then be likely that partner has length in the suit and again the hand may well be better suited to defence. (14) is hardly strong enough to compete with a strong club, particularly when it is borne in mind that 4441 hands do not play well at the best of times.

After 1♣ Pass 1◊, I suggest that better suit qualities are required for competing, in both two-suited and one-suited examples, as indicated earlier, but many would disagree so I leave it to you.

Where a positive response is made, opponents are virtually committed to game and vulnerability becomes even more important than before. Bear in mind two important points which are certainly borne out in my experience. First, if you come in, you may give away a mine of information. The point is often made that interference, notably where it takes away a lot of bidding space, is likely to force opponents to bid less accurately and thus gains in the long term.

Against that, interference which does *not* take away any significant space, for example 1♣ Pass 1♡ 1♠ is more likely to *help* opponents than hinder them. I remember a number of occasions where such interference has kept me out of 'good' but actually unmakeable slams. Three matches, against 'top-class' opposition, that swung in my favour this way immediately spring to mind – expensive gossip! Thus, if you come in, you must be confident of a reasonable chance of playing the hand successfully or for a profitable sacrifice. It is particularly dangerous to bid a broken suit under the strong 1♣. Even at favourable vulnerability, on a hand like:

♠ A Q x x x
♡ x x
◊ x x x
♣ K x x

it would be folly to come in with 1♠ after 1♣ Pass 1♡.

The strong hand can simply re- or devalue his spade holding and no bidding space has been lost. If you must come in, it should be with 2♠, prepared to take your medicine if doubled but, at least, you may have damaged their slam-bidding mechanism significantly. It costs less to come in on:

♠ K Q J 10 x
♡ x x
◊ x x x
♣ x x x

This is three points less but a near certain four playing tricks and a solid suit, especially important in this type of situation. I should have no hesitation in bidding 2♠ here and some would even risk 3♠. For a take-out double in this situation, bearing in mind the *minimum* of 24 points against you, you must have exceptional playing strength. Again this means solidity:

♠ K Q J 10
♡ –
◊ Q J 10 9 x
♣ Q J 10 x

but remember, even now, that you have warned opponents of a dreadful heart split.

There is more of a case for coming in when opponents make conventional bids asking for controls. Now you can indicate a lead without cost, but again remember a broken holding could help opponents' accuracy. This is a typical precision sequence:

1♣	Pass	1♡	Pass
2♡	Pass	2♠	?

After the strong club, the partner shows 8+ points and at least five hearts. The 2♡ support confirms the suit as trumps and asks for details of length and quality with a view to a slam (remember that they are committed to at least game in 4♡). The 2♠ response is disappointing, showing none of the top three honours. With a good solid spade holding, this would be an excellent opportunity to double for a lead. But you wouldn't, because it is your lead! The only purpose of a double here would be to suggest a sacrifice. But the supposing the auction continues:

1♣	Pass	1♡	Pass
2♡	Pass	2♠	Pass
3◇	?		

This asks about diamond control and now a double, with partner on lead, would be lead-directing. Even now, you should hesitate to do it with a broken holding like A Q or K J, which may well be more helpful to the enemy.

Where strong 1♣ players open 2♣, they are showing a long club suit and opening strength. It is usual to treat this as a one-level bid, doubling for take-out, overcalling normally and bidding 2NT with the usual strong no-trump overcall, but bear in mind that you need to be a point or two stronger or have a slightly better suit to overcall as everything is a level higher.

If the bidding goes 2♣ Pass ?, then, in both Precision and Blue systems, 2◇ is treated as a forcing relay (nothing to do with diamonds), asking the 2♣ opener to bid a four-card major or, if he can't, start to show stops in non-club suits for no-trump purposes. You can double 2◇ with a good diamond holding, say ◇ K Q 10 x x minimum, with a view to lead-direction or competing in the suit.

Similarly, with the 2◇ opener showing an approximate 4414 hand (specifically short diamonds), a double shows a good diamond holding and a minimum of overcall strength.

Where two of a major is treated as Benji, the double is for take-out as usual; where it shows the bid major and clubs with 11–15, the double is again for take-out and shows the other major and diamonds. Bear in mind that this will commit the partnership to the three-level (except over 2♡ where partner is able to answer with spades) and therefore a slightly stronger hand is required than would be appropriate over the one-level. A bid of 3♣, the opponents' announced suit, is the unassuming cue-bid, strong and forcing at least to suit agreement.

Where 2NT is played as showing 11–15 and 5–5 in the minors, there are several options and I suggest the following:

Double: About 16 points or more, balanced. Partner can cue-bid in clubs or diamonds if he wishes a further description of your hand, for example to find a 4–4 major-suit fit. The usual practice is to cue- bid the suit where he has a stop, if possible, so that 3NT can be reached if no major-suit fit is found.

3♣: A weak take-out double – say up to about 14 points.

3◊: A strong take-out double – say 15 points or more.

3 of a major: Natural overcall, non-forcing.

Failing that, on dubious hands, it is possible to pass 2NT and wait. The partner of the 2NT opener will normally show a minor and there is still the possibility to double for take-out or bid a major.

When defending against Blue Club, two main differences arise. First, there is much more scope for lead-directing doubles as their first response to the strong 1♣ is control-showing and nothing to do with the suit named.

Thus 1♣ Pass 1♠ ? shows three controls (typically an ace and a king) and you can double to show a good spade suit. Second, a problem arises in respect of the wide-range no-trump (13–17 points). This is very difficult to handle for the defender with about 15–16 points. A double, particularly without a good lead, may be expensive if the opener turns out to be strong. Against that, failure to double may be just as costly if he turns out to be weak and goes for a paltry penalty, notably non-vulnerable, while your side has a game on.

My suggestion is that, unless you have a good long suit to lead, do not double under 16 points.

In Blue Club, there are possible differences in two of a major openings. If they are not Benji-style weak bids, they will be Flannery or reverse Flannery, 5–4 two suiters and you will be told which two suits. Double for take-out to show the other two suits; use the other implied suit for the unassuming cue-bid as explained in Precision.

With the strong 3♣ opening, I suggest double for take-out (remembering that you are on the three-level but also that the opener is primarily a playing rather than a defending hand).

Defence against Weak No-trump Openings

We now turn to a far more common situation, the defence against a weak no-trump opening. Up to now, we have bid naturally at the two-level, allowing 2NT as unusual for two-suiters, but the laws specify that it must be game-forcing. It is more or less universal, in club and tournament bridge, to play two-suit overcalls and you will hear such names as Aspro, Astro, Asptro, and (less fashionable nowadays) Kelsey, Sharples and Cansino. It will be advisable to take up one of these yourself, but my concern here is to advise you how to handle them if they are played against you.

Aspro, Astro, Asptro are primarily two-suited hands:

2♣ indicates hearts (described as the anchor suit) and another suit;
2◊ indicates spades (the anchor suit) and another suit;
2♡ and 2♠ are natural.

The two-suiters will normally contain a minimum of nine cards and, in cases where both majors are possible, most pairs anchor to the longer suit; some to the shorter. Opening bid strength is usual but some pairs allow it on weaker hands, taking vulnerability into account. Remember, however, that they are always denying sufficient strength to double the 1NT bid.

In reply to the conventional minor-suit bid, assuming that the partner of the no-trump bidder passes, there will one forcing relay (*either* 2NT *or* a raise of the minor-suit named), asking for the other suit. Other bids are suggestions for final contract.

Let us illustrate with a few examples where we have opened 1NT as South.

```
S     W     N     E
1NT   2♣    Pass  2♦
```

The 2♣ bid is explained as showing hearts and another suit, anchoring to the longer major, typical hands might be:

(a)♠ K x	(b) ♠ x x	(c) ♠ Q J x x	(d)♠ K x
♡ Q J x x	♡ K Q x x x	♡ K Q J x x	♡ A K x x x
◇ x x	◇ A Q x x x	◇ A x	◇ J x
♣ A Q x x x	♣ Q	♣ x x	♣ Q J x x

In reply, East's 2◇ bid says that, if the second suit is diamonds, he wishes to play there. Otherwise, West is expected to correct to hearts if he has five or more, but bid his second suit (inevitably black) if he has only four hearts. Therefore his bid would be:
(a) 3♣;   (b) Pass;   (c) 2♡;   (d) 2♡.

If, instead of 2◇, East bids 2♡, he is showing at least a trebleton heart and wishes to play there. If he bids 2♠, he wishes to play there although West may support in the unlikely event of his second suit being spades! If East bids 2NT, announced as a forcing relay, then West is expected to bid his second suit, irrespective of length, but hearts if he has five hearts and four spades – partner can then correct. Therefore his bid would now be:
(a) 3♣;   (b) 3◇;   (c) 3♡;   (d) 3♣.
East is entitled to pass any of these responses.

How do we defend against this? The basic principle is that a double is always for penalties and the bid of the anchor suit is forcing and for take-out as clearly we are hardly likely to want to play there. A bid at the three-level is more debatable. Some play it as strong, natural and forcing. I prefer, however, to play it as preemptive, bidding the anchor first and then my natural suit with the strong hand. Again, let us take some examples. This time, we are sitting North. Partner deals and opens 1NT. West bids 2♣, explained as hearts and another, anchoring to the longer major. These are eight possible hands:

(a)♠ x x	(b) ♠ x x x	(c) ♠ Q J 10 x x	(d) ♠ K Q J x x
♡ Q x x	♡ x	♡ J x x	♡ x x
◇ Q x x	◇ Q J x	◇ A x	◇ A J x
♣ K Q 10 x x	♣ Q J 10 x x x	♣ J x x	♣ Q x x

(e) ♠ K x x   (f) ♠ A x   (g) ♠ Q J x x   (h) ♠ K x x x x x x
    ♡ Q J 10 x   ♡ x x x   ♡ J x x   ♡ x x
    ◊ x x   ◊ A Q J x x   ◊ A x x   ◊ J x
    ♣ A Q 10 x   ♣ Q x x   ♣ A K x   ♣ x x

(a) I would double, hoping partner can compete in clubs and indicating a good lead should East declare in hearts.

(b) With little defence, I should like to preempt with 3♣ (possibly even 4♣ at favourable vulnerability). Doubling 2♣ is pointless and takes no bidding space away from opponents.

(c) Here I should bid 2♠, non-forcing, hoping to play there.

(d) Here I have enough to insist on game and would cue-bid the anchor suit with 2♡, intending to bid 3♠ on the next round. This is again forcing (note that the cue-bid has committed the partnership to game or suit agreement) and leaves options open for 3NT or 4♠, according to partner's attitude to spades and stops in the other suits, notably hearts.

(e) Here a double stands out and the intention is to double 2♡ as well. Possibly partner will be able to double the other suits. Otherwise we shall be playing in 3NT.

(f) This time, 3NT is favourite if partner can stop the hearts. We set up a forcing situation with 2♡, intending to bid diamonds next round or support 2NT to 3NT.

(g) Another game-going hand, 3NT and 4♠ being candidates. Again, we bid the anchor suit, 2♡, and, if partner fails to bid no-trumps with a heart stop or show a four-card spade suit, we try a directional-asking 3♡ next round, to play in 3NT if partner has a half-stop. If he hasn't, 4♠ on a 4–3 fit or five of a minor are still possible.

(h) This time, particularly if partner has length and/or honours in spades, the defensive prospects against a likely 4♡ are very poor and now is the time to preempt with 3♠.

Kelsey, Sharples and Cansino refer to three-suited hands and the laws stipulate that at least one suit must be named. That is the suit for the cue-bid (where two suits are named, both are available; bid the one where you have a stop or the lower-ranking where you can stop both). All other bids are natural and non-forcing. Jumps are preemptive or forcing as before according to how you agree it.

Transfer Bids

We shall remain in the 1NT area to discuss a new topic – transfer bids. These are virtually a standard entry under 'special responses' on the system card and that applies irrespective of the strength of the no-trump bid. They also apply over 2NT and sequences like 2♣ 2◊ and 2♣ 2◊ as well as over 1NT and 2NT when 2NT   3NT
they have been made as overcalls.

Transfer bids were originally introduced when the strong no-trump was standard, primarily to ensure that the strong hand, in preference to the weak, could be declarer. That gives two obvious advantages:

1 The opening lead comes round to, rather than through, the strong hand.
2 The strong hand is closed, giving opponents less information than otherwise.

A third benefit is that it gives an extra round of bidding, free of charge.

Let us illustrate with a few examples. The standard major-suit transfers are:

1NT 2◊   is a transfer to hearts. Opener is expected to bid 2♡.
1NT 2◊   responder has a weak take-out in hearts but now the
2♡   Pass strong hand is declarer.

(In Marx-Sharples, the sequence 1NT 2◇ is used for certain balanced hands.)   2♡   2♠

1NT 2♡ is a transfer to spades. Opener is expected to bid 2♠.
1NT 2♡ now responder has a weak take-out in spades.
2♠   Pass

The meaning of the higher bids varies with style.

1NT 2♠ Can mean either:
    (a) A transfer to clubs – opener is expected to bid 3♣;
    (b) A simple raise to 2NT – opener is expected to sign off in 2NT with a minimum 1NT opener but bid 3NT with a maximum.

1NT 2NT can mean either:
    (a) A transfer to diamonds, in line with case (a) above. Opener is expected to bid 3◇.
    (b) An unspecified minor-suit transfer. Opener is expected to bid 3♣: now responder will pass if he wishes to play there or 'correct' to 3◇ if he wishes to play there.

Note immediately a number of important points:

1 The weak take-out to 2◇ has been lost. With these hands, responder bids in the same way as with a weak take-out in clubs (lost because of Stayman) – pass and wait to be doubled.
2 With the transfer sequence, bidding can continue as responder has another bid. It is therefore more convenient to show two-suited hands at a low level, as we shall see in a moment.
3 With the use of transfers, there is no need to jump to the three-level even with strong hands. Therefore, three-level bids are used for different purposes, as we shall see in a moment.

Let us start with the use of the transfer to show stronger hands. We have just seen that responder has the option to pass the transfer bid with the weak take-out in his implied suit. But, if he is strong, he can continue to describe his hand:

1NT 2◇
2♡   2NT
This shows about 11–12 points with exactly five hearts and an

otherwise balanced hand. The sequence is non-forcing and opener is expected to bid as follows:

(a) Minimum and a doubleton heart, or a 4333 shape where the hearts are trebleton: pass.
(b) Minimum with three or more hearts with a doubleton outside: 3♡, sign-off.
(c) Maximum with dislike of hearts or flat hand: 3NT, sign-off.
(d) Maximum with heart fit: 4♡, sign-off

1NT 2◊
2♡   2♠

Except in Marx-Sharples, this is forcing for one round and therefore unlimited, showing at least five hearts and at least four spades. Opener describes his hand in that light.

2NT: probably 3244, minimum, non-forcing.
3♡:   preference for hearts, minimum, non-forcing.
3♠:   exactly four spades, minimum, non-forcing.
3NT: probably 3244, maximum, non-forcing.

1NT 2◊
2♡   3♣

Again forcing for one round, showing at least five hearts and at least four clubs. Opener has the option to sign-off in 3♡, support the clubs or, notably with a maximum, bid 3◊ or 3♠, promising a stop in that suit, but expressing worry about the other, for 3NT.

1NT 2◊
2♡   3◊

Similar, but showing diamonds rather than clubs as second suit.

1NT 2◊
2♡   3♡

Six-card, or longer, heart suit and about 10 points, invitational.

1NT 2◊
2♡   3NT

Shows exactly five hearts and an otherwise balanced hand. Opener is expected to pass or bid 4♡, according to his attitude to hearts.

1NT   2◇
2♡   4♡

At least six hearts – sign-off.

We could go on for hours but this should be enough for you to see the idea; our concern at this stage is how to defend against these sequences. The usual approach is as follows.

A double of the transfer bid indicates the suit actually named; thus in the sequences above, a double of 2◇ would suggest a diamond suit for a lead or possibly competing.

The *immediate* bid of the suit implied by the transfer, in the above examples, that would be

S	W	N	E
1NT	Pass	2◇	2♡

is a strong take-out double against hearts. If partner can bid spades, the prime interest, we shall still be on the two-level, but he would have to bid a minor suit at the three-level with no points at all and we shall be responsible. I suggest 16 points, minimum, with the appropriate shape, ideally 4144. Remember that North is still completely unlimited and could have ambitions up to grand-slam level.

With weaker hands suitable for a take-out double against the suit implied by the transfer, pass now (remember that you are guaranteed another bid) and then make the take-out double on the next round if possible. The sequence will go:

S	W	N	E
1NT	Pass	2◇	Pass
2♡	Pass	Pass	Dble

and you can see the difference. By his pass on the second round, East has announced a weak take-out in hearts, and now it is much safer to compete in the knowledge that partner will have a reasonable hand.

An immediate overcall shows a goodish hand. The exact requirement varies with vulnerability and there is a wide range of opinion. I should expect about 11 points or more on the two-level; 13 or more on the three-level, with a good six-card suit. Again, remember that North is unlimited.

With weaker hands suitable for an overcall, pass now and hope to compete later if North proves to have the weak take-out.

2NT is unusual, showing both minors, except against Marx-Sharples transfers where, in cases when North has transferred to a minor, it shows the two lowest outstanding suits with a good hand as follows:

S	W	N	E
1NT	Pass	2◊	2NT

Shows the minors as usual.

S	W	N	E
1NT	Pass	2♡	2NT

Shows the minors as usual.

S	W	N	E
1NT	Pass	2♠	2NT

(a) If the 2♠ shows a raise to 2NT, then our 2NT shows the minors as usual (but remember there are likely to be at least 23 high-card points against us).

(b) If, as in Marx-Sharples, 2♠ is a transfer to clubs, then our 2NT shows a diamond-heart two-suiter.

S	W	N	E
1NT	Pass	2NT	Dble

Where, as in Marx-Sharples, the 2NT is a transfer to diamonds, the double shows a club-heart two-suiter.

As indicated earlier, the use of transfers leaves the three-level bids available for other purposes. This is a typical arrangement: 3♣ and 3◊ are non-forcing, indicating a six card-suit in the minor named with two top honours and about 10–11 points. This would be a reasonable example:

♠ x x
♡ K 10 x
◊ A Q x x x x
♣ J x

In reply to 1NT, this hand bids 3◊ and it is clear that 3NT will be dependent on bringing in that diamond suit. If the opener has the ◊K, he will normally be expected to bid 3NT, notably if he is maximum. With a useless doubleton, he is expected to pass. With dubious cases, including holdings like ◊ x x x and a maximum, or

◊ J 10 x with a minimum, the opener has the option to bid stops in the majors, keeping the option of 3NT open while being prepared to play in 4◊ if necessary. Therefore, in the above case, if opener rebid 3♡, he would be advertizing spade weakness and responder would have to sign off in 4◊. However, were he to bid 3♠, promising a spade stop but advertizing heart weakness, responder could try 3NT, assured of at least one heart stop.

3♡ and 3♠ are normally played as preemptive and sign-off.

My recommended defence to all these bids is the take-out double, all other suit bids being natural and non-forcing. 3NT is unusual over the minors (hearts and the other minor). Over the majors, it is more debatable as the preempter is likely to be very weak and 3NT could be on for us. I prefer to play it as natural but you can agree to play it as unusual for the minors.

Let us conclude this section with a timed test on 1NT sequences. In each case, where there are several styles in vogue, I shall give you the exact meaning of opponents' bids and, as usual, you will be expected to give a complete account of what you know so far, intend to bid now and the final contract(s) you envisage. You should be able to answer each example in under fifteen seconds to complete the nearly eighty questions in about twenty minutes. Assume throughout that South deals at Love All, playing a 12–14 no-trump, but state whether there would be any differences were the vulnerability to alter. Start your stop-watch.

(1) You are North. Partner opens 1NT and West bids 2◊, showing spades and another suit, anchoring to the longer major. What do you bid on:

(a) ♠ x x	(b) ♠ x x	(c) ♠ K Q J x	(d) ♠ K x x
♡ x x	♡ K Q 10 x x	♡ x x x	♡ J x
◊ K J x x x x	◊ A x	◊ x x x	◊ K Q J x x
♣ x x	♣ J x x x	♣ x x x	♣ J x x
(e) ♠ Q x x	(f) ♠ x	(g) ♠ A Q J x	(h) ♠ K Q x
♡ K x	♡ K Q J 10 x x	♡ x x	♡ K J x
◊ x x	◊ x x	◊ A Q J x	◊ J x x x
♣ A J x x x x	♣ J x x x	♣ x x x	♣ Q x x

(i) ♠ x x x   (j) ♠ x x   (k) ♠ K x
     ♡ K x   ♡ A K Q x x   ♡ x x
     ◇ A K Q J x x   ◇ A J x   ◇ x x x
     ♣ x x   ♣ x x x   ♣ A K Q x x x

(2) You are South in the same conditions as in (1), having opened 1NT on:

(a) ♠ A K x x   (b) ♠ x x   (c) ♠ K 10 x   (d) ♠ J x x
     ♡ Q x x   ♡ K J x x   ♡ K x x   ♡ J x x
     ◇ K J x x   ◇ A x x   ◇ x x   ◇ Q J x x
     ♣ J x   ♣ A x x x   ♣ A K x x x   ♣ A K x

What do you bid now, in each case, after the following sequences:

S	W	N	E
1NT	2◇	*	Pass
?			

* is   (i) Dble   (ii) 2♡   (iii) 2♠   (iv) 2NT
      (v) 3♣   (vi) 3◇   (vii) 3♡   (viii) 4◇

(3) You are South in the same conditions as above. The bidding goes:

S	W	N	E
1NT	2◇	Dble	*

* is   (i) Redouble (SOS – remove diamonds in all circumstances).
     (ii) 2♡, meaning that, if the second suit is hearts, East wishes to play there.
     (iii) 2♠.

What do you bid now on those same four hands?

(4) You are East. South opens 1NT, West passes and North bids 2◇, transferring to hearts. What do you bid on:

(a) ♠ K x x   (b) ♠ A K x x   (c) ♠ J x   (d) ♠ K Q x x
     ♡ K Q J x   ♡ x   ♡ x x x   ♡ J x
     ◇ K x x   ◇ A K x x   ◇ K Q J 10 x   ◇ K J x x
     ♣ x x x   ♣ A x x x   ♣ x x x   ♣ K x x

(e) ♠ A K Q x x x   (f) ♠ x   (g)♠ K Q x x x (h)♠ x x
   ♡ x x   ♡ x   ♡ x x   ♡ x
   ◊ Q x x x   ◊ Q J x x   ◊ A x x   ◊ K Q J x x
   ♣ x   ♣ K Q J x x x x ♣ K x x   ♣ K Q 10 x x

(5) You are East. South opens 1NT, West passes and North bids 2♠, transferring to clubs. What do you bid on:

(a) ♠ K Q 10 x x (b)♠ K Q J 10 x x x (c) ♠ K Q J x (d)♠ K x x
   ♡ A x   ♡ x x   ♡ K Q J x   ♡ J x x
   ◊ x x x   ◊ A x   ◊ A x x x x   ◊ A K Q J x x
   ♣ x x x   ♣ x x   ♣ –   ♣ x

(6) You are East. South opens 1NT, West passes and North bids an invitational, but non-forcing 3♣. What do you bid on:

(a) ♠ K x   (b)♠ x x   (c) ♠ K Q J x   (d)♠ A K x
   ♡ K J x   ♡ K Q J x   ♡ A x x x x   ♡ A J x
   ◊ A Q J 10 x x   ◊ A x   ◊ A x x x   ◊ K x x x
   ♣ x x   ♣ J 10 9 x x   ♣ –   ♣ J x x

(7) You are East. South opens 1NT, West passes and North bids a preemptive sign-off in 3♠. Assuming you have agreed that 3NT is to be unusual, for the minors, what do you bid on:

(a) ♠ K J x x   (b)♠ x   (c) ♠ K   (d) ♠ x x
   ♡ x x   ♡ A Q 10 x x   ♡ A x x x   ♡ x
   ◊ K x x x x   ◊ A Q 10 x   ◊ A x x x   ◊ K Q J x x
   ♣ A x   ♣ K x x   ♣ A x x x   ♣ A K J x x

(8) You are West and the bidding goes:

S	W	N	E
1NT	Pass	3◊	Dble
Pass	?		

In a situation like this, a take-out double of diamonds at a high level, although ideally 4414 or thereabouts, should be considered primarily orientated to the majors, so that the doubler can come in on 5512 type hands without fear of his partner going wild in clubs. What do you bid now on:

(a) ♠ Q x x x   (b) ♠ K Q x x   (c) ♠ J x x   (d)♠ x x
   ♡ x x   ♡ K Q x x   ♡ x x   ♡ J x
   ◊ x x x x   ◊ x x x   ◊ x x x   ◊ x x x
   ♣ A x x   ♣ x x   ♣ K Q x x   ♣ K Q J 10 x x

Let us work through the answers:

(1) (a) Opponents could well have a game on, notably if the two-suited hand is very distributional and partner is minimum. Preempting is therefore called for and I should recommend 4◊, irrespective of vulnerability. With the two-suiter likely to be a playing, rather than defensive hand, opponents will find it difficult to double for penalties. If they bid game anyway, then, in accordance with usual preempt rules, it is for *partner* to decide on any further action.

(b) Here we simply compete with 2♡, non-forcing. Partner can compete, if necessary, or even invite game if he has a fit. He will, of course, take into account his honour holdings, badly placed under the two- suiter.

(c) We have fabulous defence against spades although it is likely that opponents will choose West's other suit. We want to defend rather than play, so we pass for the time being. We will probably decide to double 2♠ if they come to rest there.

(d) This time, we can show our good diamond suit with a double. With 11 points opposite a guaranteed minimum 12, there is no need to preempt. If partner is maximum with appropriate stops, we may reach 3NT.

(e) This is similar to (b) and we bid a non-forcing 3♣, hoping to play there, or perhaps in 3NT.

(f) With a lot of playing strength and little, if any, defence, (West could be down to a void of hearts) preempting is in order and we bid 3♡, hoping to play there. If opponents compete, partner has the option to sacrifice in 5♡ against a game, which may well be worthwhile, notably at favourable vulnerability. But remember it is *his* decision!

(g) Here we have the values for game but there is no need to rush. We first double 2◊, intending to double 2♠ if they escape to that contract. Partner may be able to double the other suits. If they escape to clubs and hearts, we shall bid 3♠ to complete the picture of our hand, after which partner will probably bid 3NT if he can stop both the other suits. Failing that, it may have to be 5◊.

(h) Here there are two possible approaches. One is double now, intending to double everything else, and that is not unreasonable. We and partner both have balanced hands and it is therefore well on the cards that opponents have a misfit. In that case, the penalty could be enormous. The alternative, with stops everywhere, is to bid 2NT or possibly even 3NT with the spades likely to be well placed.

I should base the decision on vulnerability, preferring double at favourable or equal, 3NT at unfavourable, but I have little doubt that a panel of experts would offer a variety of opinions.

(i) Here we have a potentially game-going hand and 3NT will be obvious if partner can provide the necessary stops. I recommend the unassuming cue-bid of 2♠, intending to follow with 3◊, still forcing. A double of 2◊ followed by 3◊ would not be forcing. Even if partner cannot stop the spades, a doubleton in his hand might enable 5◊ to be made.

(j) Here again, we make the unassuming cue-bid of 2♠ and follow up with 3♡, forcing, leaving partner the options of 3NT or 4♡. He might even bid 3♠, directional-asking, looking for a half-stop for 3NT. On this hand, we should have to insist on 4♡.

(k) Here there are two approaches. One is to make the unassuming cue-bid and follow with 3♣, forcing, after which, with 3NT at the top of the agenda, partner should show his stops. I have to admit this is what I should do, but a reasonable alternative is to punt 3NT direct, giving as little information as possible, and let the opponents guess what to lead. West should realize that we are likely to have a spade stop and go for his other suit but this may not be clear-cut, notably if he has five spades and only four cards in that other suit.

I explained in an earlier book that my style is to prefer accurate bidding – in this case leaving the options open for 4♣ or 5♣ to wild punting, but many top-class authorities take the other view. This hand is a classic example of the controversial area.

(2) (i) Here partner has shown a diamond suit and East has indicated that, if diamonds is West's second suit, he wishes to play there.

  (a) It is obvious that West will run to clubs or hearts but there is no need to rush for the moment. Partner has another chance and may double again. If he doesn't, we shall prefer to play in diamonds rather than defend, but, if West runs to 2♡, it will cost us nothing to bid 2♠ on the way to 3◊ (remember that, with 1NT, we cannot have more than a four-card suit). This may pave the way to 4♠ or 3NT or even 5◊.

  (b) Again, we have no reason to bid at the moment. We might compete with 3◊ if 2♠ is passed round to us but otherwise I would not recommend bidding again.

  (c) Again, a pass is obvious at this point. If they run to the majors, we are close to a double, but I should take the view that the risk comfortably outweighs the potential gain.

  (d) Again, we have no reason to bid; we may compete in diamonds later.

(ii) Now partner has competed with 2♡, non-forcing. He has promised a five-card suit and about 9–11 points.

  (a) This is a maximum but our spade honours are not working and, on the reasonable assumption that West's second suit is clubs (if it is diamonds, the whole hand is a disaster), the ♣J is wasted. For those reasons, I should recommend a pass. If we do decide to try for 4♡, the best approach is probably to bid 2♠, an unassuming cue-bid asking partner for more information. If he shows a diamond interest, we might try 4♡.

  (b) Despite the minimum point-count, this is more attractive with an extra trump, top tricks in the minors and nothing wasted in spades. Nevertheless, I still prefer a pass – 3♡ is possible.

  (c) Here we have some heart support, our points are in top cards and we have a good suit outside. However, the spade holding is poor and again I prefer a pass.

  (d) With the flat minimum, we have no reason to bid.

(iii) This time, partner has forced us with an unassuming cue-
bid and we must describe our hand.
(a) With the spades well stopped, we bid 2NT.
(b) We bid our suits in the normal ascending order – 3♣.
(c) Same applies – 3♣.
(d) Same applies – 3◊.

(iv) Partner has shown an invitational balanced hand and
should have at least one spade stop.
(a) A clear maximum – 3NT.
(b) A clear minimum – pass.
(c) Middle of the point range but a good five-card suit,
likely to produce extra tricks – 3NT.
(d) A clear minimum – pass.

(v) Partner has made a non-forcing bid. If we are to look for
game, 3NT will be uppermost in our minds and, if we bid at
all, we should show stops in ascending order.
(a) This is a maximum and the ♣J can be counted as a
working card. However, the scarcity of aces implies that
we are unlikely to be able to run nine tricks before the
defenders set up five. I should recommend a pass but
we might get away with 3NT.
(b) This is very good in support of clubs but both 3NT and
5♣ are most unlikely. I recommend a pass.
(c) This is a surprise and partner should have ♣ Q J x x x x
and some points outside. Now 3NT may be on and I
recommend 3♡, indicating that partner will need a
diamond stop to play 3NT. Otherwise, we shall have to
settle for 4♣. We might get away with the punting
approach of 3NT direct.
(d) A poor minimum and, despite the club support, there is
little reason to bid.

(vi) Here partner has preempted as opposed to doubling the 2◊
bid – a sign of weakness. We have little reason to bid on any
of these hands, although, at favourable vulnerability, there
is a case for pushing the preempt up further on (d).
Particularly, if West is void of diamonds, we may not be
able to defeat game in a major and a sacrifice may be cheap.
Note that, if we bid 4◊, that is preemptive rather than

invitational to game. If we want to invite, we change suit, which must agree diamonds as we have already promised a balanced hand and there is no question of any other denomination.

(vii) Again partner has preempted and again we have little reason to bid on any of these hands. We might be tempted to try for game on (b), which will be made if partner can produce ten cards between the two majors (unlikely).

(viii) This is a big preempt and it is unlikely that West will compete further. There is little reason to bid at this stage although we may decide to sacrifice at favourable vulnerability or even Love All on (a) or (d).

(3) Partner has shown a diamond suit but is unlimited in strength.

(i) East is short of diamonds and is angling to play in spades or West's other suit. We shall certainly have another chance to bid and there is no reason to bid in front of partner on any of these hands.

(ii) In this case, East is likely to be short of spades and probably has at least four hearts. Now West may pass and we are *not* guaranteed another chance to bid.

(a) With the diamond fit, I should not recommend defending at the two-level, preferring to show the strong hand with an unassuming cue-bid of 2♠. This forces the partnership to at least 3◊ (suit 'agreement') and opens discussions for a possible game in 3NT or 5◊.

(b) Here opponents appear to be in trouble and partner is likely to have length in spades. With four trumps, top cards and ability to double 3♣, I recommend doubling 2♡ despite the minimum point-count. The expected penalty is likely to outweigh the risk of occasionally looking silly.

(c) With the diamond misfit, a heavy penalty is also possible but, with at least one major king likely to be badly placed and the possibility that West is very short of clubs, a pass is preferable.

(d) Here we have no wish to defend against either major and I would recommend competing with 3◊ – as explained in (a), this is merely competitive rather than constructive. I hardly expect to make it but it should not be doubled and is unlikely to cost much. Vulnerable, I prefer a pass.

(iii) Here East has expressed the wish to play in 2♠ and will have at least three cards in the suit.

(a) With the diamond length, it is unwise to double and I recommend looking for game in no-trumps with 2NT. Partner should appreciate that we have this type of hand and either pass, sign off in 3◊, or bid 3NT.

(b) With poor spades and good diamond support, it could well be right to compete with 3◊ here, but partner can still have four spades or a suit of clubs or hearts for that matter. With a minimum hand and no strong feeling in any direction, I recommend passing to leave it up to partner.

(c) Same applies – we should not rush to compete in clubs or no-trumps with a misfit for diamonds – leave it up to partner.

(d) Here I would compete with 3◊, non-vulnerable, as explained above.

(4) (a) Here we are delighted to defend against a heart contract and have no reason to bid either now or later.

(b) This is an excellent take-out double against hearts and we show it with 2♡.

(c) Here we want a diamond lead against either hearts or no-trumps, played by South. We show it with a double.

(d) This is a poor take-out double against hearts and, with North unlimited to date, it would be lunacy to enter the bidding. We pass and, if South's enforced 2♡ is passed round to us, we can *then* reopen with a take-out double, confident that North has a weak take-out and partner is bound to have some points.

(e) Here we have a good suit of spades and I would recommend a 2♠ overcall at any vulnerability. At unfavourable, the pessimist might prefer to pass, intending to come in only if 2♡ is passed round to him.

(f) Here we have plenty of playing strength but little or no defence – preempting time. How far is much more debatable. My view would be 5♣ at favourable, 4♣ at equal and 3♣ at unfavourable, but expert opinion would vary considerably.

(g) This is a dubious hand and it is wisest to pass, intending to compete with 2♠ if 2♡ is passed round to us.

(h) With plenty of playing strength and poor defensive prospects, we should compete here – 2NT unusual is ideal. Even at unfavourable vulnerability, it is unlikely to cost much.

(5) (a) Here we double – as in (4c) above.

(b) Now we want to preempt. I recommend 4♠ at favourable; 3♠ otherwise.

(c) On this huge take-out double against clubs, we bid 3♣ – similar to (4b) above.

(d) We bid our excellent diamond suit with 3◊. If partner can stop clubs, 3NT may be on.

(6) The important point to realize in this sequence is that *both* opponents are now limited and we are in a very good position to judge how far to compete.

(a) We bid 3◊, hoping to play there, at the same time being assured of the right lead if they do play in 3NT.

(b) Here partner is void of clubs and South will have a doubleton honour. We shall pass now and, when he bids 3NT, we can confidently double, having a dreadful surprise for him in clubs – no credit unless you appreciated this point.

(c) Here we have a good playing hand in any non-club suit and it seems a pity not to compete with a take-out double. Opponents are most unlikely to double us into game at this level when North has indicated a playing hand.

(d) With 16 points balanced, it is clear that partner is looking at next to nothing (or less) and we have no reason to bid. Take extra credit if you appreciated that, with clubs breaking, we are most unlikely to defeat 3NT; we shall have terrible discard problems on the run of six or more rounds of clubs.

(7) (a) We are happy to defend and have no reason to bid.

    (b) This is a close decision – it could easily be wrong to bid but just as expensive not to. Even if we do decide to bid, it is then a question of whether to double, offering all three non-spade suits but risking missing the most likely game, 4♡ on a 5–3 fit; or risking 4♡, which could be doubled for an enormous penalty while four or five of a minor is lay-down. My choice would be a double, as this carries the lower risk.

    (c) Of our 15 points, three are wasted and now partner is going to be that much weaker in terms of useful cards. Vulnerable, I should certainly recommend a pass. Non-vulnerable, it is less clear and a case could be made for a take-out double, but I should still prefer a pass, deeming game unlikely and, if North has the ♠A, there is every chance that we shall defeat 3♠.

    (d) With considerable playing strength, I recommend 3NT for the minors.

(8) (a) We choose our longer major, 3♠.

    (b) This is strong enough to warrant trying for game and I should suggest leaving the choice of major to partner with a cue-bid of 4◊. He could have a shape like 4315 or 3415.

    (c) Here 4♣ could be right but, as explained in the question, it is preferable to bid 3♠.

    (d) This time, we bid 4♣, prepared to play there, even opposite a doubleton or less – partner should respect this and only move with about eleven or more cards in his suits.

The Double and Other Conventions

We now turn to the next section of the convention card, dealing with action after opponents have interfered. When we filled in our own card, we observed the rule that a double is for penalties (because partner has already bid) and bids (except, of course, by a passed hand) are forcing as usual. However, on the tournament scene, a different approach is almost universally adopted. Some years ago, my namesake Alvin, a New Yorker, was the pioneer of the negative double and we shall now introduce it and examine its applications in competitive bidding.

In practice, it is rare that a player will want to double a low-level contract for penalties, even if his partner has already bid. This particularly applies at the one-level.

Problems continually arise in the following kind of situation. Partner opens 1♣, the next hand overcalls with 1♠, and we are looking at something like:

♠ x x
♡ K Q x x
◊ Q x x x
♣ J x x

There is hardly a satisfactory bid. 1NT is ruled out for lack of a spade stop and 2♣ virtually commits us to clubs on what may be a poor 4–3 fit. Ideally, we would like to offer all non-spade suits as alternatives and we do so by sacrificing the penalty double. A double with his kind of hand is for *take-out*. This is known as the *negative* or *Sputnik* double, the latter name deriving from that of the early Russian satellites which circumnavigated the Earth from

1957. The bid is forcing and the auction *goes round* again (except in the most unlikely event of partner's having a solid spade stack *under* the overcaller when he may wish to pass, converting it into a penalty double). The negative double, in the first place, shows interest in the other major but also likely tolerance for partner's bid suit and the other unbid suit. But suppose that, this time, we hold something like:

♠ x x x
♡ x x
◊ A Q 10 x x x
♣ J x

It seems a pity to pass, but 2◊ would be forcing and show a much stronger hand. However, playing negative doubles, we can play 2◊ as non-forcing and bid it here with little risk. In practice, rules vary between partnerships in respect of whether 2◊ is forcing in this situation – there are three schools of thought:

1 It is always forcing unless, of course, the hand has passed previously;
2 It is never forcing;
3 It is forcing if a level *has not* been lost, but non-forcing if a level *has* been lost.

Some examples will clarify this point. In the above case, had the spade overcall not been made, we could have answered with 1◊. Therefore a level *has been lost* and 2◊ is considered non-forcing. On the other hand, consider the sequence: 1♣ by partner, 1♡ by opponents, 1♠ by us. Here we would have bid 1♠ anyway and a level *has not* been lost, so that third group would play the bid as forcing.

Practice also varies in how high negative doubles go. Some play them on the one-level only to show hearts after partner has bid a minor and opponents have bid spades. Others go up to game-level. This solves a lot of problems against preemptive bidding. Partner opens 1◊ and the next hand preempts with 3♠. What are we to bid with something like:

♠ x x
♡ A Q x x
◊ J x x
♣ K x x x

We certainly want to compete, but anything could be right. The negative double describes this 'good – but do not know what to do' type of hand.

Playing negative doubles, of course, rules out the immediate double for penalties. It is accepted practice that, with a hand suitable for a penalty double, the player passes (avoiding the telling long think!) and the opener (particularly with shortage in the overcalled suit) is expected to reopen with a double (take-out in all systems). The responder will then pass to convert it to penalties. Note that, contrary to what we learnt before, the reopening double now promises *no extra strength*.

In the future, I have little doubt that you will want to adopt this kind of bid, but we are not concerned with that at this stage. Our concern is to understand its implications and to learn how to combat it. Let us first listen to our opponents' bidding, assuming that all doubles of suit bids are negative, up to and including 3♠. Note that doubles of no-trump bids are still normally played for penalties. These are common sequences. (Assume that we are sitting West and South deals at Love All):

(1) S   W   N   E
    1♣   1◇   Dble

North will have at least one, possibly both, majors and tolerance for clubs.

(2) S   W   N   E
    1♣   1♡   Dble

North almost certainly has a four-card spade suit and is prepared for his partner (forced to speak) to bid either minor.

(3) S   W   N   E
    1♣   1♡   1♠

Playing negative doubles, North is now likely to have five or more spades – a useful distinction.

(4) S   W   N   E
    1♣   1♠   Dble

North almost certainly has four hearts and tolerance for either minor.

(5) S W N E
 1◊ 2♣ Dble

North is likely to have four cards in both majors or, if he has only one, he is prepared to play in 3◊ if South has no major or picks the 'wrong' one!

(6) S W N E
 1♡ 2◊ Dble

North almost certainly has four spades.

(7) S W N E
 1♡ 2◊ 2♠

North almost certainly has at least five spades.

(8) S W N E
 1♠ 2♡ Dble

North is likely to be at least 4–4 in the minors and is prepared for his partner to rebid 2♠.

(9) S W N E
 1♠ 2◊ Pass Pass
 Dble Pass Pass

North wanted to double 2◊ for penalties but could not do so in this system. He waits for his partner to reopen and converts the take-out double to penalties. The important point now is that, if East removes to another suit, any double by either North or South is for penalties. Having stated the desire to defend, they do not now go back to declaring, particularly after East–West have announced a misfit!

(10) S W N E
 Pass 1♡ 1♠ 2♡
 Dble

One can also play negative doubles opposite an overcall. Here South is prepared to compete in spades but probably has two long minor suits and would prefer a 4–4 or 5–4 fit in a minor to a 5–2 fit in spades.

The negative double can also be used, with correction or further information, to offer the choice of two suits, no-trumps and/or game or slam. Let us go through some of the above situations (where negative doubles were used) again and listen to a further round of bidding.

(1)

S	W	N	E
1♣	1◇	Dble	Pass
1♠	Pass	2♣	

North has a four-card heart suit but no interest in spades. When his partner chooses the 'wrong' major, North reverts to clubs.

(2)

S	W	N	E
1♣	1♡	Dble	Pass
2◇	Pass	3♣	

South does not have a four-card spade suit but has a diamond suit. North clearly has hearts and clubs. Note that *North*, rather than South, takes the responsibility for going to the three-level. South's bid of 2◇ is merely answering the double and does *not* guarantee reversing values.

(4)

S	W	N	E
1♣	1♠	Dble	Pass
2◇	Pass	2♠	

North, in the first place, was looking for a heart fit. When that failed to materialize, his 2♠ is directional-asking, looking for no-trumps. North must have the values to cover 2NT or three of either minor.

(5)

S	W	N	E
1◇	2♣	Dble	Pass
2♠	Pass	2NT	

North was looking for a heart fit and should have a potential double-stop in clubs. 2NT is non-forcing.

(6)

S	W	N	E
1♡	2◇	Dble	Pass
2♠	Pass	4◇	

A fit has been found and North shows a void of diamonds. His initial negative double was slightly risky in that South might have left it in, but this is extremely rare against a two-over-one overcall. The overcaller should have a good suit and therefore it is most unlikely that South will have a strong enough holding (badly-placed) to leave it in. North will probably be 4306.

(8) S   W   N   E
     1♠   2♡   Dble   Pass
     3♣   Pass   3◊

North is offering the choice of diamonds or spades – he probably has six diamonds and three spades.

(10) S   W   N   E
     Pass   1♡   1♠   2♡
     Dble   Pass   3◊   Pass
     3♠

South was offering clubs as an alternative to spades but settled for spades when North failed to show a club suit.

My recommended defence against the negative double is to treat it just like a take-out double, as explained in the beginners' book. Six positions were distinguished:

1 Weak with misfit in partner's suit;
2 Weak with fit in partner's suit and
   (a) many points in partner's suit,
   (b) few points in partner's suit;
3 Strong with misfit;
4 Strong with fit – same subdivisions as in (2).

In (1), we consider moving to another contract if we think it is likely that the double will be left in and that the alternative (bearing in mind whether or not that involves raising the level of bidding) will be a better contract.

In cases (2a) and (4a), we are frightened of defending and support partner's suit immediately as far as we can go, possibly stretching a level to cause maximum disruption at the risk of a small penalty.

In (3), we definitely want to defend and redouble.

In (2b) and (4b), we pass and support partner later (or bid another suit to show that suit and support for partner's) as we do not mind defending and want to warn partner against sacrificing.

There are, however, two very important differences. With the take-out double, partner's original opening bid may be down to a weak four-card suit and therefore the case in (1) can occasionally arise. Where partner has overcalled, he has promised a good five-card suit and therefore running away from a negative double to another suit for fear that the double will be left in, particularly by a player who has already shown length in another suit, is virtually never right. Similarly, with partner's overcall having shown playing strength rather than high-card points, it is very rare that the partner will be strong enough to double everything, even with a bad misfit, and therefore the redouble is also very rare. For that reason, some authorities use it for other purposes, usually as support for partner of exactly three cards, and I have to admit that, on frequency, they are certainly using the bid more often than I am. Nevertheless, I recommend keeping the redouble for its normal meaning, if only to prevent frivolous competitive bidding, which is common nowadays.

I mentioned at the time and repeat now that many top authorities handle the take-out double differently and, if you wish to follow them, fair enough. However, for this next test, I should like you to assume that my above recommendations apply. In each case, I should like you to state what you know about the hand so far, what you intend to bid and what final contract(s) you envisage. You should complete the fifty questions at the usual rate of fifteen seconds per example – comfortably under thirteen minutes. Assume South deals at Love All but state any differences a change of vulnerability would make. Start your stop-watch.

(1) You are East and the bidding goes

S	W	N	E
1♣	1♠	Dble	?

What do you bid on:

(a) ♠ K Q x
   ♡ x x x x
   ◇ x x x x
   ♣ J x

(b) ♠ x x x x
   ♡ A K x x
   ◇ K x x
   ♣ x x

(c) ♠ K Q x x
   ♡ K x
   ◇ J x x x x
   ♣ x x

(d) ♠ K x x x
   ♡ K Q x
   ◇ K x x x
   ♣ x x

(e) ♠ K Q x x x
   ♡ x x x x
   ◇ x x x x
   ♣ –

(f) ♠ x x x
   ♡ A K J x x
   ◇ K x x
   ♣ x x

(g) ♠ –
   ♡ Q J 10 9
   ◇ A J 10 9
   ♣ Q J 10 9 x

(h) ♠ x x x
   ♡ A x
   ◇ A K Q x x x
   ♣ x x

(2) You are West and the bidding goes:

S	W	N	E
	1♡	2◇	Dble	3◇
	*	?		

* is (i) Pass (ii) 3♡ (iii) 3♠ (iv) 4♣ (v) 4◇ (cue-bid: first round control – almost certainly a void) (vi) 4♡ (vii) 4♠

What do you bid now on:

(a) ♠ K J   (b) ♠ x x x   (c) ♠ K x   (d) ♠ x x
    ♡ x x x x   ♡ –   ♡ K x x   ♡ K Q x
    ◇ A K x x x   ◇ K Q J x x x   ◇ A K J x x x   ◇ Q J 10 x x x
    ♣ J x   ♣ A x x x   ♣ x x   ♣ K x

(3) You are East and the bidding goes:

S	W	N	E
1♡	2◇	Pass	Pass
Dble	Pass	Pass	?

What do you bid now on:

(a) ♠ K Q x x   (b) ♠ x x x   (c) ♠ K Q x x x   (d) ♠ K J 10 x x x
    ♡ x x x x   ♡ K Q J 10 x x   ♡ x   ♡ Q x
    ◇ x   ◇ x   ◇ x   ◇ x x
    ♣ J x x x   ♣ x x x   ♣ Q J x x x x   ♣ x x x

(4) You are South and the bidding goes:

S	W	N	E
1♠	2♡	3◇	Dble
?			

What do you bid now on:

(a) ♠ A K Q J x   (b) ♠ A K x x x   (c) ♠ A Q J x x   (d) ♠ A K x x x
    ♡ x x   ♡ K Q x x   ♡ –   ♡ x
    ◇ K x x x   ◇ x x   ◇ A x x x   ◇ K Q x x
    ♣ x x   ♣ x x   ♣ Q x x x   ♣ J x x

(e) ♠ K Q J x x x   (f) ♠ A K x x x   (g) ♠ K Q x x x   (h) ♠ A K J x x x
    ♡ x x   ♡ x x x   ♡ K Q x x   ♡ x x
    ◇ A Q x x   ◇ K Q x x x   ◇ x   ◇ K x x
    ♣ x   ♣ –   ♣ K J x   ♣ x x

(i) ♠ A K Q x x x   (j) ♠ A Q x x x x
    ♡ x x   ♡ x
    ◇ A x x   ◇ K J x x x
    ♣ J x   ♣ Q

Let us work through the answers:

(1) (a) With nearly all our points in spades we are keen to play, rather than defend, and preempt as far as possible with 2♠; some would even risk 3♠. Remember this is purely obstructive rather than a constructive attempt to reach 4♠.

(b) Here we have enough for 3♠ but, with all our points outside the spade suit, we are happy to defend at a high level. I therefore recommend a pass followed by 3♠ next round to show this type of hand.

(c) This is certainly worth a preemptive raise to 3♠ and some might even risk 4♠. However, with the ♡K likely to be badly placed under the opener, there are likely to be too many losers to make this worthwhile, even at favourable vulnerability. Opponents, after all, have neither bid nor made a game yet.

(d) This is a good raise to 3♠ and we show it with 2NT in the normal way after a take-out double. Partner can accept (with 4♠); reject with 3♠; or make a long-suit trial at the three-level if he is not sure.

(e) Here we preempt to the limit with 4♠, non-vulnerable, 3♠ vulnerable although some would go to 4♠ at any vulnerability and a good case can be made for this as opponents could be cold for anything up to 7♣. The danger of bidding 4♠ is that partner will turn up with values in clubs, in which case opponents may not be even be able to make game, while we are losing 500 or 800.

(f) Here I recommend a pass, intending to bid hearts next round, probably at the three-level, to show the good suit with support for spades. Partner can take it from there and we shall probably finish in 3♠ or 4♠.

(g) With a very unpleasant surprise for opponents in all three non-spade suits, we are prepared to double anything at the two-level. Here I would recommend a redouble, intending to double anything they say. It is most unlikely that they can make anything at that level and the penalty could be heavy.

(h) This is similar to (f), but we are prepared to play at the four-level here. I recommend a pass followed by 4◊ to clarify this type of hand. Partner will then know whether to sacrifice and, if he decides to defend, what to lead should the bidding climb to the five-level.

(2) Here partner has made a modest preempt to his limit and should not bid again unless we force him to do so.

   (i) South has left any further action to his partner, thereby advertizing a probably minimal opening bid. We have little reason to bid on any of (a), (c) and (d) but might push the preempt up a further level to 4◊ on (b), particularly when non-vulnerable. Short of trumps, it will be very difficult for opponents to double us and we shall have made it harder for North, who clearly has a big hand, to bid accurately.

   (ii) This time, South has made a free bid (non-forcing) and therefore shows extra values and probably a six-card (or at least very good five-card) suit. Before considering bidding on any of these hands, one very important rule should be emphasized. If we decide to bid 4◊, we should decide *now* what we are going to do if opponents compete with 4♡. There will be three obvious choices: pass or double, intending to defend; or sacrifice in 5◊. If we intend to sacrifice, it will be worth considering bidding 5◊ immediately; it then may not be clear to opponents whether we hope to make it or our bidding is an advanced sacrifice.

     On (a), (c), and (d), we have some defensive prospects and any sacrifice is going to be far too expensive at any vulnerability. There is therefore no need to bid – we are unlikely to make even 4◊ and opponents haven't yet bid 4♡. (b) is less clear. It is certain that opponents will reach at least 4♡ and, if one of them is void of diamonds, they could well bid and make 6♡. Irrespective of partner's club holding, we are unlikely to lose more than five tricks in 5◊, losing 500, non-vulnerable, and I should recommend it, certainly at favourable vulnerability and possibly at Love All. Vulnerable, I should recommend 4◊ and pass subsequently.

   (iii) Here South has bid even higher but need not be as strong as a reverse as he has guaranteed a fit in at least one of his majors. Indeed, some players take the view that they will not be 'talked' out of the auction by a 'pathetic' 3◊ preemptive support and compete with little or nothing above their opening bid. The first point is that, as the bid is merely answering a take-out double at the cheapest possible level, it is non-forcing. Now that South has offered both majors, game in either becomes a possibility for opponents' final contract.

On (a) (c) and (d), there is little reason to bid but on (b), much will depend on whether opponents finish in hearts or spades. With hearts, the position is as in (ii) above but, with spades, there are defensive prospects in that we can put partner in with his assumed ◊A for a heart ruff. There are a number of possible approaches but my recommendation is to pass and wait. Now: if they settle for 4♠, I would try a double and lead the *queen* of diamonds, forcing partner to overtake and hopefully he will realize what is going on. If they settle for 4♡, we still have the option to sacrifice in 5◊ should the vulnerability warrant it. It may well be that, particularly if South is the type who refuses to be talked out by the 3◊ bid, the opponents will shoot for a slam. In this case, with the poor heart break and a certain defensive trick in the ♣A, I recommend letting them play it.

(iv) Again there is little reason to bid on (a), (c) and (d). With (b), opponents can still play in 4♡ and we have the same options as before. However, although it is unlikely, they may go for 5♣. In that event, we have the option to defend and play a forcing game with the diamonds or, with partner virtually guaranteed to hold, at most, a singleton club, bid 5◊, confident of at least nine and probably ten tricks, giving partner no more than ◊ A x x x. Eleven would require partner to hold something useful in spades (he will certainly have length and holdings like ♠ Q 10 x are not impossible, enabling 5◊ to be made if North has the ♠J and one or both top honours). My recommendation is to wait, if only to find out if North thinks that his partner is stronger than he is and goes slamming.

(v) The announcement of a void in South's hand – and he is probably very strong as he has committed the partnership to game – throws a very different light on the matter.

(a) The sacrifice is still likely to be too expensive and we still pass.

(b) We cannot put partner in for a heart ruff (if spades are trumps) and therefore our defensive prospects are reduced. It is almost certain that opponents will reach a slam and I recommend 5♦ (non-vulnerable) to reduce opponents' bidding space. Vulnerable, it is probably best to pass and hope the bad heart split will bring about opponents' downfall.

(c) All hangs on the positions of the major aces. With South having announced a strong hand, I should elect to defend the slam rather than sacrifice at the seven-level. However, non-vulnerable, it is probably worth bidding 5♦ now to crowd the bidding.

(d) We shall still want to defend in all circumstances and therefore pass throughout.

(vi) Here South has shown a suit which he is happy to play opposite a useless doubleton, the minimum expectation of the negative doubler.

(a) That gives South six or more hearts and partner a singleton at most. Our four trumps will be useless in defence and it may be worth considering a sacrifice at favourable vulnerability. It will probably be too expensive otherwise. I should take the view that, with our major-suit holdings, it is unlikely that North will want to go any higher.

(b) This time, North might well go higher and it could be a question of a possible sacrifice in 7♦ against 6♥. We are likely to lose two club tricks and three spade tricks – five off – which is 1100 non-vulnerable and 1400 vulnerable. Such a sacrifice is therefore only a serious proposition at favourable vulnerability. However, even here, with no guarantee that opponents will either bid a slam or make it, I recommend a quiet 5♦ (non-vulnerable only), awaiting further developments.

(c) There is a lot of defence here and it is probably not worth sacrificing.

(d) We are delighted to defend and pass.

(vii) (a) We have some defence; a sacrifice is likely to be too expensive and we have no reason to bid.

(b) Here there are chances to defeat 4♠ although partner may not realize what is happening unless we double. The double, however, would be unwise as opponents are unlimited. There is no guarantee of defeat, even if we do get a heart ruff, and opponents may well go higher. My suggestion is 5◊, intending to double 5♠ but prepared to give up if they compete in hearts – there is no guarantee that they will have stopped at the correct level and they face a bad trump split anyway.

(c) Similar arguments apply as to (a).

(d) As before, we wish to defend and pass.

It should be said that the handling of these very difficult competitive situations is very much a question of judgment, and I have no doubt many more respected authorities would disagree – possibly strongly – with many of my answers. These divergences of opinion are, of course, half the fun of the game, but I feel that the important factor at this stage is to understand how I approach a problem. If you get that far, you will, at least, save yourself many decisions which are way off the mark and, particularly at high levels, could be very expensive.

(3) This time, a take-out double has been converted to penalties by a hand which clearly would have doubled for penalties had they not been playing negative doubles.

(a) This is a nightmare but there is nowhere to go so we pass and take our medicine.

(b) Here, despite the heart bid on our left, it is worth rescuing to 2♡ as the hand will be worth several more tricks with those hearts as trumps. Even with a void, partner should respect our decision.

(c) Here we can offer two alternative contracts and make a Kock-Werner SOS redouble to invite partner to choose a black suit.

(d) We have two diamonds this time but the argument here is that the diamonds are heavily stacked while the spades may or may not be. To be realistic, South ought to have four spades for his reopening take-out double, but he could reasonably be 3514. The chances are that 2♠, particularly as it is on the same level, stands to gain more than it loses.

(4) This is one of those hands where there appear to be 50 or more points in the pack. Partner has forced to game while East, having made an effective take-out double against spades and diamonds, has shown support for hearts and a good club suit. A highly competitive auction is likely and vulnerability may well be a critical factor in who sacrifices against whom.

(a) We have two options: to repeat the spades – a good idea because it could well be that we have to play 4♠ on a 5–2 or 5–3 fit in preference to 5♢ on a 5–4 or better fit; or to support diamonds at once. I prefer 3♠, intending to support diamonds later if necessary. Note that the absence of a redouble implies that we have at least some tolerance for diamonds.

(b) Here the heart bid on our left has devalued our hand considerably and, having a minimum opener anyway, we pass and await further developments.

(c) With good support for partner, we are prepared to go to at least 5♢ and a slam could well be on. The most important piece of information is the heart void and we show it with 4♡.

(d) This is similar but we have a singleton. My suggestion is 3♡. For the time being, partner will take it that we are looking for 3NT, being able to stop hearts and asking him if he can stop clubs. When we remove 3NT to 4♢, he will realize that the 3♡ bid was an advanced cue-bid in support of diamonds and elect to play in game or slam in diamonds or spades accordingly.

(e) Here the same applies but we have a singleton club and we bid 4♣.

(f) With the void of clubs, we bid 5♣ – which may lead to a small or grand slam in diamonds or spades.

(g) With a lot of points in opponents' suits and an intense dislike of diamonds, we redouble, showing our wish to defend. Partner can still remove to 3NT or 4♠ if his hand is more suited to declaring.

(h) This is similar to (a) but now 3♠, hoping for game or slam in spades (unless partner has long diamonds and short spades) is clear-cut.

(i) Similar to (h) but stronger and I recommend showing the solid suit with 4♠.

(j) Here there are a number of approaches. We could start cue-bidding opponents' suits as (d) and (e) above to show singletons, but this hand is very poor for defence and we are likely to be interrupted. Alternatively, this hand is a rare example of one suitable for Blackwood, although the ♠K could be offside with the opening bid. My choice would be a direct 5◇ and partner might well realize that we have this sort of hand. (With exactly *one* singleton or void, we could have cue-bid).

So far, we have learnt three types of double:

1 Take-out or informative;
2 Penalty;
3 Negative.

In fact, there are several more types played on the tournament bridge scene, notably at top level but, for the time being, it will be sufficient to learn about two more.

Responsive double

Especially in these days of very obstructive bidding, the type of situation that follows crops up regularly. South opens 1◇ and West doubles (normal take-out); North preempts with 3◇ and East is looking at something like:

♠ K x x x
♡ K J x x
◇ x x
♣ Q x x

Undoubtedly, he will want to compete, but with what? A straightforward 3♥ risks finding partner with a shape like 4324 when spades would clearly be better. There are similar dangers in bidding 3♠. To surmount this problem, many pairs sacrifice the penalty double in this position on the grounds that, once the opener's suit has been supported (notably with a jump) a heavy trump stack suited to a penalty double is unlikely. They therefore use the double as take-out to describe this type of hand. The take-out double in response to partner's take-out double after the opener's suit has been supported is called a *responsive* double (i.e. a double by the responder).

When a responsive double is played against you, simply treat it as a take-out double, observing the same guides as above. The exception arises in that, with a suit agreed, there is no running away to a new suit for fear that the responsive double will be left in. That is most unlikely by a hand that has announced shortage in our suit! The only exception would arise if the doubler has a strong, no-trump hand (18+ points) and intended to bid no-trumps next round. In practice, the situation virtually never arises; the doubler's partner will usually have a long suit to bid and is unlikely to make a responsive double. Therefore the sequence:

S	W	N	E
1♠	Dble	2♠	Dble
3◊			

is a long-suit trial, asking for help with diamond losers as usual, with the intention of finishing in 3♠ or 4♠.

Competitive double

The fifth type of double to be learnt occurs when the two pairs have both found fits and a competitive tussle results. Let us look at a typical example with South as dealer:

S	W	N	E
1♥	1♠	2♥	2♠
3♥	?		

First, consider South's bidding. His 3♥ bid is merely competitive, i.e. intending to play there, and in no way an invitation to game. Had he wanted to invite game, he could have made a long-suit trial in one of the minors or bid 2NT with spade values. Now, how about West's position? The bidding has been crowded and he has no room to invite game with a long-suit trial or other bid indicating a hand intermediate between 3♠ and 4♠. To cover this situation, many pairs take the view that, having established a spade fit, it is most unlikely that they will want to double 3♡ for penalties. They therefore stipulate that a double is a serious game-invitational raise to 3♠. A 3♠ bid is merely competing for the part-score and may well be stretched.

This type of double is called a *competitive* double, i.e. a double occurring in a competitive auction. Returning to the above auction, many pairs would play a double by South (instead of 3♡) as competitive, lacking an obvious long-suit trial. Some, however, only play competitive doubles in positions where (as for West above) there is no room at all between the opponents' bid and the competitive bid. To illustrate this point, suppose the auction above had been:

S	W	N	E
1◇	1♠	2◇	2♠
3◇	?		

then this school would play a double from West as penalties. 3♡ would be a serious game-invitational raise (unspecified rather than a definite long-suit trial in hearts). 3♠ is merely competing as usual.

Our concern here is how to play against competitive doubles. There are a number of possibilities as the redouble and pass (in a forcing situation) have now become available. I suggest:

Pass followed by double:
   Penalties (it is senseless to warn them with a redouble in this position as they seem to be contemplating game!).
Pass followed by competing:
   Prepared to go that far but wish to defend at a higher level.
Immediate competing:
   Suggests reluctance to defend and a possible sacrifice.
Redouble:
   A serious game invitation in our suit (rare because partner was only 'competing') – after that, leave it to partner.

New suit:

> Prepared to play our suit at the cheapest level now available but lead-directing, showing values, useful if we defend and partner is going to be on lead.

Let us have a short test on playing against responsive and competitive doubles. As usual, state your suggested bid with full justification, indicating the final contract(s) anticipated. Assume South deals at Love All but indicate any changes in your answers were the vulnerability different. Again, each example should take about fifteen seconds, so that you complete the eighteen-question test in well under five minutes. Start your stop-watch.

(1) You are South and the bidding goes:

S	W	N	E
1♠	Dble	2♠	Dble
?			

What do you bid now on:

(a) ♠ A K x x x x
♡ x x
◊ K x x
♣ J x

(b) ♠ J 10 x x
♡ K Q 10
◊ K Q x
♣ A Q J

(c) ♠ Q J x x x
♡ A x
◊ Q x x
♣ K J x

(d) ♠ A K Q x x
♡ K Q x
◊ x
♣ Q x x x

(e) ♠ A K J x x x
♡ –
◊ K Q x
♣ K x x x

(f) ♠ A K J 10 x x
♡ Q 10
◊ K Q x
♣ x x

(2) You are North and the bidding goes:

S	W	N	E
1♠	Dble	2♠	Dble
Rdble	3♣	?	

What do you bid now on:

(a) ♠ K Q x x x
♡ x x x
◊ x x x x
♣ x

(b) ♠ K 10 x x x
♡ x x x x
◊ Q J 10
♣ x

(c) ♠ J x x
♡ x x
◊ Q x x x x
♣ K J x

(d) ♠ Q x x x
♡ Q x x
◊ Q x x
♣ x x x

(3) You are North and the bidding goes:

S	W	N	E
1♡	1♠	2♡	2♠
3♡	Dble	?	

What do you bid now on:

(a) ♠ Q J 10 9	(b) ♠ x x	(c) ♠ x x x x	(d) ♠ J 10 9 x
♡ x x x	♡ K Q 10 x	♡ A x x x	♡ Q J x x
◇ x x	◇ x x	◇ K x	◇ x
♣ K J x x	♣ x x x x x	♣ J x x	♣ K x x x

4) You are North and the bidding goes:

S	W	N	E
1♡	Dble	2♡	2♠
3♡	Dble	?	

West's first double is a normal take-out; the second is competitive, i.e. a game-invitational raise to 3♠. What do you bid now on:

(a) ♠ x x	(b) ♠ A K x	(c) ♠ x x x	(d) ♠ x x x x
♡ K 10 x x	♡ x x x x	♡ J x x x	♡ Q J x x
◇ Q x x	◇ x x x x	◇ Q x x x x	◇ x
♣ J x x x	♣ x x	♣ A	♣ Q J 10 x

Let us work through the answers:

(1) (a) With long spades and most of our points in that suit, we have poor defensive prospects and should preempt with 3♠, hoping to play there. Remember that this is preemptive rather than an invitation to game.

   (b) This hand is at the other extreme with very strong defensive prospects. There are two approaches. One is to redouble, intending to double any escape while being prepared for partner to overrule if he has long spades and no outside defence. The other is to bid 2NT, as usual, hoping to finish in 3NT or 4♠ but being prepared for partner to sign off in 3♠. Vulnerability is important here and we might well take the view that, at favourable, we should redouble and hope for a big vulnerable penalty. At unfavourable, we should prefer 2NT, aiming for a vulnerable game in preference to a relatively modest non-vulnerable penalty. At equal, it is less clear-cut. I should prefer the redouble as this is a defensive type of hand with points in the short suits. Our honours are badly placed under the doubler and, for that reason, it could well be right to redouble even at unfavourable vulnerability.

(c) With this poor hand, further devalued by the double on our left, we have no reason to bid again.

(d) Here we have enough to invite game and make a long-suit trial with 3♣, prepared to play in 3♠ or 4♠.

(e) This hand is likely to be worth 4♠ but it costs nothing to cue-bid our heart void on the way with 4♡. Give partner no more than:

♠ 10 x x x

♡ x x x x

◇ A x x x

♣ x   and 6♠ is excellent.

(f) This is less clear. The heart holding could hardly be worse and our defensive potential will largely depend on the position of the ◇A. At favourable vulnerability, one possible approach is to bid a 'confident' 4♠ and let West guess whether this is a serious bid or advance sacrifice. A second is to bid 3♠ and hope West does not compete. A third is to pass and hope they do not reach game; we may decide to compete if they stop in 3♡. My choice would be 4♠ at favourable, 3♠ at equal and pass at unfavourable.

(2) Here partner has shown the sort of hand in (1b) above.

(a) Opponents are likely to have a nine-card fit and, with no defence whatsoever, it is safer for us to bid 3♠, hoping to play there, or in 4♠ if partner is very strong.

(b) This is a similar hand to (a) but it costs nothing for us to show our diamond feature with 3◇, on the way to 3♠. That may help partner to decide whether to bid 3♠, 4♠ or possibly 3NT.

(c) With poor spades and splendid defence against the clubs, we are happy to double 3♣ for penalties.

(d) With a very poor minimum hand, we have no right to bid again, and should pass, leaving any further action to partner.

(3) Here West has invited game in spades.

   (a) We have a very unpleasant surprise for opponents in trumps and I should be prepared to double 3♠ for penalties. We pass now and see if they bid 4♠!

   (b) This is at the other extreme, a virtually defenceless hand. The first point we have to consider is what we are going to do if they reach 4♠. A sacrifice in 5♡ may be worthwhile at favourable vulnerability but, with those doubletons in spades and diamonds, it will probably be too expensive otherwise. The second question is whether it is worthwhile competing with 4♡ if they stop in 3♠. This may well be allowed to be played undoubled, non-vulnerable, and should be cheap against the value of a certain part-score. My policy would be to pass now, prepared to go to 5♡ against 4♠ at favourable vulnerability but not otherwise. If they stop in 3♠, I should suggest still passing, for fear of pushing them into an unbeatable 4♠ – possibly East will misjudge a close decision.

   (c) The bidding has improved this hand considerably in that partner will have a singleton spade at most and therefore all our points are likely to be working. I should suggest a redouble here to suggest a game in hearts. Partner should realize that we have this type of hand and he will then be well placed to take a decision over 3♠.

   (d) Again the opponents' bidding has improved this hand. I should take the view that I am prepared to play 4♡ but defend against 4♠. I suggest passing now, intending to bid 4♡ over 3♠ but clarifying to partner that I should prefer to defend 4♠ rather than go to 5♡.

(4) This is similar to (c) but the subtle difference is that partner will be on lead against a spade contract.

   (a) We have a poor hand and little reason to bid any more.

   (b) Again we shall want to defend and pass.

   (c) This time, we are prepared to go to 4♡ and we can see a defence to 4♠ provided partner leads a club. We shall win and hopefully put partner in with hearts for a club ruff. To inform partner of this, we now bid 4♣.

(d) Here we might have a good sacrifice on, especially if partner, as is likely, has a singleton or void spade. I suggest an immediate 4♡, irrespective of vulnerability, intending to leave any further decision to partner.

We conclude this section with the variations you are likely to meet in handling your take-out double. It was explained in the beginners' book that there at least two other approaches to my policy of trying to distinguish six types of hand. Some players simply ignore the double and bid as though the hand had passed, using the redouble to show about 10+ points, replacing 2NT which is still used as the good raise to three of the opener's suit. Others merely use the redouble to show about 9+ points, irrespective of attitude to opener's suit, and bid normally otherwise, although there is a division of opinion on whether a change of suit is forcing or not. A third group plays a jump in a new suit as splinter, showing a good raise in the opener's suit to the cheapest level available with a singleton or void in the suit named. So 1♠ Dble 3◊ would show something like:

♠ K x x x
♡ K Q x
◊ x
♣ Q x x x x.

You can simply double that bid to show diamond values.

We shall conclude this section with some miscellaneous conventions which you are likely to meet and of which you should be aware.

Defence against preemptive bids

There are a number of ways of handling preemptive bids. I recommended using the double for take-out, all other bids natural and the cue-bid for strong hands, notably one- and two-suiters which might be deemed unsuitable for a take-out double, notably at a high level. In order to combat preemptive bids on very poor hands, an increasingly common feature of the modern game, many pairs like to play the double for penalties, notably when sitting over the preemptive hand. They therefore use one of the following for take-out:

1 Next suit up (known as *Fischbein* or *Herbert*), i.e. 3◊ over 3♣
                                                          3♡ over 3◊
                                                          3♠ over 3♡
                                                          4♣ over 3♠
   Pairs who use this in the direct position only but use the take-out double in the protective position are said to play FOXU, Fischbein Over, Double Under.

2 Lower minor, in order to keep major-suit bids natural, i.e. five-card or longer, the cheapest *minor-suit* available is used as take-out double: 3◊ over 3♣
                                                            4♣ over 3◊, 3♡ or 3♠
   Pairs who use this in the direct position only but use the take-out double in the protective position are said to play LMX.

3 3NT: partner may leave it if he has the preempt suit well stopped.

The Acol gambling 3NT

While we are on the subject of preemptive bidding, there is one in common use which we have not discussed – the *Acol gambling 3NT*. This is done on a long solid minor suit with, in principle, not more than a queen outside. In that area, there are differences of opinion on what is required. Most agree that it should be at least a seven-card suit; some demand a minimum of A K Q J x x x; others allow A K Q x x x x. As it is unlikely that you will run into a loser with the latter holding, I agree with that view. Regarding outside holdings, some allow up to a king outside the suit; others rigidly adhere to a queen, arguing that, once there is a king or more, the hand is strong enough to open at the one-level. Most agree, however, that in fourth position the hand can be considerably stronger as partner is bound to have a few points and the opponents are unlikely to be able to take five tricks quickly. The partner of the gambler will either pass if he thinks the contract will be made; otherwise he bids 4♣, which opener can pass or correct to 4◊ according to which minor he has. Alternatively, responder can bid 4◊ himself if it is obvious that his partner has diamonds (i.e. he, himself has club honours) so that responder's tenaces in the side-suits are protected.

How do we defend against this? There are a number of approaches; my suggestion is:

Double:
    For penalties in principle, general values, probably about a good opening bid or more.
Suit bid:
    Natural and non-forcing.
Pass and then double (once minor suit has been identified):
    Take-out – primarily for the majors.
Double and then double again (once minor suit has been identified):
    Penalties – but primarily showing high-card strength rather than a trump stack – partner may remove to game in a major if his hand is more suited to declaring than defending.

Baron roll

While on the three-level, you should know that the Stayman convention is usually modified after an opening bid of 2NT or the sequences:

2♣	2◇	and	2♣	2◇
2NT			3NT	

With a big hand announced, a minor-suit slam is a possibility and Stayman is modified to cater for this. The convention is known as the *Baron roll*. After the no-trump bid, 3♣, rather than specifically asking for majors, asks the no-trump bidder to show his four-card suits in ascending order. Responder does the same until a 4–4 or better fit is found, or the partnership realizes that it has no such fit and agrees to play no-trumps. Therefore

2NT	3♣
	3◇

guarantees at least four diamonds but does not deny four of a major. Responder now bids three of his own major (hearts if he has both) and opener supports or continues the roll with 3♠ or 3NT. Let us listen to a few example sequences:

2NT	3♣
3◇	3♡
3♠	3NT

Opener has at least four diamonds and four spades but does not

have four hearts. Responder has four hearts but does not have four
spades.

2NT   3♣
3♡   3♠
4♠
Opener has at least four hearts and four spades but has denied
four diamonds. Responder has four spades. In practice, rather
than merely bidding 4♠, opener could cue-bid a non-spade ace at
the four-level at no cost.

2NT   3♣
3NT
This means that opener's only four-card suit is clubs.

As far as defending against this is concerned, there is little to
worry about as it is most unlikely that you will want to enter the
auction. The major difference is that, whereas with Stayman, the
diamond bid did not guarantee a suit and could be doubled for
lead or sacrifice, with the Baron roll, it does guarantee a suit;
therefore it is unlikely to be wise to bid with a diamond holding.

There are further variations of Stayman around but there is no
need to worry about them at this stage.

Baron 2NT

We turn to strong hands replying to an opening bid. In the earlier
books, we learnt that a sequence like 1♡ 2NT shows 11–12 points
balanced, non-forcing. In modern tournament bridge, this still
holds for the passed hand but is seldom used otherwise. Problems
arise with very strong (say 16+ points) balanced hands. A jump in
a new suit shows a one-suited hand, while a simple change of suit,
though forcing, presents problems in catching up afterwards with
what is a likely to be a slam-going hand.

Nowadays, the common solution is another invention of Baron,
the Baron 2NT. This shows 16+ points, balanced, or an intention to
support opener's suit on the next round to initiate cue-bidding for
a slam. Opener, forced to game at least, continues to describe his
hand naturally. There is little need to have a defensive convention

against this as there is likely to be a minimum of 30 points against you. Thus you should not be entering the bidding without fabulous distribution and, almost certainly, favourable vulnerability. I suggest all suit bids are natural and very long suits. A double of the 2NT or any higher no-trump bid offers the two lowest outstanding suits (discounting the opener's bid suit) and a cue-bid of the opener's suit shows a two-suiter, subject to correction, other than the two lower. It is extremely rare that one enters the auction at all in this situation.

Crowhurst

In the beginner's book, we learnt that the sequence: 1◇   1♠
                                                                                1NT

shows 15–16 points and indeed, that is still played by most pairs. Some, however, notably those frightened to open a weak no-trump vulnerable and/or with a suit wide open (notably a useless doubleton) prefer to open one of a suit and rebid 1NT, which now shows a point-count of 12–16. This puts responder in a quandary whether to go on and the solution is to use 2♣ as a forcing enquiry rather than natural. This convention is known as *Crowhurst*. It is best illustrated with some examples after the above sequence.

1◇   1♠
1NT   2♣
2◇

Shows a minimum hand (12–14), probably five diamonds, and denies a trebleton spade.

1◇   1♠
1NT   2♣
2♡

Shows a minimum hand, natural.

1◇   1♠
1NT   2♣
2♠

Shows a minimum hand with exactly three spades.

1◇   1♠
1NT 2♣
2NT

Shows 15–16 points and denies three spades.

1◇   1♠
1NT 2♣
3♠

Shows 15–16 points with three spades.

There are a number of variations to the above, but you can see the idea. All that you need to remember is that the 2♣ bid is forcing and therefore, if you pass, you are guaranteed another bid (unlikely that you will need it anyway as you did not come in on the first round). I recommend using the double to show a strong club holding for a lead as opponents may well finish in 3NT.

Slam conventions

Finally, in the slam zone, for those who have not been cured of Blackwood, there a number of variations, including *Roman* Blackwood and *five-ace* Blackwood (in which the king of trumps is considered an 'ace'). There are also a number of other conventions. These need not be detailed here – the important point to remember is that, where an unnatural bid is made, you have the double available to indicate a lead to partner (if you are sure that partner will be on lead!). Before using it, however, beware two important points. First, you give them an extra round of bidding in that both pass and redouble are available to the hand on your left. Second, particularly if you double on a broken holding, like A Q or K J, the information given may be more helpful to opponents than to partner.

Defensive signalling

It remains to discuss the varieties of defensive signalling methods being used. I described them all in great detail in my book, *Signal Success in Bridge* (Gollancz 1989; reprinted as paperback 1993) and you are well advised to read it before playing in a tournament. The important variations you are likely to meet are:

1 Lead of third or fifth highest from long suits. In these cases, whereas you use the rule of eleven for fourth-high, you use the rule of twelve for third-high and rule of ten for fifth-high – fifteen being the total to remember (4 + 11, 3 + 12, 5 + 10).

2 Honour leads vary. Some play *Roman* leads (the lower of touching honours, i.e K from A K, Q from K Q, etc.) Others play the ten as a *strong* card, guaranteeing two higher honours, e.g. A J 10 or K J 10, and they have the advantage that the lead of a jack *denies* a higher honour.

3 In following suit and discarding, practices vary. Some give the count all the time, either in the *normal* manner (high even, low odd); or in the *reverse* manner (low even, high odd). You will always be told of the meaning of a discard.

That, I think, will be enough for the time being. There is a great deal to learn, but do not be put off. Once you have played a few friendly duplicate evenings, you will wonder what all the fuss was about. Soon, when you are well into the swim of duplicate, you will be in a position to go on to further studies.

Index